Urban Poverty in Asia

A Survey of Critical Issues

Edited by
Ernesto M. Pernia

Hong Kong
Oxford University Press
Oxford   New York
1994

Oxford University Press

Oxford   New York
Athens   Auckland   Bangkok   Bombay
Calcutta   Cape Town   Dar es Salaam   Delhi
Florence   Hong Kong   Istanbul   Karachi
Kuala Lumpur   Madras   Madrid   Melbourne
Mexico City   Nairobi   Paris   Singapore
Taipei   Tokyo   Toronto
and associated companies in
Berlin   Ibadan

Oxford is a trademark of Oxford University Press

First published in 1994

Published for the Asian Development Bank by Oxford University Press

British Library Cataloguing in Publication Data
available

Library of Congress Cataloging-in-Publication Data
Urban poverty in Asia : a survey of critical
issues / edited by Ernesto M. Pernia.
p. cm.
Includes bibliographical references.
ISBN 0-19-586770-X
1. Urban poor--Asia. 2. Urbanization--Asia. I. Pernia, Ernesto M., date.
II. Asian Development Bank.
HV4131.85.A5U72 1994   94-41610
362.5'095'091732--dc20   CIP

Printed in Hong Kong

Published by Oxford University Press (Hong Kong) Ltd.
18/F Warwick House, Taikoo Place, 979 King's Road, Quarry Bay, Hong Kong

Foreword

While the poverty problem in Asia has commonly been perceived as largely a rural phenomenon, accelerating urbanization and higher urban population growth rates are making urban poverty increasingly more prominent and poignant. Regardless of economic growth performance in the short to medium term, urban poverty in many Asian countries will remain a formidable challenge for years to come. It is important, therefore, to sharpen our understanding of the intricate dynamics of the problem and to effectively disseminate the results of analysis and research on the subject. This process should contribute to the formulation of progressively better policies and programs for poverty reduction.

The Asian Development Bank is committed to the reduction of poverty as a strategic objective in its mission. To this end, the Bank has actively encouraged and funded policy-oriented research in the area of poverty. Besides paying greater attention to poverty-related aspects of development projects, the Bank has carried out two major research undertakings: the first on rural poverty and the second on urban poverty.

The present volume contains a set of issues papers which emanated from the research project on urban poverty. It comes as a sequel to an earlier volume which was the outcome of the research on rural poverty. The two volumes together should serve as a convenient reference on critical poverty issues in developing Asia.

The views and opinions expressed in this volume are those of the authors and do not necessarily reflect the views and policies of the Asian Development Bank.

V.V. Desai
Chief Economist
Economics and Development Resource Center
Asian Development Bank

Preface

This book is an outcome of the Bank's regional technical assistance project, Critical Issues and Policy Measures to Address Urban Poverty, which came on the heels of an earlier research undertaking on rural poverty. The project was co-sponsored by the Directorate General for Development Cooperation of the Ministry of Foreign Affairs, Government of the Netherlands. The project had two parts: one part dealing with critical issues, and the other part consisting of country case studies.

This volume is principally devoted to the critical issues papers. Besides introducing the subject of urban poverty and the issues papers, the Introduction and Overview chapter gives the highlights of the country studies. More complete versions of these studies appear in the *Asian Development Review*, Vol. 12, No. 1 (1994). A list of these studies and their respective authors is given at the beginning of this volume.

About two years have passed since the beginning of the project—which is not unusual for an undertaking of this nature. The commencement meeting was held in early August 1992 at the Bank's Headquarters in Manila, to collectively plan the scope, emphasis, and methodology of the research. The second and final meeting took place again in Manila in late March 1993 to present, discuss, and critically review the draft papers. Apart from the respective authors of the papers, government officials participated in the final meeting to help address the more practical aspects of urban poverty and related policies. These included Abuzar Asra, D.N. Basu, Dante B. Canlas, In-Geun Kim, Sawai Prammanee, Badiur Rahman, and R.M.K. Ratnayake. The Netherlands Directorate General for Development Cooperation was represented by Fon Van Oosterhout who also made a valuable contribution to the deliberations. From the Bank's Programs and Projects Departments, discussants included Shamshad Akhtar, Patricia Alexander, Evelyn Go, David J. Green, Bong Koo Lee, Ivan Ruzicka, Asad Ali Shah, Jeffrey R. Stubbs, Allan Williams, and Peter Von Brevern.

At various phases of the project, from its conceptualization to its completion, M. G. Quibria and Min Tang lent insightful advice and invaluable assistance. J. Malcolm Dowling, Jr. provided important moral backing and guidance on various aspects of the project. Hakchung Choo and S.C. Jha extended general direction and encouragement.

Emma M. Banaria supplied superb technical assistance and took charge of administration and coordination matters. Helen K. Buencamino, my efficient, imaginative, and indefatigable secretary, saw to it that nothing was amiss, besides processing the numerous versions of the manuscripts. She was ably assisted by Annie Angeles. Last but not the least,   Lynette R. Mallery provided excellent editorial assistance and seasoned advice on production and related matters.

Ernesto M. Pernia
August 1994

Contents

Chapter One
Introduction and Overview
Edwin S. Mills and Ernesto M. Pernia

Chapter Two
Issues of Urban and Spatial Development
Ernesto M. Pernia

Chapter Three
Urban Poverty and Labor Markets
Dipak Mazumdar

Chapter Four
Social Infrastructure and Urban Poverty
Paul J. Gertler and Omar Rahman

Chapter Five
Urban Shelter, Municipal Services, and the Poor
Emiel A. Wegelin

Chapter Six
Improving Urban Environmental Quality: Socioeconomic Possibilities and Limits
Peter Nijkamp

List of Tables

Chapter Four

List of Figures

List of Boxes

List of Contributors

Paul J. Gertler
Associate Director and Senior Economist
Family in Economic Development Center
RAND Corporation
Santa Monica, California

Dipak Mazumdar
Principal Economist
World Bank
Washington, DC

Edwin S. Mills
Director, Center for Real Estate Research
  and Gary Rosenberg Professor of Real Estate and Finance
J.L. Kellogg Graduate School of Management
Northwestern University
Evanston, Illinois

Peter Nijkamp
Professor
Faculty of Economics
Free University
Amsterdam

Ernesto M. Pernia
Senior Economist
Economics and Development Resource Center
Asian Development Bank
Manila

Omar Rahman
Associate Director and Social Scientist
Population Center
RAND Corporation
Santa Monica, California

Emiel A. Wegelin
Head
Human Settlements Economics Department
Netherlands Economic Institute
Amsterdam

List of Country Studies

The country studies which were a major part of the Asian Development Bank's regional technical assistance research project "Critical Issues and Policy Measures to Address Urban Poverty" are listed below. They appear in *Asian Development Review*, Vol. 12, No. 1 (1994) which serves as a companion volume to this book.

Urban Poverty in Bangladesh: Trends, Determinants, and Policy Issues
By Nasreen Khundker, Wahiddudin Mahmud, Binayak Sen, and Monawar Uddin Ahmed

The State of India's Urban Poverty
By Om Prakash Mathur

Urban Poverty in Indonesia: Trends, Issues, and Policies
By Carunia Mulya Firdausy

Urban Poverty in Korea: Critical Issues and Policy Measures
By Jong-Gie Kim

Urban Poverty in the Philippines: Nature, Causes, and Policy Measures
By Arsenio M. Balisacan

Urban Poverty in Sri Lanka: Critical Issues and Policy Measures
By Godfrey Gunatilleke and Myrtle Perera

Urban Poverty in Thailand: Critical Issues and Policy Measures
By Somchai Ratanakomut, Charuma Ashakul, and Thienchay Kirananda

Acronyms and Abbreviations

ADB	Asian Development Bank
ADC	Asian developing country
ASEAN	Association of Southeast Asian Nations
ASKES	*Asuransi Kesehatan*, Indonesia
BMR	Bangkok Metropolitan Region
CBO	Community-based organization
CFC	Chlorofluorocarbon
DFI	Direct foreign investment
DGIS	Directorate General of International Development Cooperation
ESCAP	Economic and Social Commission of Asia and the Pacific
FELDA	Federal Land Development Authority
FY	Fiscal year
GDP	Gross domestic product
GIS	Geographic Information Systems
GNP	Gross national product
IBT	Increasing block tariff
KALIM	Kalimantan-Timur
LAO PDR	Lao People's Democratic Republic
lcd	Liters per capita per day
LSD	Local sustainable development
NGO	Nongovernmental organization
NHA	National Housing Authority
NIE	Newly industrializing economies
NTB	Nusa Tengara Barat
OECD	Organisation for Economic Co-operation and Development
PHB	*Perum Husada Bahkti*, Indonesia
PRC	People's Republic of China
SD	Sustainable development
SSE	Small-scale enterprises
SUSENAS	National Social and Economic Survey of over 60,000 households in Indonesia
UNCHS	United Nations Centre for Human Settlements
UNDP	United Nations Development Programme

UNESCO	United Nations Education and Social Commission
UNICEF	United Nations Children's Fund
US	United States
USAID	US Agency for International Development
VIP	Very important person
WCED	World Commission on Environment and Development
WHO	World Health Organization

Chapter One

Introduction and Overview

Edwin S. Mills and Ernesto M. Pernia

Among the most conspicuous phenomena in developing Asia during the last two to three decades has been the accelerating pace of urbanization in various countries of the region. The 1980s, which was a decade of economic dynamism for many Asian developing countries (ADCs), saw the highest rate of urbanization[1] for the region as a whole, not only historically but also in comparison with the other developing regions. For instance, while Africa was urbanizing at an annual rate of about 2 per cent, and Latin America at roughly 1 per cent, Asia's urbanization level was rising by 2.7 per cent per annum during the decade. Although the pace of urbanization is likely to slacken in coming years, the region's urban population is expected to continue to grow at more than 3 per cent per annum until the early part of the next century.

Urban Asia comprises one billion people—more people than there are in all of the high-income countries of the world or in the urban and rural areas of Latin America, the Caribbean and Sub-Saharan Africa combined. The only area of the world with more people than urban Asia is rural Asia, which has a population of approximately 1.6 billion.

Asia as a whole is roughly a third urban. However, given its vastness and heterogeneity, this regional average masks wide variations across subregions and countries, as is shown in the next chapter of this volume. Most East Asian countries have virtually completed their urban transitions.[2] The Republic of Korea, for example, is nearly three-fourths urban and is projected to be more than 80 per cent urban by the year 2000. At the other extreme are countries in South Asia where levels of urbanization are about 25 per cent; exceptions are Pakistan, which is on the high end, and Nepal, which is on the low end of the range. Hence, in South Asian countries, there is still enormous potential for further urbanization and urban growth. Southeast Asia occupies an intermediate position at about 30 per cent urban, and countries in this subregion are undergoing the most rapid urban transformation in Asia. Malaysia and the Philippines are likely to be more than 50 per cent urban in the year 2000, while Indonesia is expected to be about 37 per cent urban, and Thailand just under a third urban. The potential for additional urbanization and urban growth in Southeast Asian countries is thus also considerable.

While urbanization, which is an integral part of the development process, presents opportunities and new possibilities, the problems it poses are often formidable and frequently more acute and complex than problems in rural areas. Urban problems are usually more intense and highly charged and can often lead to social and political instability. There tends to be a higher sense of deprivation and demoralization among the poor in the city than in the countryside, despite generally higher living standards. For one thing, rural residents generally have access to food both directly and through trade, while those in cities have access only through trade. For another, urban living entails many more nonfood needs, which can easily be accentuated by the demonstration effect (Pernia 1985). Urban poverty is commonly both a major cause and consequence of urban problems.

On the whole, poverty incidence has been on the decline in both rural and urban areas in developing Asia. Data from the United Nations show that the incidence of urban poverty in Asia (excluding the People's Republic of China [PRC], for which figures were not available) had fallen from 42 per cent in 1970 to 34 per cent in 1985, while the corresponding figures for rural poverty were 61 per cent and 47 per cent. These figures indicate about a 20 per cent lower poverty rate in 1985 than in 1970 in both urban and rural areas.

Nevertheless, because of continuing urbanization and urban population growth, poverty will increasingly become an urban phenomenon and, regardless of economic growth performance in the short to medium term, will remain a formidable problem in many countries for years to come. This problem requires a concerted effort by the government and the private sector in each country, as well as appropriate support from international organizations.

This chapter first provides a quick review of the concept and measurement of poverty. Next, it discusses briefly the characteristics and correlates of urban poverty, as well as the link between poverty and economic growth. Then, the chapter presents summaries of the critical issues that are the topics of the remaining chapters. The discussion of critical issues is complemented by summaries of the country studies that were a main part of the urban poverty research project but are published elsewhere.[3] The main points of the chapter are then summarized.

CONCEPT AND MEASUREMENT OF POVERTY[4]

Poverty is basically the inability to achieve a politically acceptable potential living standard. "Living standard" is a near-synonym for "real income, appropriately measured." Real income starts with money income and makes comparisons through time or across space by adjusting money income for price level changes or differences. To money income must be added income in-kind which refers to goods and services produced and consumed in households or to earnings which are paid in-kind, such as when farm workers are paid a share of the crops they produce or harvest. In both cases, income is produced, and adds to living standards, but no financial transactions occur. Real income includes earnings, property income, and transfer payments.

"Potential" refers to the fact that some people devote themselves to activities that generate lower living standards than would other activities they could undertake. Students who accept low living standards so as to add to their human capital are the most common example. People who accept low living standards to engage in religious pursuits are another example. Such people should not be regarded as poor insofar as their low living standards are voluntary. Some people experience temporary reductions of real income because of sickness, accidents, or involuntary unemployment and are able to maintain an acceptable living standard by reducing their savings or assets. This phenomenon is important in high-income countries, but is probably not significant for those below or slightly above the poverty line in developing countries, given that poor people in developing countries have few assets and little savings at the same time that they lack access to credit markets.

The setting of an acceptable living standard for use in defining poverty is an important policy matter. However, while a poverty line serves as a guidepost for a government to adopt policies that enable its citizens to achieve living standards above that line, the basic reason for antipoverty policies is to enable people to live with some measure of comfort, security, and dignity.

Another issue concerning living standard measurement concerns biological and activity differences among demographic groups. Children require less food and living space than adults, and adult women require less food than adult men since they are about 20 per cent lighter and may be less active. Many countries employ adult-equivalent standards, by which a child may, for example, be counted as half an adult.

A final issue concerning living standard measurement is scale economies with respect to household size. Two adults living together require less than twice as much space to achieve a given living standard as each would need if they were living separately. Likewise, large households can specialize among activities, and thus achieve scale economies (Atkinson 1991). A common procedure in this regard is to define $y=\bar{y}/n^s$, where $\bar{y}$ is measured household income, y measures living standard per capita, n is number of household members and s is an empirical parameter to measure household scale economies. $s = 1$ implies no household scale economies, and y is just household income per capita. At the other extreme, $s = 0$ implies that only household income matters, not household size. Most estimates of s are between 0.25 and 0.75, implying that y falls less than proportionately as n increases, for fixed $\bar{y}$. For example, if $s = 0.5$, a doubling of household size for fixed $\bar{y}$ reduces y by a factor of $1.414 = \sqrt{2}$. This adjustment is ad hoc but can approximate a variety of empirical situations.

Country poverty studies typically employ a nutrition-based poverty line, with the urban cost of a minimum healthy diet being raised by a factor that represents the cost of housing and clothing needed for safety and decency. Though informative, actual estimates of poverty incidence are often not directly comparable across countries because of differences in definitions and quality of data. Accordingly, the focus of attention should not be on poverty levels at points in time but rather on trends over time.

The most commonly used poverty measure is the head-count index, defined as

$$H_p = N_p / N$$

where H_p is the ratio of the population in poverty N_p to the total population N. This index is more popularly known as a measure of poverty incidence.

A second measure is the poverty gap, defined as

$$YG = \sum_{n=1}^{n=Np} (Y_p - Y_n)$$

where Y_n is the income of the nth poorest consumer unit and Y_p is the poverty line. The poverty gap measures the additional incomes needed by the poor to rise above the poverty line. Although the head-count index and the poverty gap are related, neither implies the other, and they can move in opposite directions.

A third measure is the Foster-Greer-Thorbecke (FGT) index which is calculated in a manner similar to that of the poverty gap, except that the weights used are simply the squared values of the income short-falls. This index falls whenever an income transfer occurs from a poor household to a poorer one. One drawback, however, is that this distribution-sensitive measure of poverty is not as easy to interpret as the other two indices.

CHARACTERISTICS OF URBAN POVERTY

Urban and rural poverty have much in common in terms of their characteristics and etiology. They are also related in that the poor move between rural and urban areas, though primarily from rural to urban areas. Nevertheless, the incidence, economics, demography, and politics of poverty differ between urban and rural areas. There-fore, the analysis, formulation, and implementation of policies should be differentiated, although policy coordination is obviously needed for optimum effect.

In general, the urban poor can be identified and surveyed at lower cost and probably with greater accuracy than the rural poor, given the higher densities and literacy rates in urban areas. To the extent that the urban poor are spatially segregated, they may be still easier to identify than the rural poor, although poor people are often inter-spersed among the nonpoor in cities. The more extensive monetization of the urban economy also makes urban poverty easier to measure. In many cases, data on social indicators are more plentiful for urban than for rural residents.

Income in-kind, mainly in the form of subsistence farming, is more important in rural than in urban areas. Subsistence farming is closely associated with lack of access to land, the chief income-producing asset in rural areas. The urban counterpart to subsistence farming is the low-income segment of the urban informal sector. Both sectors contain large numbers of poor people, and a part of rural-urban migration comprises poor subsistence farmers moving to somewhat less poor urban informal occupations.

Poverty incidence is typically less in urban than in rural areas (World Bank 1990; Quibria 1993). Moreover, for a given per capita gross national product (GNP), the overall incidence of poverty is lower the more urbanized a country is (Mills and Becker 1986). In most developing countries, real per capita urban incomes are higher than those in rural areas. Surveys from many countries report that those who migrate from rural areas generally improve their living standards although they may still be classified as urban poor. However, the poorest rural residents, as well as discouraged migrants who return, are probably not sufficiently represented among rural-urban migrants, given that migration is an undertaking that involves risks and requires a minimum of capital.

Rural-urban migration is theoretically viewed as an equilibrating mechanism that reduces urban earnings and raises rural earnings. Nevertheless, the excess of urban over rural earnings may persist for decades owing to imperfect markets and information, among other factors. Rural-urban migration may increase urban poverty. Not only are many migrants poor, though perhaps not among the poorest rural residents, but also migration keeps down the earnings of both poor and nonpoor urban residents. However, in a dynamic context, rural-urban migration is an important process that tends to improve the general well-being of both rural and urban households.

Government services and transfers are less expensive to deliver in urban than in rural areas. High urban population densities permit provision of government services and transfers at a large enough scale to keep transportation costs low. Even if the easier availability of government services and transfers induces more rural-urban migration than would otherwise occur, the lower cost of government services and transfers in urban areas provides an offsetting benefit. A different view is that of Lewis (1978) who claims that high infrastructure costs necessitated by urbanization are an important cause of fiscal problems in developing countries. However, it may be argued first, that most of these costs, including those for education and health care, are necessitated by economic development, not specifically by urbanization; and second, that infrastructure costs which are necessitated by urbanization, such as those for commuting, are justified by the increases in land values and can be financed by taxing part of the increments in land rents.

In any case, the above arguments must be tempered by the recognition that the rapid influx of migrants to urban areas poses severe stress in many developing countries. Because many migrants are poor and illiterate, they have limited capacity in dealing with the complexities of urban life. Many problems would be less serious if governments could provide inexpensive sites and minimal services where the poor could build or have built legal housing with secure tenure. However, government budgets and administrative capacities are severely strained by demands in other sectors and by continuing urban population growth itself (Pernia 1991).

The basic demographic characteristic of urban poverty is that its incidence is highest in households in which the dependency ratio is greatest. The poorest households tend to be those with the largest numbers of consumers relative to income earners. Frequently, the most disadvantaged urban residents are children, their mothers and grandparents in households in which there is no paid worker. Begging, prostitution, and child labor may be the only sources of income. Also, recent migrants from rural areas are among the poorest, although there appears to be no study indicating that a significant group has become worse off as a result of rural-urban migration.

While subsistence farmers generally consume what they produce and produce what they consume, the urban poor are more likely to earn money and purchase the goods and services they consume. The most important type of subsistence production in urban areas usually relates to housing. The poorest urban residents live in self-built, usually illegal housing. Living costs may be 10–25 per cent higher in urban than in rural areas. Food is comparatively more expensive. But housing costs are typically much higher in urban areas, not only because of high land costs but also because government controls often prohibit the only housing that the poor can afford. In effect, governments tend to exacerbate rather than alleviate poverty and add to the other hazards that the urban poor must face.

Most of the urban poor who earn incomes do so in the informal sector. Although the informal sector is not precisely defined, it typically consists of workers with poor education, experience, and skills who retrieve and sell wastes, sell new or used products on the street, or perform minor personal services. Many day laborers in manufacturing or construction firms are also part of the informal sector. While their earnings do not have as large a seasonal component as those of the rural poor, their incomes are probably almost as unstable because they have little protection from sickness and injury and the unpredictable demand for their services. The poor possess little human capital and almost no physical capital that can be sold or consumed when there is a sudden dip in their earnings. Having no assets that can be used as collateral, they also lack access to credit markets.

Some of the urban poor receive government or private transfers. While the latter may come from rural connections, especially for recent rural-urban migrants, most transfer payments appear to be in the reverse direction, i.e., from urban to rural residents. Private transfers to the urban poor may also come from urban relations or from informal social security networks. Government transfers may be pure transfers or pay for work.

The urban poor are often discriminated against in the provision of government services. Illegal squatter settlements are typically not provided with schools or health services on the same basis as are legal residents. In many cases, because governments intend to eventually relocate squatters to permanent and legal sites, they do not provide even minimum services to squatter settlements. Unfortunately, this situation may persist for years if governments lack the resources or the will to provide the permanent settlements, or if the squatters resist being moved. Also, in some cases, shortly after squatters are relocated to legal settlements, they return to the illegal sites after selling or subleasing the subsidized housing provided by the government.

URBAN POVERTY AND ECONOMIC GROWTH

To a large degree poverty incidence at a point in time is a reflection of previous economic growth performance, as illustrated with data for several Asian developing countries in Figure 1.1. Similarly, as is depicted in Figure 1.2, the speed of decline in poverty is contemporaneously associated with gross domestic product (GDP) growth over time. The direction and strength of the associations are virtually the same when data specific to urban poverty are used.

Why does economic growth reduce the incidence of poverty, including urban poverty? Economic growth results from the adoption of new technology as well as human and physical capital accumulation, all of which create employment opportunities and raise worker productivity and hence wages. In addition, economic growth provides public and private resources that can be used to improve education and health care, both of which are crucial to increasing worker productivity in the long run.

Urban workers with the lowest productivity may not benefit directly from new technology and capital accumulation in the short run inasmuch as their skills do not qualify them for the available high-paying jobs. But they benefit indirectly as low-skill jobs that were formerly held by workers who now qualify for better jobs become available to them. Also, as their education and health improve, they qualify for jobs that require more skills.

Not all groups benefit equally from economic growth, especially in the early stages. In some countries, income distribution becomes more unequal as per capita GNP increases from around US$200 to about US$1,000 per year. During that period, which may be long or short depending on the growth rate, incomes of the poorest groups increase, but more slowly than the average. At higher income levels, the incomes of the poor typically increase faster than the national average.

Much of the job creation that accompanies economic growth occurs in urban areas. The urban population increase that accompanies economic growth results partly from natural increase, but in large cities, normally more than half of urban population growth comes from rural-urban migration.[5] As mentioned earlier, massive urban in-migration of relatively low-income rural workers tends to reduce

Figure 1.1
Poverty Incidence and GDP Growth

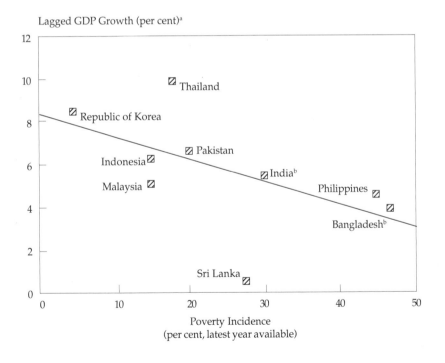

[a]Average growth during the five-year period preceding the latest year for which data on poverty incidence are available.
Sources: Country papers under the Asian Development Bank's Regional Technical Assistance Project on Critical Issues and Policy Measures to Address Urban Poverty; World Bank 1990.

rural poverty, though not extreme rural poverty. However, it may slow the reduction of urban poverty and may contribute to increased urban inequality. This is a critical link between urban and rural poverty, suggesting that economic growth and urbanization have a larger national effect on poverty than might be judged by merely tracking urban poverty trends.

The empirical record shows that more economic growth can be expected to help all income groups, including the poor (Fields 1994). The poor benefit in absolute terms when growth occurs, even under an initial condition of highly unequal income distribution. However, it is also clear that the poor can benefit to a greater or lesser extent

Figure 1.2
Poverty Incidence Decline and GDP Growth
(annual per cent change)[a]

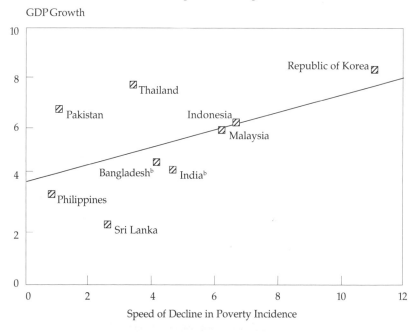

GDP Growth

Speed of Decline in Poverty Incidence

[a] Bangladesh, India, Malaysia, and Philippines—circa 1970–1990; Republic of Korea - 1970-mid-1980; Indonesia and Thailand—mid-1970–1990; and Pakistan and Sri Lanka—1980–mid-1980.
Sources: Country papers under the Asian Development Bank's Regional Technical Assistance Project on Critical Issues and Policy Measures to Address Urban Poverty; World Bank 1990.

from economic growth depending on the *type* of economic growth achieved. For example, labor-intensive growth—in contradistinction to capital-intensive growth—tends to be *broad-based* and, hence, benefits the poor to a greater extent. In the experience of the more advanced Asian economies, labor-intensive, broad-based growth has also been export-oriented, implying a foreign exchange bonanza.

Thus from the perspective of a decade or two, economic growth is not only the most important antipoverty strategy but is also the only strategy that can generate meaningful poverty reduction in very poor countries. Without substantial economic growth, these countries simply lack the resources to have a significant impact on urban or rural poverty, by providing the poor with improved education and health care, by tax and transfer programs, and by improved public services, in addition to employment creation.

Besides providing the infrastructure and policy environment conducive to rapid economic growth, governments can do other things as well to reduce poverty. However, specific antipoverty programs should be viewed as ancillary, not as alternatives, to growth-promoting policies (Behrman 1993). If specific antipoverty programs conflict with the promotion of economic growth, such programs should be seriously questioned. Nonetheless, whatever the national growth rate, poverty reduction can be accelerated if governments adopt specific complementary and efficient policy measures. These are taken up in later chapters.

CRITICAL ISSUES

The subsequent chapters of this book deal with selected topical issues relating to urban poverty. These issues are urbanization and economic development, urban labor markets and poverty, social infrastructure and urban poverty, urban shelter and municipal services, and the urban physical environment. A summary discussion of these issues is presented below by way of introducing the chapters.

Urbanization and Economic Development

As mentioned at the outset, urbanization is an essential aspect of development and is closely related to poverty patterns and trends. Pernia (Chapter Two) provides this context for an analysis of urban poverty. He shows that the degree and pace of urbanization can be predicted to some extent from the level of economic development and rate of economic growth. Thus, the more progressive economies in

East Asia, as well as those in Southeast Asia, have urbanized rapidly and appear to be in a transition not only to a slowdown in urban population growth but also to a diffusion of urban primacy (concentration in one or two large cities), accompanied by remarkable reductions in both rural and urban poverty.

He observes that a problem in the less developed of the Asian economies has been rapid urban population growth, especially in terms of absolute increases on top of already large urban demographic bases, not to mention the growth momentum inherent in young populations. Another critical issue concerns the excessive spatial concentration in the primate cities that have become, or are fast emerging as, megacities. This is a prominent issue as it manifests itself in terms of the highly-charged problems of poverty and inequality, unemployment and underemployment, inadequate infrastructure and housing, deficient social services, and environmental degradation.

Evidently, these persistent urban ills indicate that urban population is growing faster than the economic absorptive capacity and fiscal means of cities. In all likelihood, this continuing gap between urban growth and capacity largely stems from market failure that is further compounded by policy failure. This is probably because while the majority of governments in the region have continuously expressed the need for policy intervention on the spatial distribution of population, difficulties remain in clarifying the specific nature, extent, and timing of intervention.

Pernia notes that population distribution and urbanization policy is obviously a country-specific matter, and a broad cross-country analysis can, at best, only lay down some general considerations. First, such a policy should be formulated and implemented as a functional part of national development strategy, such that conflicts with other policies are minimized, and complementarities optimized. Second, the implicit spatial biases of economywide and sectoral policies, such as fiscal and monetary, trade, industrial, and agricultural policies, should be sufficiently understood. Policy reforms for economic restructuring toward labor-intensive export industries, as well as for deregulation and decentralization, may have the beneficial side effect of reducing the large-city bias.

Third, explicit dispersal policies should be thoroughly re-evaluated for their relevance, timeliness, and overall effectiveness. Research and experience show that locational controls and fiscal incentives have generally not been effective and are also costly. Access to markets, adequate power and water supply, and communication facilities are more important considerations in determining the location of industries. Any new spatial policy schemes, if warranted, should be formulated in consonance with the broader economic and other development policies. Fourth, urban management policy tools that directly tackle such problems as congestion, pollution, transport, housing, and basic social services are strongly recommended as part of the solution to the overall urbanization problem. But more important perhaps than the preceding, Pernia stresses, is a determined policy to improve basic infrastructure and services in towns and rural areas toward raising economic efficiency and living standards. Unless this is done, national development strategy will continue to address merely the symptoms of a broader malaise that is partly manifested in urban ills. Furthermore, given the important role played by the demographic factor, an effective policy for slowing population growth, especially in the less progressive countries, should form part of the package of policies.

Urban Labor Markets and Poverty

Mazumdar (Chapter Three) notes that, rural-urban migration has been largely profitable for the individual migrant in terms of improving economic conditions. However, certain basic factors, such as the "migrant stock" effect, prevent migration from being an equilibrating process, and the social effects of rural-urban migration could indeed be less beneficial than the private gains. Few migrants reach the high-wage formal sector of the urban market. Kinship ties in the process of recruitment ensure that these lucky few are not the migrants from the poorer rural families. A low degree of intersectoral mobility ensures that a large majority of those starting in the low wage sector fail to make it to the high wage sector within a reasonable period. Thus, rural poverty translates itself into urban poverty despite higher incomes in the urban sector.

Mazumdar takes exception to the Harris-Todaro model which postulates relatively easy movement of workers from the informal to the formal sector after a period of waiting. He presents an alternative view, namely, that the urban labor market is segmented in the sense that, although new workers may find it relatively easy to enter the informal sector, their further progress into the formal sector is restricted. This view has serious implications for the distribution of income in the urban labor market. The large difference in earnings between the two sectors along with limited entry into the high-wage sector creates a "labor aristocracy" in the urban labor market. A relatively small proportion of the labor force employed in the sector shares in the high income generated in the modern economy, whereas a large number of workers are left more or less permanently in the low wage-low productivity sector.

Labor movement into the high-wage formal sector may be restricted, notes Mazumdar, owing to institutional factors such as the "closed shop" practices of unions. However, it is unusual for such restrictions to exist in formal collective bargaining agreements. If employers are found to depend heavily on union representatives to fill vacancies, there must be strong economic reasons for that dependence. Employers attach great importance to the social solidarity of the work force in large establishments. Where unions are strong, union leaders and management both tend to want to achieve a socially integrated and motivated work force. Managers might well depend on unions to introduce new recruits. Nonetheless, a closed shop might also operate without unions. If employers attach more importance to the productivity-augmenting effects of a cohesive work force than to getting new workers at the lowest wage possible, they will depend on the foremen and senior workers to assist in recruitment. Accordingly, the field of new recruits may be restricted to those with close kinship or community ties to those already employed.

A second factor inhibiting mobility from the informal to the formal sector is the operation of internal labor markets in large establishments. Firms that encourage a lifetime commitment from their workers typically recruit young employees who are at a relatively low point on the career structure. Vacancies higher up the structure are filled through promotions rather than through outside recruitment. Thus, the opportunity to move into a formal sector job decreases significantly with the number of years spent in the informal sector.

The foregoing factors represent the demand side of the labor market. Segmentation can also occur when labor with different attributes is offered to the market. When these attributes are used as "labels" in the hiring of employees, the labor market may split into noncompeting groups. The most important of these supply-side attributes are sex and education.

Because of the traditional concentration of women in the service sector, especially in domestic service, a disproportionate number of women work in the informal sector. Even when women workers are employed in the large-scale manufacturing sector, they are usually concentrated in certain occupations or industries. Young unmarried females in Japan, for example, tend to work in textile industries. In

India's textile industry, women workers are employed only in specific occupations labeled *magi* (female) jobs. The proportion of females in industrial employment in the formal sector has been small and has declined over time.

When jobs are labeled in this way, remarks Mazumdar, female job seekers are crowded into certain occupations. Occupational crowding drives down the supply price of women's work throughout the economy, so that even the relatively small number who manage to get jobs in other parts of the labor market have lower earnings than men in the same occupation.

The informal sector contains a heterogeneous collection of workers with different degrees of entrepreneurial skills and capital. Those who sell their labor power with little entrepreneurial assets find substantial barriers to movement to the high-wage segment, while entry into the self-employed sector showing high returns to enterprise is limited by the need for prior acquisition of a minimum amount of human and financial capital. But segmentation in the capital and product markets may be even more serious than in the labor market.

The heterogeneity of earnings in the informal sector suggests that there is considerable dynamism within this sector and the acquisition of skills and entrepreneurial activity by the workers in this sector offer perhaps the best prospects for reducing urban poverty. This is particularly true because of the low elasticity of employment with respect to output growth in the formal sector in recent economic history. Toward the reduction of poverty, Mazumdar also recommends the promotion of small-scale enterprises and changing the sectoral and spatial composition of public investment and social overhead capital.

Social Infrastructure and Urban Poverty

Governments need to develop well-targeted poverty reduction programs. Gertler and Rahman (Chapter Four) make the case for increased investments in the human capital of children of the urban poor so as to help the next generation climb out of poverty. They argue that expanding and improving education, health care and family planning programs are important vehicles for urban poverty reduction. However, Asian countries face two interconnected problems in terms of the delivery of social services: (i) they need to generate more resources in order to expand and improve the quality of services; and (ii) public subsidies are typically regressive in that more subsidies accrue to the nonpoor than to the poor.

Governments can raise additional resources through increased user fees at public facilities and by promoting the private sector. Both methods have great potential for generating substantial revenues. However, unless careful safeguards protecting the poor's access to social services are established at the same time, both of these financing proposals could exacerbate the existing inequities between poor and nonpoor.

The major obstacle to large increases in user fees is that a vast segment of the poor population may be priced out of the market. Gertler and Rahman analyze four methods of price discrimination that would allow the government to raise prices to the nonpoor and lower them to the poor: individual, geographic, self-selection, and wealth indicators. They propose that a further investigation of the feasibility of individual price discrimination is warranted because individual price discrimination, if administratively inexpensive, is the optimal level at which to implement a system of differential fees. Indeed, it is worth pilot testing several different alternatives to gain information about the potential of each.

The second method investigated is geographic price discrimination, i.e., charging lower prices at facilities that serve poorer populations and higher prices at facilities that cater to wealthier people. Feasibility studies in two Indonesian provinces indicate that this method is likely to be highly successful in areas where the poor are heavily concentrated. However, information on price elasticity of demand and how the price elasticity differs by income is needed for full-scale implementation. A pilot test of geographic price discrimination would be a major step forward in its implementation.

While geographic price discrimination is feasible in some areas where public facilities are located far apart, other methods must be tried in urban settings, remark Gertler and Rahman. Because public facilities are located close to one another, it is all but impossible to identify facilities that serve only the poor. An alternative to geographic price discrimination is self-selection. In health care, the government would maintain a set of facilities (health subcenters) with low prices that triage patients. Those requiring sophisticated care would be referred at a reduced fee to health centers and hospitals. Those not willing to spend the time at the health subcenters could bypass them by paying a higher fee; the nonpoor would pay this fee and thereby self-select out of the health subcenters. Another form of self-selection is through differential pricing of frills (such as VIP rooms). The success of self-selection, however, requires getting the price differentials between the levels of service right. Achieving the right levels depends on being able to estimate the price and time elasticities of demand for the various levels of care, the cross-price elasticities and how these vary by income.

The fourth method of targeting services to the poor is to use indicators of wealth for charging higher prices. For health care, one such indicator is insurance status, note Gertler and Rahman. Evidence suggests that Indonesian *Asuransi Kesehatan* (ASKES) insurance members are generally better off economically, use more public health services than the general population, and are charged lower fees. As a result, the relatively well-off ASKES population is receiving a larger than proportional share of public health care subsidies. Insurance status, such as ASKES, could be used to charge the better-off the full cost of care. In this way public subsidies could be retargeted to the poor. However, if the prices charged for the care of ASKES members are increased, ASKES must be allowed to raise its premium so as to be able to cover the increased liabilities.

While the development of health insurance represents a huge potential for generating the resources necessary to expand the health sector, care must be taken in structuring the design so as not to exacerbate the regressivity of public subsides. Indeed, as insurance coverage grows and consequently prices rise, the government needs to guarantee the poor access to insurance or provide low price alternative care. Moreover, as increased insurance coverage raises the flow of nongovernmental resources into the health care sector, mechanisms must still be found to better target these resources to the poor. While insurance may generate additional resources, there is no guarantee that these will reduce the regressivity of public subsidies. Indeed, if the new resources are simply added to the current system, then benefits will accrue in substantially greater proportion to the nonpoor. The authors suggest that methods must be found to retarget public subsidies toward the poor, possibly by increasing the public subsidy to the rural health care system and to the low end public urban facilities. They caution that the position of the poor would be further eroded if government subsidies were reduced as nongovernmental resources increased.

Gertler and Rahman also discuss a promising method of better targeting public subsidies to the poor, i.e., the promotion of the private sector. Promotion of the private sector will expand the private market, making it accessible to a wider class of individuals. If a large enough proportion of households currently served by the public sector shifts to the private sector and the current subsidies to the public sector are not reduced, then it is possible for the public expenditure per person to rise. In this case, the users of the public facilities would be the poor and there would be less need for incorporating price discrimination mechanisms in publicly-provided services.

Urban Housing and the Poor

Urbanization and the associated shift of poverty from rural to urban areas translate into enormous requirements for urban shelter. In the absence of significant subsidized housing schemes, points out Wegelin (Chapter Five), this amounts to virtually all effective demand in the various housing submarkets that can be identified, ranging from squatter housing to legal and illegal low-income housing subdivisions, to "regular" developer-provided middle-class housing and higher-income housing. Typologies vary from city to city but typically about one third of the urban population in major Asian cities live in slums and squatter settlements, and about 60–80 per cent of housing supply is provided and financed through informal mechanisms.

Wegelin argues that realistic options in housing and urban services for the urban poor will be variations on the theme of the "enabling approach." Generally this will amount to finding ways and means to allow the informal sector shelter delivery to function more effectively, such that access for the poor is improved and shelter costs lowered. The important role for governments is to ease supply constraints in the market and exercise strategic interventions to strengthen the position of the urban poor therein. The precise mix of policy instruments will necessarily vary from country to country, but the author recommends a number of major elements for consideration.

Housing policy program. Approaches to assist the urban poor in obtaining suitable shelter are best formulated as part of an overall medium-term housing policy program, in which the housing sector is considered as part of the national economy, and in which low-income housing demand and supply are seen as part of aggregate housing demand and supply. This is because decisions on housing by other groups directly impact on housing opportunities for the poor, and many of the enabling actions required of government are not necessarily in the housing area per se but must be considered in a broader perspective, including land issues, housing finance and subsidies, and the regulatory framework.

Review of regulations on urban land supply. The foregoing policy program will have to contain a review of the regulatory framework covering planning and building controls, land expropriation and land transfer, land/property tax, public land disposal policies and procedures, and land titling procedures, in order to remove barriers to effective and affordable land supply.

Enhancing the quality of housing finance. Housing finance institutions must be authorized and strengthened to compete for savings with other financing institutions at market rates of interest; access of the poor to housing finance must be enhanced by ensuring that the relevant institutions are physically accessible, offer housing loans which meet the demand of the lower-income groups; in many cases this will require a link-up with informal housing finance systems effectively capitalizing such systems and making use of their network and organization. The range of financial instruments should be broadened to include small loans for upgrading/extension of homes. This may only be possible through the institutions of incentives for savings and loans associations/credit unions, with appropriate provisions for systems of uncollateralized loans through group and/or mutual guarantees. Secondary mortgage markets may also need to be established. The government may be required to stimulate the development of the housing finance system through the institution of a guarantee system or through fiscal facilities.

Neighborhood infrastructure and services. Provision of municipal infrastructure and services such as local roads, electricity, water supply, drainage, sewerage/sanitation, garbage collection and disposal, and public transport needs to be carried out in conjunction with and in support of new residential land development. Provision should be carried out in an integrated fashion to maximize the benefits of infrastructure and services and to facilitate efficient land utilization. Through infrastructure and services provision/denial the local government will be able to guide the direction and pattern of urban growth away from areas where settlement is dangerous (e.g., hillsites where there are substantial risks of landslides) or where provision of services is prohibitively expensive. This policy needs to be unambiguous and consistent, and must be supported by the regulatory framework concerned with land titling/subdivision and planning and building controls.

Rental housing and inner city rehabilitation. In many cases the (local) government may not be institutionally strong enough to undertake positive action to stimulate supply of rental housing and to ensure sensitive redevelopment of inner city areas to protect the interests of the urban poor. In those cases, the government should at least desist from regulations and actions which run counter to the development of rental housing supply (e.g., rent control regulations) and which may adversely affect the position of the urban poor.

Minimizing relocation. To the extent that the poor use their shelter for more purposes than just having a roof over their head, the location of their shelter vis-a-vis employment opportunities, infrastructure and services is of paramount importance. Forced relocation must therefore be avoided as much as possible. Where this cannot be avoided, simple, transparent and enforceable rules dealing with forced relocation will be required, based on the principle that relocatees will be at least as well off after relocation as before.

Targeted subsidies. Housing and municipal services delivery systems in almost any country contain explicit or implicit subsidies. More often than not these subsidies would be unaffordable to the government, if the housing and municipal services programs actually met demand. In this situation there is a case for abandoning such subsidies altogether. Where there is room for subsidies, they should be as well targeted to the specific target (low-income) groups as possible (see Gertler and Rahman, Chapter Four). Generalizations are difficult in this area, except that there is a *prima facie* case against price subsidies (e.g., interest subsidies, below market land prices, rent control, below-market service charges for such services as water or solid waste) on two counts: (i) they distort the pricing system, often resulting in the opposite of what was intended; and (ii) they tend to be preempted by nondeserving groups.

Direct income supplements to deserving households do not distort the pricing system and may be easier to target, but have the drawback that they are open-ended from a budgeting point of view. In the services area, specific subsidized provision may be considered for common facilities well-targeted to poor neighborhoods, such as water standpipe provision, but such subsidy provision needs to be explicit, transparent, and not at the expense of the financial sustainabilty of the overall water supply operations.

Incentives for the commercial and noncommercial private sector. Experience has shown that both the private commercial sector (formal and informal) and the nongovernmental organization (NGO) sector have important roles to play in the development of shelter and associated infrastructure. The role of the private commercial sector is profitable activities, which obviously may include design, building activities, building materials production and housing finance. The government's role is to promote transparent competition in all these areas, to ensure functional building standards (with realistic minimum standards relating to the prevention of fire and other natural hazards), and to ensure and promote the commercial attractiveness of environmentally and technologically appropriate building materials.

Improving the Urban Environment

Nijkamp (Chapter Six) draws attention to the increasing gap between the need for economic progress and urban quality of life in cities in the developing countries. He attempts to identify critical success factors for urban sustainable development, based on empirical illustrations from Asian countries.

After a background sketch of growth and environmental issues in the developing countries, Nijkamp introduces the notion of local sustainable development (LSD) as a policy strategy. He argues that urban sustainability indicators ought to be developed to provide guidelines for effective policy-making. He discusses several experiences from both the developed and the developing world, giving particular attention to the triangular relationship among efficiency, equity, and sustainability.

A main part of the chapter is devoted to the assessment of urban sustainability in the developing countries by using a pentagon prism with critical success factors, comprising in particular: hardware, socioware, orgware, ecoware, and finware. The feasibility of various sustainability policies may be judged by investigating four important fields: (i) urban resources and waste management; (ii) urban quality of life; (iii) urban transport; and (iv) financing urban sustainability policies. The author analyzes and illustrates each of these fields from the perspective of the pentagon prism.

Nijkamp remarks that the nodal position of cities in all economies, including those in developing countries, necessitates a careful analysis of and thorough policy attention to the socioeconomic potential of these cities. Urban sustainability may be regarded as an appropriate motive for effective and efficient strategies to find a balance between growth, equity, and environment. This means that local government capacity has to be strengthened, so that environmental considerations are integrated in urban development plans.

Nijkamp argues that the particular situation of cities in the developing countries—characterized by rapid urbanization, widespread poverty, low levels of public services, and a dual economy—makes them very vulnerable, so that indeed the issue of sustainability is at stake. The close connection between urban poverty and urban environmental conditions will reinforce the common tendency to seek short-term solutions without alleviating the long-term trends. Governments are faced with extremely difficult and delicate choice problems in finding a balance between the fulfillment of urgent needs and the necessity to work on a sustainable city. A paradoxical situation tends to emerge in many developing countries, namely, that the increase of welfare levels of the poor will lead to more pollution and waste, and hence will erode the urban basis for sustainable development. In this context, an appropriate combination of hardware, socioware, orgware, ecoware, and finware measures has to be found.

It is evident that, besides an improvement of welfare prospects and related behavioral changes, technology development in the area of environmental management and pollution abatement is a *sine qua non.* At both national and local levels, effective steps have to be taken to discourage the use of polluting technologies. At the same time, many abatement technologies and other industrial or household technologies with a polluting nature are acquired from abroad and, hence, part of the solution to the pollution problem in cities in the developing countries has to be found in the developed economies. This means that there is a need for an international code preventing the transfer, trade, or export of polluting technologies and products. It also means that the development of agreements with multinational companies or exporting companies would deserve high priority to safeguard urban sustainability in the developing countries, especially regarding those activities involving aid-funded projects. Also, the use of polluting products by households at the local level (e.g., plastic bags, chlorofluorocarbons [CFCs]) has to be strictly discouraged. Thus hardware and ecoware would have to lead to a mutually supportive mechanism, for instance, by developing products incorporating indigenous natural raw materials and by favoring recycling schemes. This strategy would also reduce urban poverty and unemployment and thus favor socioware.

Nijkamp also emphasizes the active role to be played by local actors (both private and public) to reduce pollution from all economic activities and energy use. Price and tax schemes on fuel, electricity, and gas have to be properly applied so as to ensure an efficient use of scarce resources, making such resources also available for the low-income groups. In general, inappropriate pricing of environmental resources and services has to be avoided. Moreover, positive stimuli have to be given to safeguard the urban environment, such as replantation schemes, maintenance of urban parks, selective (controlled) disposal of waste and garbage, installation of drainage and sewage systems, and construction of flood control systems.

Finally, the author underscores the positive role of the city in Asia. A city is a node of economic activity, entrepreneurial spirit, and social renewal. Not only industrial and service activities should be promoted in the city, but also many other activities which increase urban sustainability. For instance, many Asian cities house collections of monuments and cultural amenities which could attract foreign tourists. While some cities have been successful in exploiting this indigenous resource, in others, such resources remain largely untapped. In this context, a more market-oriented approach to the development of tourist amenities would have a great potential. Thus, a proper mix of ecoware, finware, and socioware would greatly improve the competitive position of cities in the developing world.

Nijkamp concludes that cities in developing countries need not be concentration points of socioeconomic despair, but rather can be focal points of sound sustainable development. The five critical success factors mentioned in the chapter, namely, hardware, socioware, orgware, ecoware, and finware would need to be implemented and regarded in a proper combination to ensure long-run success. Thus urban sustainability policy in developing countries is a formidable task, which requires keen political attention and strong political will.

COUNTRY STUDIES

Case studies of selected ADCs constituted an integral part of the research project on urban poverty. These countries were Bangladesh, India, Indonesia, the Republic of Korea, the Philippines, Sri Lanka and Thailand. The country studies are published under another cover.[6] Summaries and highlights of the studies are presented below as an essential complement to the above summary discussion of critical issues.

Table 1.1
Poverty Head-Count Ratios in Selected Asian Developing Countries
(percentages and numbers)

	Total		Urban		Rural	
	percentage	thousands	percentage	thousands	percentage	thousands
Bangladesh						
1973/74	72.7	55,675	63.2	4,415	73.7	51,260
1988/89	47.1	48,483	33.4	6,348	43.6	42,135
India						
1972/73	51.5	291,550	41.2	47,330	54.1	244,220
1987/88	29.9	237,670	20.1	41,700	33.4	195,970
Indonesia						
1976	40.1	54,200	38.8	10,000	40.4	44,200
1990	15.2	27,200	16.8	9,400	14.4	17,800
Korea, Rep. of						
1970	23.4	7,544	16.2	2,105	28.3	5,439
1984	4.5	1,818	4.6	1,216	4.3	602
Philippines						
1971	52.2	19,764	40.6	4,948	57.7	14,816
1991	44.6	28,039	36.7	9,967	50.7	18,072
Sri Lanka						
1978/79	22.3	3,306	19.4	620	23.1	2,686
1986/87	27.4	4,414	12.3	418	31.4	3,996
Thailand						
1975/76	31.7	13,360	17.6	1,600	35.6	11,760
1990	18.0	10,100	10.1	1,700	21.4	8,400

Sources: Country Studies under the Asian Development Bank's Regional Technical Assistance Projects on Rural and Urban Poverty published in *Asian Development Review*, Vols. 10 and 12, No. 1 (1992 and 1994); and *World Development Report 1990*.

Table 1.1 provides a numerical context for a discussion of urban poverty in Asia. The data are total, urban, and rural poverty head-count ratios and the corresponding numbers of poor in the selected countries for two periods, mostly the early 1970s and late 1980s. As indicated in the section on measurement of poverty above, the data are not strictly comparable across countries; actually more instructive are the intertemporal trends.

Bangladesh

The cities of Bangladesh face an overwhelming problem of population growth and extreme poverty. Urban poverty in Bangladesh must, however, be viewed within the context of a predominantly agrarian economy characterized by extreme conditions of generally low living standards, low productivity and widespread unemployment. The country is still mainly rural, with only about 16 per cent of the population living in urban areas. The urban population is estimated to have grown at around 6 per cent annually over the last three decades, compared with the national population growth rate of 2.5 per cent per annum in the 1960s, 2.7 per cent in the 1970s and about 2 per cent in the 1980s. The urban population is expected to increase rapidly because of continued rural-urban migration and the territorial extension of existing urban areas. In physical terms, the growth of the cities is taking place both in the densely built-up core areas and in the peripheral areas. In the latest population census of 1991, the population of the capital city, Dhaka, was estimated to be about 3.6 million; but the greater Dhaka area including the adjacent urban settlements accounted for more than 6 million of the country's total population of about 110 million. With increasing urbanization especially centered around bigger cities, the problem of providing employment, shelter and basic services to the urban population has become an important policy concern.

For more than a decade there has been a significant reduction in urban poverty in Bangladesh insofar as income is concerned. However, the gains are modest in light of the underlying weakness of the survey data used for the calculations, and of other indicators such as real wages, levels of unemployment, and per capita cereal consumption. This declining trend in poverty is also incompatible with macro indicators, which show a deceleration in agricultural and overall economic growth, and a decline in public sector investment and savings ratios over the same period.

Urban poverty, therefore, continues to be a major problem. The problem stems from (i) the low level of public expenditures and their inefficient allocation for services such as education; (ii) the skewed pattern of landholding due to past policy biases; and (iii) the inefficient distribution of health services, especially in terms of the geographic location of facilities. Some gains have, however, been made in urban poverty reduction, thanks to innovative approaches by NGOs in the areas of nonformal education and health delivery services, although the coverage of these schemes remains limited. There is considerable scope for improving the delivery of various services by charging user fees or setting a price-discrimination mechanism, given that the poor and the nonpoor can be differentiated even in slums, and that the poor usually pay very high charges for such things as water and housing, supplied mostly by informal sources.

There is a close link between rural and urban poverty owing to the process of rural-urban migration. Migration is a heterogeneous process, both in terms of the motives of migrants and the economic consequences of migration. For some migrants, the move to the cities has a positive impact on living standards and employment, and allows occupational mobility over time. Others, however, experience a worsening of their lot, and often end up as beggars or prostitutes. They are eventually cut off from their rural origins. A similarity also exists between the premigration status of migrants and their postmigration status. The poor's disadvantaged position in rural areas due to polarization or natural calamities recreates some of the conditions of rural poverty in urban areas in that unskilled migrants without any assets engage in unskilled and low-paying occupations. This implies that urban poverty should be addressed in conjunction with interventions in rural areas to stimulate agricultural growth and productivity and to improve income distribution.

The persistence of poverty in Bangladesh should also be seen within the context of poor economic growth and limited employment opportunities in the formal sector of the economy. Most of the labor force in urban areas are in the informal sector. There has, however, been some expansion of remunerative employment in new industries such as garments, which have absorbed a sizable portion of the predominantly female migrant labor force. This has had the effect of putting upward pressure on the wages of other segments of the informal labor force, such as those of maids. A similar upward pressure on wages in construction has been due to the international migration of unskilled labor.

The urban labor market is segmented, with significant differentials in earnings between the formal and informal sectors, among occupational categories, and among informal sector workers with varying skills and access to capital. A similar wage gap exists between male and female workers. Skill formation in the informal sector takes place almost entirely through apprenticeship or on-the job training, and the supply of skilled labor is quite elastic. Demand-side considerations are thus more important in terms of labor absorption. In this context, small-scale industries have an important part to play, and the focus of policy should be on reducing the productivity differentials between large and small industries by stimulating the innovative potential of the latter through, among others, improved supply of raw materials and credit intervention.

Political economy issues have a bearing on urban poverty. Most of the poor, being in the unorganized sector and not within the purview of state patronage, are less able to exercise leverage in the shaping of policies and setting up of institutions for their benefit. The current political scene in Bangladesh is such that there is no well-articulated or well-formulated development agenda on the part of major political parties or the government that addresses the issue of poverty. Rather, cultural and ideological issues have overshadowed key concerns, creating an atmosphere of divisiveness.

A well-integrated strategy of poverty reduction is called for. This strategy would require an emphasis by NGOs and the government on improving the provision of social infrastructure through better targeting and pricing of services. It would also require credit intervention to make an impact on the nonwage income of the urban poor. This necessitates the steps to legalize squatters and informal settlements on public lands. Adequate attention should also be paid to affordable housing for the poor, keeping in mind that many income-generating activities are located in households. Similar steps should be taken to service "informal" industrial areas adequately. Particular care should be taken so as not to unduly dislocate informal businesses while planning for urban development.

A significant reduction in poverty will, however, not be possible without expanding employment opportunities by stimulating industrial and agricultural growth. The interlinkages in the economy are such that efforts at urban poverty reduction should be matched by those to improve conditions in the rural economy in terms of agricultural growth, income distribution, and more productive employment in off-farm activities.

India

Over the last two decades, the incidence of poverty has declined in India. Indeed, using the official data on poverty incidence without any form of adjustment, the decline would appear to be dramatic, with the head-count index dropping from 51.5 per cent in FY1972/73 (ending on 31 March) to 29.9 per cent in FY1987/88, and the absolute numbers of the poor from 291.6 million to 237.7 million during the same period.

The decline from 41.2 to 20.1 per cent in the head-count index of *urban* as distinct from *rural* poverty during FY1972/73 to FY1987/88 is even more dramatic, as it coincided with a period of relatively rapid urbanization and urban population growth. Between 1971 and 1980, for instance, the urban population in India increased by a record 46 per cent. Although this rate of increase subsided in the subsequent decade it was still high enough to cause serious population pressures.

The decline is also notable in that it took place during a period when labor market conditions in the country were highly depressed; for instance, employment in the factory sector registered a fall rather than an increase in absolute terms, while formal (organized) sector employment rose only marginally by 2.1 per cent annually during the period FY1972/73 to FY1987/88.

The decline in urban poverty incidence amid trends normally expected to lead to greater pressures and marginalization raises a number of important issues. First is the issue of the definition and method(s) of measurement of poverty. How is poverty, and specifically urban poverty, defined in India, and how is it measured and aggregated to yield head-count and poverty gap ratios? To what extent are the existing definition and method of measurement able to capture the nature and magnitude of poverty in the urban areas? Could the reduction in the incidence of urban poverty be explained by the way in which poverty is defined and measured? Or could the decline be just statistical jugglery and illusion?

The second issue is concerned with the relationship between poverty *and* income growth and distribution. Is the reduction in urban poverty that the country experienced during FY1972/73 to FY1987/88 in any way attributable to income/GDP growth and its distribution? Is it at all possible that the annual average real GDP growth of 3.3 per cent during the 1970s and 5.5 per cent during the 1980s (up to FY1988/89) could have resulted in a fall by 20.1 percentage points in urban poverty? Could it be explained by the changes in the share of different population quintiles, especially of the bottom quintile, in incomes or expenditures?

The third issue concerns the policy framework for poverty reduction. What is the existing macro and sectoral policy framework for poverty reduction, and could this in any way explain the recent fall in poverty incidence? Could poverty reduction be the result of any shift in the pattern of investments in sectors such as health and education, or of any changes in policies concerning shelter and services, which have a direct bearing on poverty? Could the fall in poverty incidence be the result of specially designed and targeted programs?

The importance of sound macroeconomic policy and sustained growth for poverty reduction has long been recognized; even so, the poor face a variety of barriers caused by various kinds of institutional structures and regulations. Issues relating to the impact of stabilization and structural reforms on the urban poor are important. Although the process of adjustment in India began in the early 1980s, it picked up only during the past two years; hence, its impact is still obscure in a quantitative sense.

As the processes of urbanization and urban population growth gain momentum, the poverty agenda will assume greater significance in the country. Even assuming that poverty incidence can be held at the FY1987/88 level and not be allowed to deteriorate, the prospects of adding by the year 2000 anywhere from 20 million to 35 million people to the already large base of urban poor are frightening. This is particularly so since tackling poverty has so far proved to be difficult and complex, being bound up with several issues and priorities (rural versus urban; directly productive sectors of agriculture and industry versus education and health), institutional roles (governments versus the market), and financial systems (subsidies versus the beneficiary-pay principle).

The prospects of poverty reduction under these circumstances are crucially dependent on five factors: (i) the extent to which the process of future economic growth can shift to labor-intensive employment strategies by appropriately pricing capital, on the one hand, and by instituting labor market reforms, on the other; (ii) the extent to which the various rigidities that characterize the land and shelter markets can be eliminated so as to increase the access of the poor to such markets; (iii) the extent to which investments can be directed to education and health sectors and used efficiently and equitably; (iv) the extent to which various programs such as the Nehru Rozgar Yojna, urban basic services for the poor, and shelter-related programs can be consolidated and accessed via a single source of funds, e.g., a development fund for the poor as opposed to current multiple sources and multiple administrative arrangements; and (v) the extent to which information on the poor, e.g., what they consume and what they produce, and the sensitivity of their consumption and production patterns to price changes, can be generated and used in monitoring progress.

The agenda for addressing urban poverty seem to fit in with the philosophy underlying the current economic reforms in the country, as reflected in a recent discussion paper of the Government of India entitled *Economic Reforms: Two Years After and the Task Ahead*. What is important is the convergence of strategies rather than their divergence, as has often been the case in India. This will be possible when the respective roles of the government, nongovernmental partners, communities, markets, and international organizations are clearly defined and delineated.

Indonesia

Urban poverty is among the great challenges confronting Indonesia in the 1990s and beyond. One reason for this is that urbanization is likely to accelerate, while efforts to deal with it will remain inadequate. This inadequacy is due not only to the lack of development funds for the provision of goods and services to meet basic urban needs, but also to the government's limitations to create urban employment opportunities. In addition, policies to meet rapid urbanization tend to benefit the nonpoor more than the urban poor.

The statistics on the urban poor vary widely depending on the poverty lines used. Using the official poverty line approach of the Central Bureau of Statistics, it is estimated that the proportion of the urban poor declined from 39 per cent in 1976 to 17 per cent in 1990. This calculation is based on 2,100 calories and an allowance for essential nonfood expenditures. However, in terms of absolute numbers, the number of the urban poor did not change much over this period. In 1976 the urban poor numbered 10 million people, while in 1990, the figure was 9.4 million, accounting for more than one third of the total poor.

As in other countries, the problem of urban poverty involves many complex issues. While rapid economic growth and increased efficiency of resource use are necessary to reduce poverty, they should be complemented by some direct policy interventions in favor of the urban poor. These direct policy measures include improvements in the access to basic infrastructure and services, as well as in the access to productive employment both in urban and rural areas. Given the composition of the urban population living in poverty, the strategy to reduce poverty has to be differentiated. The development of urban agriculture and of activities in the informal sector are among those that deserve government attention.

The roles of the government, private sector, NGOs, local community, interest groups, aid agencies, and urban poor themselves are critical in shaping institutional arrangements toward the mitigation of urban poverty. The predatory behavior of bureaucrats and politicians, and administrative incompetence in policy-making and implementation should end. A strong political commitment is needed to achieve efficiency and effectiveness in the implementation of urban poverty programs.

Republic of Korea

The economic development of the Republic of Korea (henceforth Korea) has been among the most rapid and sustained in the world. By pursuing an industrialization-led development strategy since 1961, Korea has achieved considerable economic growth and structural transformation from a largely agricultural, subsistence economy into a newly industrialized one, despite the lack of significant natural resources and the burden of high defense expenditures. In the promotion of economic development through mass industrialization, the distribution of the labor force underwent a drastic change. From 1960 to 1990, the agriculture sector was reduced to less than a third of its former size, while the mining, manufacturing, and construction sectors together more than tripled in magnitude.

Urbanization has accompanied industrialization, and Korea's cities have grown largely in response to the rapid growth of the industry sector. Since 1960, large numbers of people have moved from rural to urban areas, and urbanization has risen rapidly. In 1960, less than 30 per cent of the population lived in urban areas; by 1990, about 74 per cent could be found in urban areas. Korea experienced rapid urban growth between 1965 and 1980, with the annual growth rate averaging 5.7 per cent, a figure much higher than in other developing countries.

During 1965–1980, Korea showed a net urban population growth rate of 3.8 per cent, which was about double that in other developing countries. However, from 1980 to 1990, Korea's net urban population growth slowed to 2.7 per cent annually, approximating the growth rate in other developing countries. Korea had by this time almost reached a mature stage of urbanization. One of the main features of urbanization was the concentration of the population in large cities (especially Seoul), from 2.6 million in 1960 to almost 11 million in 1990.

This rapid urbanization and heavy population concentration in large cities has resulted in various social and economic problems including traffic congestion, pollution, housing shortages, unemployment, and a proliferation of slums. In particular, the urban poor posed one of the most serious problems during the early stages of development. In the early 1960s, almost 55 per cent of the total urban population was estimated to be living in absolute poverty. Widespread urban poverty created a multiplicity of social problems, including legal complications due to the numbers of those living in unlawful dwellings in slum areas, health problems brought on by poor water and sewage systems, fire hazards due to the close proximity of houses and the lack of egress for fire trucks, increased family disruptions arising from cramped living quarters and unstable incomes, and increased public disorder stemming from growing conflicts between classes.

The Government formulated and implemented domestic policies and programs to deal with those serious problems. These programs, coupled with substantial benefits arising from strong economic growth over three decades, functioned to reduce the number of the urban poor to less than 5 per cent of the total urban population in the mid-1980s. But to formulate and execute such policies successfully over the years, the Government had to be responsive to economic shifts and the changing characteristics of poverty. Urban poverty in the early period of economic development in the 1960s to the early 1970s was attributable mainly to large-scale rural-urban migration. In the late 1970s and 1980s, as the number of the urban poor decreased with greater economic prosperity in the country, the Government's major policy concerns focused on preventing the transmission of poverty from generation to generation and improving the poor's ability to live solely on their own through job training programs and the opening up of more educational opportunities.

Although the causal relationship between various government policies and poverty is not easy to determine, some explanations are plausible. First, while substantial reduction of urban poverty in Korea resulted in part from government policies to help the urban poor, the most important factor in this decline has been the overall growth of the economy. The country's industrialization-led economic development strategy generated enough employment opportunities to absorb rural-urban migrants, who constituted most of the urban poor. Aside from the Government's development strategy based on the promotion of employment opportunities, the sharp decline in urban poverty can be attributed to the absorption of relatively younger and more educated rural-urban migrants in the formal employment sector.

Second, beginning in the late 1970s, various policy measures were implemented either to reduce urban poverty or to help the urban poor. These measures were pursued in accordance with the living conditions of two groups. The first group consisted of those whose conditions could be drastically improved by general policies such as income security programs, labor market programs, and housing programs. The second group was made up of those who could not make a living without government support through public assistance and social welfare programs.

The major thrust of the measures for the first group was not merely to provide temporary relief. The programs placed a high priority on creating employment opportunities for the urban poor or improving their skills, thus enabling them to be self-reliant. The services provided included education, job training, and job placement.

For the second group, the Government has provided charity and relief. The problem now is how to provide more assistance and how to establish a workable service delivery system for social welfare. Private firms and religious organizations are being encouraged to establish social welfare institutions or to contribute to existing facilities.

Third, while the general living conditions of the poor have improved significantly, there are areas in desperate need of improvement. One such area is housing for the urban poor, which has become one of the most pressing political issues of the country. Various policy measures have been instituted to solve the urban poor's housing problems, but with only limited success. As a result, the urban poor have frequently been forced to relocate, often to unsuitable locations and far from their work places. Most government projects did not pay much attention to the financial constraints of the poor. Distortions in the housing market characterized by extremely high prices and chronic shortages have worsened the housing conditions of the urban poor. Foremost among the reasons for the scarce and unbalanced supply of housing is the shortage of urban land sites that has resulted in high prices. These problems have been caused mainly by government policies which—in combination with the greenbelt policy—restricted the conversion of agricultural, forest, and other nonurban land uses to urban use. It seems imperative to revise the land use policy first to solve the urban poor's housing problems.

Philippines

The accelerating pace of urbanization in the Philippines is shifting the burden of poverty from rural to urban areas. The proportion of the population living in urban areas rose from about 30 per cent in 1960 to 38 per cent in 1980 and 49 per cent in 1990. However, unlike in many developing countries where high levels of urbanization reflect a shift in the economy's dynamic comparative advantage from one initially based on agriculture to one based on industry and services, the country's high urbanization level has not been matched by a correspondingly high per capita income or by a significant shift in labor employment from low to high productivity areas. Its real GDP per capita at the beginning of the 1990s was not much different from that in the late 1970s. The share of the industry sector in total employment remained virtually unchanged at about 16 per cent during the last three-and-a-half decades. The employment share of the manufacturing sector, which is the hub of dynamic growth in the fast-growing neighboring countries, even contracted from 12 per cent in the mid-1950s to 10 per cent in the early 1990s.

The urban poor have become an increasingly substantial proportion of the country's total poor population, rising from only 28 per cent in 1961 to 45 per cent in 1991. At the current level of urbanization and urban deprivation, poverty has ceased to be merely a rural phenomenon.

The maintenance of economic growth is crucial to the reduction of poverty. However, even with economic growth sustained at the rate experienced in 1986-1989—that is, at an average real GDP per capita growth of 3.2 per cent—it will take many years for the average poor person to cross over the poverty line. How long depends much on whether the growth will be accompanied by changes in the size distribution of income. Assuming that income distribution remains essentially unchanged, as indeed it has over the last three decades, it will take about 15 years for the average poor person to cross over the poverty line. A faster growth of 5 per cent—not a far-fetched possibility, given the experience of neighboring Asian countries—will shorten the cross-over time to about 10 years. The implied (point) elasticity of the distributionally-neutral growth is about –1.8; that is, a 10 per cent growth in GDP per capita would reduce the average poverty gap by 18 per cent.

If the growth is accompanied by an improvement in income distribution in favor of the poor, the average poor person will, for a given growth rate, move up the poverty line in a much shorter time. The elasticity of the poverty gap index with respect to the Gini index is about 2.4 per cent; that is, a reduction in the Gini index by 1 per cent will decrease the average poverty gap by 2.4 per cent. Clearly, income growth accompanied by a decrease in income inequality will go a long way toward reducing Philippine poverty.

The roots of urban poverty can be traced to (i) industrialization policies that unduly encouraged the concentration of infrastructure and social services in major urban centers, particularly Manila; (ii) trade and macroeconomic policies that severely penalized agriculture, labor-intensive exports, and small-scale and medium-scale manufacturing establishments; and (iii) public spending policies that accorded little attention to human capital formation for the poor. This policy environment engendered industrial "enclaves" that have little linkage with the rest of the economy, dampened the expansion of high-paying employment opportunities for the fast-growing labor force, and limited the access of the large majority of the urban poor to basic infrastructure and social services.

The economic welfare of the poor can be secured only by comprehensive economywide policy reform aimed at correcting the disincentives against the production (and consumption) of labor-intensive goods, particularly labor-intensive exports, and at promoting backward integration and balanced urban-rural growth. In particular, the reform has to allow for rapid and sustained growth of employment outside the agriculture sector and the urban informal sector. The reform also has to permit infrastructure and institutional development outside Manila.

Political support for the institution of pro-poor, pro-market, and pro-growth reform has to be enhanced. Beneficiaries of the *status quo*, who are typically well organized, can mount strong opposition to policy reforms. On the other hand, those who would gain from policy reforms, who are usually unorganized, spatially dispersed, lowly educated, and often uninformed about the benefits (and costs) of policies, are politically weak, even though they may be a numerically large group. The influence of pro-reform advocates in government is seldom enough to bring about reforms. The academic community and social action groups play a critical role in this struggle. Policy analysis can help shape perceptions among the actors in the political arena about the costs and benefits of government action (or inaction). Organizing the diverse, export-oriented industries into a powerful lobby that can support the position of pro-reform advocates in government would also be helpful in enhancing the success of reforms, especially in countering the protectionist pressure exerted by import-substituting industrialists. The process requires the pro-reform advocates to explain to the public why the reforms are needed, how they are supposed to work, and why and how they can benefit the majority of the population.

Balanced rural-urban growth and economic development require a strong complementarity between the state and the market. The state not only institutes and enforces the long-term rules of the game that empower and constrain economic actors but also provides complementary public goods for the efficient operation of markets. In recent years, the state missed performing its major functions—the financing and public-sector coordination of investments in social and physical infrastructure, the promotion of rules ensuring incentive compatibility in government and in the private sector, and the pursuit of an egalitarian distribution of assets in the private sector—in laying the foundation for long-term economic growth and development.

Pro-poor policies should be designed in such a way as to provide a clear blueprint for achieving poverty reduction as well as explicitly specifying penalties and rewards, thereby ensuring that private and public actors will find it in their interest to behave in a poverty-reducing manner. A necessary element of this design is a contingent renewal scheme: public agents would be given high salaries and benefits, with a credible threat of their withdrawal if they do not meet clearly specified standards of satisfactory performance. However, for many basic services, this scheme might not work. In health delivery and education, for example, it is difficult to measure a public agent's performance, since the intended beneficiary's health status and progress in learning and skill formation also depend on a host of other factors affecting the individual, the family, and the physical and social environment. Moreover, certain groups with strong stakes in the public agent's decisions have an interest in offering him or her alternative incentives: a lucrative job in the private sector, "gifts" during special holidays, and threats. Finally, rent-seeking behavior may lead to the preemption of the benefits of poverty-focused programs by unintended groups.

Contingent renewal, therefore, needs to be complemented by other incentives aimed not only at eliciting the participation of the poor in the design and implementation of poverty-focused programs, but also at making unintended beneficiaries realize that it is not worth their while to preempt the benefits of these programs. Locating basic services in areas where the poor live is, for example, one effective way of reducing their participation cost while at the same time raising the participation cost of unintended beneficiaries. Thus, publicly provided curative health centers in the nation's capital are hardly pro-poor programs. Similarly, public programs with attributes that are also highly valued by unintended beneficiaries (e.g., socialized housing units in high-income neighborhoods, general food price subsidy) seldom succeed in reaching the intended beneficiaries.

Finally, the provision of efficient information systems is critical in raising the effective demand of the poor for poverty-focused policies and programs. The articulation of this demand can be enhanced by bringing together the poor and the nonpoor groups that have a stake in poverty-reducing reforms. The political power and administrative machinery of nongovernment organizations and private volunteer groups can be harnessed for this purpose.

Sri Lanka

An unusual feature of Sri Lanka's development during the four decades after independence has been the relatively slow growth of the urban sector. According to census data, the share of the urban population in the total population increased from 15.4 per cent in 1946 to 21.4 per cent in 1981. These data, which are based on the administrative definition of what is urban, tend to underestimate the actual extent of urbanization. But even after making corrections for this, the level of urbanization remains low. The slow expansion of the urban sector has been the result of a combination of economic, social, and political factors.

The economic development strategy focused on import substitution in agriculture, primarily in rice (the staple food), which is produced by peasant farmers. This led to a major investment to improve peasant agriculture and to expand rice cultivation. Large agricultural settlements were established in sparsely populated regions, and the landless rural poor were transferred from regions that were experiencing the mounting pressure of population on land. These policies mitigated some of the push factors that might have produced a larger rural-urban migration. Growth in the industry sector, which would have provided the base for urban expansion and stimulated rural-urban migration, was comparatively slow. The share of manufacturing in GDP had grown only marginally from about 14 per cent in 1950 to about 15 per cent in 1980, mainly because the changes in the basic structure of the economy during this period were negligible. It was only after 1978 that those changes gathered momentum and the manufacturing sector began to grow rapidly. The post-1978 policies liberalized the economy and gave high priority to industrialization, thus changing the macroeconomic context of urban poverty.

In the social sectors, the Government undertook a major welfare program, which provided free health care and education to the entire population. Large investments were made in establishing a countrywide network of services for education and health care and in improving the rural infrastructure. All this helped to reduce rural-urban disparities. Infant mortality rates, for instance, fell dramatically from 141 per thousand live births in 1947 to 57 in 1960 and 21 in 1989. Adult literacy increased from about 57 to 87 per cent during the same period. The political processes at work as manifested in national policies were strongly biased in favor of the rural sector. Universal franchise and democratic political institutions were introduced in the first half of the 1930s. From that time on, democratic institutions began to function without interruption, resulting in a vigorous multiparty system that made possible several orderly changes in government. In this competitive political system, the rural electorate had the largest weight numerically. Political parties, therefore, gave high priority in their agenda to satisfying the needs of this electorate. Consequently, the main political parties did not target the urban electorate, particularly the urban poor, in the same manner they did the rural poor electorate.

The mix of policies and its rural bias, on the one hand, contributed to the conditions that resulted in slow urban growth and an unusual rural-urban balance. This, in turn, prevented a large rural-urban migration and the worsening of urban poverty on the scale now being witnessed in most other developing countries. On the other hand, past strategies, with their emphasis on import substitution in both agriculture and industry, retarded the growth of the urban economy, resulting in very high rates of unemployment of the urban work force, which exacerbated poverty.

The strategy based on the expansion of agriculture and the import substitution of rice is reaching its limits for a number of reasons. The new development strategy has given a central place to export-led industrialization, which will bring on rapid urbanization and generate greater pulls and pressures for migration from rural to urban areas. Some aspects of the economic reforms and structural adjustments that are being undertaken, such as the removal of a wide range of subsidies and the reining in of high inflation, will have an adverse impact on the urban poor. The problems of poverty are likely to assume new dimensions in this changing context unless appropriate policies are formulated to deal with them.

The problem of urban poverty in Sri Lanka is of lesser magnitude and intensity than poverty in the rural sector. Although the flow of rural-urban migrants has been relatively small, the character of the prevailing urban poverty is closely related to the migration of the rural poor to urban areas. The majority of the urban population who are below the absolute poverty line can be found among those who have migrated during the last two to three decades. As a result, there are several easily identifiable characteristics of urban poverty—overcrowded human settlements in unsanitary environments that lack the basic amenities, housing of very poor quality, and informal sector employment. At the household level, the urban poor share the general characteristics of poverty in terms of income, household size, educational attainment, and gender. There are, however, conditions that are specific to the urban context. These include the lack of capital assets and the dependence on personal labor and skills, the absence of some of the supportive kinship networks found among the rural poor, the almost exclusive dependence on cash incomes and the vulnerability to inflation, the higher cost of nonfood components essential for subsistence, large household size, and greater vulnerability to undernutrition. These characteristics of urban poverty, which relate to the capacity of households to move out of poverty, are crucially important in the formulation of strategies to reduce urban poverty.

Those strategies are being formulated on three levels. First, at the macro level, development strategies and policies will preserve the positive elements that helped maintain the unusual rural-urban balance, thus avoiding as much as possible the processes that augment and intensify urban poverty in developing countries. The present national strategy to industrialize rapidly (with consequent urbanization) poses a new set of challenges. The scope for the expansion of agriculture and of new agricultural settlements will be curtailed after the completion of the Mahaveli Scheme. The present forest cover has already reached critical proportions because of deforestation. Therefore, the past strategy of transferring the population from overpopulated rural areas to new agricultural settlements is no longer feasible. It is in this context that the Government's policies for regional and spatial development could contribute toward an orderly pattern of urbanization that could contain the processes that exacerbate urban poverty.

Second, at the sectoral level, the development of urban infrastructure is an essential condition for improving the access of the poor to

basic amenities. This task assumes high priority in the public investment program, as it is integrally linked with the industrialization
strategy. Equally important are two other aspects of urban policies.
The pricing policies of public utilities must be such that they generate
adequate resources for maintenance and replacement, and make possible the provision of a sound financial base for future expansion
programs; the present thrust of government policy is in this direction.
Another essential condition is the growth and development of efficient local government institutions that would undertake the complex
task of urban management. The inefficiencies of poorly managed
urban local authorities lead to conditions that aggravate the deprivation of the urban poor, particularly as they relate to the provision of
basic amenities and housing.

Third, national and sectoral policies and programs will have to be
sensitive to and specially designed to deal with the specific characteristics of urban poverty. Any poverty-oriented strategy for the urban
sector should target the informal sector and the needs of the informal
labor market. Planned infrastructure improvements such as new facilities and any relocation schemes would need to take into account
the character of the informal market, its location, the cost structure of
informal enterprises and the economic base that accounts for its
competitiveness, if any. There is great potential for growth in the
informal sector if it could forge links with the formal sector for
markets, the improvement of technology, and the diversification and
expansion of production through such mechanisms as subcontracting. Another avenue for strengthening the informal sector is institutional credit. Here it is necessary to overcome the present barriers and
extend the innovative adaptations of institutional credit taking place
in the rural sector to urban informal borrowers. The NGOs that are
beginning to be active in the urban sector can play a major role in
developing institutional credit for the informal sector.

In health and nutrition, as well as in education and skills development, the urban poor, again, have needs arising out of their special
conditions of vulnerability that are different from those of the rural
sector. The monetized economy, the dependence on cash incomes,
and the lack of income-earning assets tend to make the urban poor
more vulnerable to inflation and the loss of real income. The incidence
of malnutrition also tends to be higher among them. Problems such
as environmental sanitation and the lack of safe drinking water require immediate solutions. Changes in the urban environment are
continually exposing the urban poor to new health hazards. Especially

disadvantaged groups such as street children and destitute elders in urban areas need help. In the past, the special characteristics of urban poverty did not receive due consideration, largely because the problem of rural poverty, on account of its magnitude, was the primary concern of policymakers. Future strategies to deal with urban poverty should correct this bias. Such strategies would have to be based on more complete information and knowledge of the causes and characteristics of urban poverty than are currently available.

Thailand

The Thai economy has gone through various phases of development and transformation. Bangkok is not solely a product of the culture of Thailand. It is inextricably bound up with the world system, with all its sectors (from banking to labor migration) affected by economic and social forces that are increasingly transnational in scale—a reflection that modern technology has transformed the traditional concepts of space, territory, and nation. During the 1980s, Bangkok entered an era in which it was increasingly shaped by these factors. Its economic base thus became closely tied to international economic, social, and political forces.

Thailand is still primarily a rural country, with approximately 70 per cent of its people living in rural areas. It is not surprising, therefore, to find that more than one half (55 per cent) of all migrants had moved to villages, and that a substantial number of recent migrants came from nonurban areas. About 20 per cent of all migrants moved to Bangkok, followed by 15 per cent who went to various other cities, and 11 per cent to urban and rural districts.

The richest 20 per cent of households in Thailand earned about 49.3 per cent of total income in FY1975/76, with the proportion rising to about 54.9 per cent in FY1987/88. The poorest 20 per cent earned only about 6.1 per cent of total income in FY1975/76, which fell to 4.5 per cent in FY1987/88.

Even with the country's rapid growth, the important issue of income distribution has remained. For the Bangkok Metropolitan Region (BMR), poverty incidence was 3.4 per cent in 1990 based on the head-count measure. Bangkok accounts for 31 per cent of the urban poor, who lack job security, put up with poor conditions, and are unable to get any help from the Government. About 81 per cent of these people live in slums, and about 60 per cent are unskilled. Some 90 per cent of them have had formal education only to fourth grade or lower. Their incomes are too small for them to be able to afford the rent for standard housing, which is about B4,000 per month. It is estimated that their average annual income is B6,324, or a little over US$200. About 40 per cent of them rent their living quarters and in many cases are saddled by high water bills; the rest trespass on public land or live along small waterways or under bridges. Most are street vendors who borrow from private sources to keep up their trade. Lending to them is considered a high risk, so that if they are given loans, the interest is high.

Between 1980 and 1988, Thailand's urban population increased from 12.5 million in 508 areas to 15.8 million in 660 locations. The level of urbanization is estimated to have increased from 26.5 to 28.7 per cent, with Bangkok's share in the total population declining from 41.4 to 36.2 per cent but with its share in urban population remaining high at 56.8 per cent—such that it was 27 times larger than Nakhon Ratchasima, the second largest city.

The BMR also accounted for almost 75 per cent of total value added in manufacturing between 1981 and 1988. Twelve of the country's 23 industrial estates were within its confines, and Board of Investment data show that the BMR's five inner provinces attracted the bulk of approved projects. Besides providing income and employment opportunities for a large number of people, the BMR also constituted the biggest consumer market (9 million people) for durable and nondurable products. It was also the major transport hub with the best infrastructure (e.g., piped water, telephones, hospitals, and leisure facilities).

During the period 1987–1991, the BMR attracted almost 92 per cent of total investments in infrastructure and 96 per cent in transport. With the sudden economic boom in the late 1980s, however, problems associated with inadequate infrastructure emerged.

There appears to have been no extensive poverty reduction program for the urban poor. In contrast, since 1982, which marked the beginning of the Five-Year Development Plan, the Government has been implementing a rural development program to reduce poverty in 12,888 villages throughout the country.

A strategy for urbanization and sustainable development should include at least four policy components, namely: a policy for labor-intensive industrial production; a policy for the provision of essential social services; urban management policies (e.g., those dealing with transport, water supply, sanitation, and housing); and finally, a policy on the environment. At the same time, a strategy for urban poverty reduction should include the following:

(i) *Infrastructure development* (such as an urban transit system, better housing, town planning, and satellite towns). However, a poverty reduction program should be carefully implemented, considering that not only physical solutions but also socio-politico-economic solutions are needed.

(ii) *Improvement of urban labor productivity.* The urban and rural economies are intertwined in many ways, and rural-urban migration is one of the main linking factors. Programs to improve urban labor productivity and employment would reduce poverty not only in the urban areas but in rural areas as well.

(iii) *Promotion of the agriculture sector.* Rural poverty reduction programs should continue the policy to promote agricultural industries in the rural areas and to render public assistance in the training and education of the rural folk.

(iv) *Job creation and the promotion of the subcontracting system.* Since the urban informal sector plays an important role in absorbing the labor supply, feasible solutions for the urban poor might lie in the development of the subcontracting arrangements.

(v) *On-site upgrading of slums.* This is needed because the economic survival of slum dwellers centers around urban nodes just outside the slum settlements, while maintaining only limited exchange relations with their home villages.

The urban informal sector has contributed positively to the development process in many developing countries. Thailand is no exception. In these countries, it is the subcontracting system generated by export growth and various services (e.g., housekeeper, urban food stall helper, street vendor) that has created the demand for unskilled labor.

The Seventh Five-Year Development Plan (1992–1997) emphasizes continuous economic growth, equitable income distribution and regional growth, improved quality of life, and the development and preservation of natural resources. According to the Plan, poverty-reducing measures include job creation, housing improvement, upgrading of the quality of life and the environment, and raising of the efficiency of NGOs.

The National Housing Authority (NHA) has lined up four programs to cope with the critical problem of housing for the urban poor, namely: (i) the provision of housing to low-income families by making construction costs affordable; (ii) the optimal use of available land for the improvement of legitimately situated communities; (iii) the relocation of congested communities that are illegitimately located; and (iv) the provision of housing to fire victims. NHA has finished the improvement and remodeling of 53,314 housing units and the relocation of 4,965 housing units, while over 10,013 units are in various stages of remodeling or relocation. Despite this, NHA cannot cope with the rapidly increasing requirements of the poor.

Local governments (i.e., BMR and the municipalities) and NGOs also have an important role to play in Thailand. However, with their limited resources, they cannot do much as far as housing is concerned. Nonetheless, the NGOs have contributed significantly to (i) efforts at organizing harmonious relations among community members in caring for the environment; (ii) activities of youth and child care programs; (iii) health care, nutrition and family planning services; (iv) the eradication of crime, drugs, and gambling; and (v) the promotion of self-reliance and community participation activities. Indications are that most of the congested communities in the big cities now have a better environment, improved walkways, and waste disposal systems.

Institutional factors have a strong impact on urban poverty. First of all, most of the urban poor who work in the informal sector are not assured of regular incomes. Their earnings are usually lower than the minimum wage rates in the formal sector. Those who earn their livelihood from petty trading, scavenging, and other daily laborious jobs are even worse off. While they probably earn enough for food requirements, there is no immediate prospect of improving their condition.

The booming economy of Thailand has seen a rapid increase in the demand for land. This has prompted landowners and government enterprises to evict squatters from their properties. And since squatters normally do not get any subsidy or compensation and have nowhere to go, they often invade and build new slums in other unattended areas, particularly in the outskirts of Bangkok. There are informal land transactions in the suburbs that are not registered as required by law. This allows landlords to exploit the poor and get around the requirements to provide infrastructure and services.

Land ownership is probably not a must for the urban poor in Thailand since they generally cannot afford land, and even if they could, they could not possibly maintain it. However, housing security, as well as other possible alternatives such as an affordable rental scheme, should be applied to the poor. Also, since slums are being demolished because of the growing demand for land development among landlords, the provision of low-income housing in the suburbs is now mandated. Many low-income families are willing to engage in a long-term housing investment that would ensure security for themselves and their descendants. The Government can help in this regard by encouraging private sector initiatives and simplifying bureaucratic procedures.

Health care and nutrition are also important concerns. Preventive and curative health care are generally provided to the urban poor. However, self-prescription is still frequently practiced among them, and this oftentimes complicates matters. Therefore, institutional arrangements should be set up that would make possible full subsidy to primary health care so that the poor would no longer be burdened by high medical costs, and an information system on the adverse impacts of self-prescription and self-medication.

Finally, in most cases, the lack of access to basic infrastructure, services, and schooling has been due to improper household registration. Regulations should be modified so that the poor could gain access to these services.

CONCLUSION AND POLICY IMPLICATIONS

The research in this volume confirms the important functional relationship between economic growth and poverty reduction shown by earlier works, notably those at the World Bank (1990) on poverty in general and at the Asian Development Bank on rural poverty (Quibria 1993). The evidence indicates that the decline in poverty (including urban poverty) has been unambiguous and quite pronounced in countries experiencing high rates of economic growth and urbanization, such as the Republic of Korea, Malaysia, and Thailand. Nevertheless, these countries have still to tackle relative income inequality that is becoming increasingly visible, besides pockets of hard-core urban poverty.

In countries with relatively poor-to-modest economic performance, such as those in South Asia and the Philippines, poverty reduction has been correspondingly slow and somewhat unclear. Given the link of urbanization (i.e., changing balance between rural and urban populations) to economic growth *cum* structural transformation, urbanization as such in these countries has also been relatively slow. However, urban population growth (from both natural increase and migration) has been and continues to be substantial, resulting in slow poverty reduction and, in some cases, even an increase in the numbers of urban poor.

Although rural-urban migration generally improves the economic condition of the individual migrant, further mobility into the high-wage formal sector may be restricted owing to labor market segmentation. Besides imperfect markets, other factors, such as "migrant stock" effect, faulty information, and migrants' poor qualifications prevent migration from being an equilibrating mechanism. Thus, the social consequences of migration are likely to be less beneficial than the private gains.

The causes of urban poverty and many urban problems can be traced to policy failure and government neglect, as reflected in inappropriate macroeconomic and sectoral policies. Among other things, these policies have favored large-scale, capital-intensive and metropolis-based industrialization. Public investment in infrastructure has also favored urban areas, particularly large cities, encouraging as well heavy migration to these cities. Economic growth and public infrastructure have, accordingly, mostly benefited the nonpoor. Further, public subsidies for human capital accumulation (especially education and health) have been directed largely to the tertiary levels of service, thereby benefiting the affluent much more than the poor.

The empirical record not only from Asia but also from other developing regions shows that more economic growth can be expected to help all income groups including the poor. The poor benefit in absolute terms when growth occurs, even under an initial condition of highly unequal income distribution. But it is also clear that the poor can benefit to a greater or lesser extent from economic growth depending on the *type* of growth achieved. For instance, labor-intensive growth—in contradistinction to capital-intensive growth—tends to be broad-based, and hence benefits the poor to a greater extent.

Rapid economic growth and structural transformation in East and Southeast Asian countries were essentially the result of a labor-intensive and export-oriented development strategy. This type of growth was broad-based, generating substantial employment and raising the living standards at all socioeconomic strata, including the lowest stratum. Thus, a central theme of this volume is that economic growth —especially *broad-based* growth—plays a pivotal role in poverty reduction in both rural and urban areas.

Broad-based growth must also be the overriding theme of development strategy. However, this alone is not sufficient and the overall thrust must be complemented by suitable sectoral and spatial policies. An important example is investment in social infrastructure—such as education, health and nutrition, and family planning—which can raise the quality and productivity of labor and enhance human development. If these social investments are judiciously allocated or targeted sectorally and spatially according to equity criteria, they can go a long way toward poverty reduction, both intra-generationally and inter-generationally.

In addition, social safety nets are often called for to reduce poverty of a chronic and structural nature. However, safety net programs entail a significant fiscal expense that must be financed internally through taxes or externally through foreign aid. Without rapid and sustained economic growth, it is extremely difficult for these programs to be viable, inasmuch as there are invariably numerous claims on limited government revenue and foreign aid cannot always be relied on.

A great deal of caution is needed for government intervention in terms of antipoverty programs. Besides the budgetary constraints, government spending influences resource allocation to the extent that the immediate recipients of the expenditure affect subsequent spending in ways that would be different in the absence of the intervention. Often the consequence on resource allocation is distortionary. There is a common tendency to identify a "problem" and propose a "solution" by way of a government intervention without analyzing carefully the benefits and costs of alternative interventions, including no intervention. This propensity must be tempered or corrected.

Moreover, there is increasing evidence that some programs of public spending, taxation, and regulation only serve to encourage "rent seeking," and thus benefit the politically influential groups at the expense of the interest of the majority. Although many studies on rent-seeking activities in developed and developing countries have been reported, no comprehensive estimates of their extent and social costs are available. Estimating specific effects on the urban poor appears to be a very difficult task. But a reasonable conjecture is that rent-seeking interventions have been detrimental to economic growth in general, and that the poor are highly unlikely to be beneficiaries of such activities.

In general, direct poverty reduction programs suffer from imprecise targeting, resulting in wastage due to leakages. These programs could be made less costly if the extent of their coverage is restricted (say, to the "poorest of the poor") and targeting is improved. There are increasing attempts at adopting such methods as individual price discrimination, geographic price discrimination, self-selection, and wealth indicators. But more pilot-testing and refinements are needed. Moreover, poverty reduction projects (e.g., public works, housing infrastructure, and skills training) should be formulated and executed within the framework of policies and strategies for national development.

The spatial concentration of the urban population in general and the urban poor in particular has advantages and disadvantages. The advantages are scale economies and logistical and administrative efficiency, such as more convenient delivery of infrastructure and basic social services. The disadvantages are negative externalities and social costs, including environmental and health costs, which tend to afflict the poor more deleteriously than the nonpoor. On balance, it appears that diseconomies of agglomeration and congestion have risen to such a degree in a number of Asian primate cities that more serious efforts to promote regional growth centers are warranted. Such a strategy would contribute to narrowing interregional disparities in economic growth and living standards, while enhancing rural-urban linkages. This strategy should be complemented by the promotion of small-scale enterprises in the regional urban centers to which the poor have easier access.

Environmental degradation is frequently associated with poverty, but this link reflects, in large part, the nature of incentives created by market failures and the nature of property rights. It is possible to establish incentives and property rights that will improve the environment and the conditions of the poor. For instance, extending land rights to squatters increases their opportunities for raising their earnings through investments with long gestation, as well as encourages them to improve their housing and surrounding environment.

Finally, strong complementarity between the government and private market and nonmarket organizations is required in the pursuit of economic growth and poverty reduction efforts. At the very least, government policies should not run at cross purposes with private enterprise and initiatives. Private sector participation and enterprise are indispensable owing to the fiscal constraints of governments. The government should provide an "enabling environment" and encourage self-reliance in poor communities while, at the same time, enforcing rules and regulations fairly toward achieving sustainable development in both rural and urban areas.

Notes

1. Rate of urbanization is defined as the average annual rate of change in percentage urban.

2. This is completed in terms of having a preponderant majority, say, two thirds, of total population residing in urban areas.
3. The research project was under the ADB's regional technical assistance (RETA), "Critical Issues and Policy Measures to Address Urban Poverty." The country studies are published in *Asian Development Review*, vol. 12, no. 1 (1994).
4. Poverty concepts and measurements are discussed extensively in Quibria (1991) and Srinivasan (1993), among others. This section provides a brief summary of the main points.
5. A part of urban growth from natural increase and/or migration is accounted for by the reclassification of villages near urban centers as occupations and segments of the work force change from agricultural to nonagricultural categories.
6. See endnote number three.

References

Ahmad, Ehtisham. 1991. "Social Security and the Poor: Choices for Developing Countries." *World Bank Research Observer*. vol. 6. no. 1. pp. 105–127.

Atkinson, Anthony. 1991. "Comparing Poverty Rates Internationally: Lessons from Recent studies in Developed Countries." *World Bank Economic Review*. vol. 5. no. 1. pp. 3–22.

Balisacan, Arsenio M. 1994. "Urban Poverty in the Philippines: Nature, Causes, and Policy Measures." *Asian Development Review*. vol. 12. no. 1.

Behrman, Jere R. 1993. "Macroeconomic Policies and Rural Poverty: Issues and Research Strategies." In *Rural Poverty in Asia: Priority Issues and Policy Options*, edited by M. G. Quibria. Hong Kong: Oxford University Press for Asian Development Bank.

Fields, Gary S. 1994. "Income Distribution in Developing Economies: Conceptual, Data and Policy Issues in Broad-Based Growth." In *Critical Issues in Asian Development*, edited by M.G. Quibria. Forthcoming.

Firdausy, Carunia Mulya. 1994. "Urban Poverty in Indonesia: Trends, Issues, and Policies." *Asian Development Review*. vol. 12. no. 1.

Gunatilleke, Godfrey, and Myrtle Perera. 1994. "Urban Poverty in Sri Lanka: Critical Issues and Policy Measures." *Asian Development Review*. vol. 12. no. 1.

Khundker, Nasreen, Wahiddudin Mahmud, Binayak Sen, and Monawar Uddin Ahmed. 1994. "Urban Poverty in Bangladesh: Trends, Determinants, and Policy Issues." *Asian Development Review*. vol. 12. no. 1.

Kim, Jong-Gie. 1994. "Urban Poverty in Korea: Critical Issues and Policy Measures." *Asian Development Review*. vol. 12. no. 1.

Krueger, Anne. 1974. "The Political Economy of the Rent-Seeking Society." *American Economic Review*. pp. 291–303.

Lewis, W. Arthur. 1978. *The Evolution of the International Economic Order*. Princeton: Princeton University Press.

Mathur, Om Prakash. 1994. "The State of India's Urban Poverty." *Asian Development Review*. vol. 12. no. 1.

Mayo, Stephen, Stephen Malpezzi, and David Gross. 1986. "Shelter Strategies for the Urban Poor in Developing Countries." *World Bank Research Observer*. vol. 1. no. 2. pp. 183–204.

Mills, Edwin, and Charles Becker. 1986. *Studies in Indian Urban Development*. New York: Oxford University Press for the World Bank.

Pernia, Ernesto. 1985. "Implications of Urbanization for Food Policy Analysis in Asian Countries." NUPRI (Nihon University Population Research Institute) Research Paper Series, no. 26. (Tokyo: Nihon University).

_____ . 1991. "Aspects of Urbanization and the Environment in Southeast Asia." *Asian Development Review*. vol. 9. no. 2. pp. 113–136.

Quibria, M. G. 1991. "Understanding Poverty: An Introduction to Conceptual and Measurement Issues." *Asian Development Review*. vol. 9. no. 2. pp. 90–112.

_____ . 1993 (ed.). *Rural Poverty in Developing Asia: Priority Issues and Policy Options*. Hong Kong: Oxford University Press for Asian Development Bank.

Ratanakomut, Somchai, Charuma Ashakul, and Thienchay Kirananda. 1994. "Urban Poverty in Thailand: Critical Issues and Policy Measures." *Asian Development Review*. vol. 12. no. 1.

Srinivasan, T. N. 1993. "Rural Poverty: Conceptual, Measurement and Policy Issues." In *Rural Poverty in Developing Asia: Priority Issues and Policy Options*, edited by M.G. Quibria. Hong Kong: Oxford University Press for Asian Development Bank.

World Bank. 1990. *World Development Report 1990*. Washington: World Bank.

Chapter Two

Issues of Urban and Spatial Development

Ernesto M. Pernia

INTRODUCTION

Conventional thinking behind urbanization and spatial population distribution essentially derives from the relationship between economic growth and structural change. Economic growth involves rising levels of productivity which result in structural changes with accompanying spatial shifts. Labor migration occurs in response to changing demands in the agriculture, industry, and service sectors. Since the demand for agricultural output is relatively inelastic while that for nonagricultural products is relatively elastic, the flow of labor is from rural to urban areas, given rising levels of productivity in agriculture. Improvements in productivity are then translated into increases in income which, in turn, result in a changing composition of spending in favor of nonagricultural and urban goods.

A principal consequence of structural and spatial shifts was expected to be the equalization of incomes between rural and urban areas, as well as among regions in a country. However, such equalization has generally not occurred for several reasons. A country's historical, geographic, and demographic factors are among the reasons. Imperfect markets and labor market segmentation are also important factors. Additionally, implicit and explicit spatial policies of the government are considered part of the explanation.

In an analysis of urban poverty (or poverty in general), issues of urbanization and spatial development form an essential part for a number of reasons. First, urbanization is associated with economic growth which, in turn, underpins the process of reducing poverty in the long run. Second, rapid urbanization—a common fact in many Asian developing countries—is creating severe pressures on cities and straining urban absorptive capacity, thereby slowing poverty reduction or even aggravating urban poverty in many cases. Third, an emerging consensus among development analysts and policy experts is that more balanced regional and rural-urban development is a critical element in a long-term strategy for poverty reduction.

This chapter provides a broad context for the analysis of urban poverty, more specific aspects of which will be taken up in the subsequent chapters. The chapter first reviews trends and patterns of urbanization and population distribution in Asia, and discusses important underlying forces besides the market mechanism. It also examines such issues as the pace of urbanization and urban population growth and the role of migration in this growth, the characteristics of urban systems, the effects of income and sectoral growth differences and of population growth on urbanization, and the relative efficacy of spatial policies. The chapter then presents some policy implications and approaches to spatial and urban problems.

TRENDS AND PATTERNS OF URBANIZATION

Official definitions of the term *urban* vary and the quality of data may be uneven; both will have a bearing on comparisons of urbanization trends and patterns among countries. There are also differences among countries in the definitions of large and small cities or towns. The definitions used in this chapter are those of the countries concerned (a practice adopted by the United Nations), since national statistical offices are considered the appropriate judges in this regard. It is important, moreover, to be clear about the distinction between *urbanization* and *urban population growth*. Following accepted practice in the literature, the former is here defined as the rise in the proportion (percentage share) of the total population living in urban places. It connotes the changing balance between rural and urban populations brought about by spatial shifts (migration) of people from rural to urban areas and by differences in the rates of natural increase of the population in the two areas. Hence, *urbanization*—a structural phenomenon linked in some way to structural economic change—should not be confused with *urban population growth*—a measure of absolute change which refers only to urban areas and has no reference to rural population growth. It is obvious, nonetheless, that urbanization and urban population growth are closely related.[1]

Level and Pace of Urbanization

Asia as a whole is, by world standards, not yet highly urbanized. In 1990, the region was slightly less than a third (31.2 per cent) urban,[2] similar to Africa. This level of urbanization was far below that for Latin America (71.5 per cent) and even lower than the average for the less developed regions (34.3 per cent). However, because Asia is by far the largest region, its comparatively low average urbanization level hardly reflects the wide variation across subregions and countries (Table 2.1).

Among the Asian subregions (excluding the special case of the South Pacific), South Asia has the lowest urbanization level at 24.9 per cent, with India, the largest country in the subregion, very close to this level. Notable deviations from this mean are Bhutan (5.3 per cent), Nepal (10.9 per cent), and Pakistan (32 per cent). South Asian countries can expect accelerated urbanization in the years to come. This will especially be true of such countries as Bangladesh, India, and Pakistan although their urbanization levels will be only in the 30–45 per cent range by 2010. The levels could be higher if economic growth and structural change speed up as a consequence of economic reforms that are underway in these countries.

Southeast Asia's urbanization level is not much higher (29.2 per cent) than that of South Asia, and countries in this subregion expectedly also exhibit a wide range from about 12 per cent for Cambodia to 43 per cent for Malaysia, to 100 per cent for Singapore. Many Southeast Asian countries, mainly those in the Association of Southeast Asian Nations (ASEAN), are apt to maintain their rapid pace of urbanization in conjunction with sustained rates of economic growth and structural change. Lao PDR and Viet Nam are likely to follow in the trail of the ASEAN countries, given the transformation of their economies to the market system. Nevertheless, by 2010, countries in Southeast Asia, except Malaysia and the Philippines, will remain below the 50 per cent urbanization mark.[3]

East Asian urbanization (29.1 per cent level) is predominantly reflective of the PRC which is 26 per cent urban, in contrast to the other countries in the subregion which are well past the 50 percent level. While these other countries will continue their urban deceleration in the years ahead, the PRC will tend to urbanize at a faster pace, especially if its liberalization and deregulation policies continue. However, by 2010, the PRC is projected to be only 43 per cent urban.

Although there are many factors involved in the urbanization process, as will be discussed below, the above trends and patterns tend to show that the smaller Asian countries have generally urbanized faster than the larger ones, such as the PRC, India, and Indonesia, which will remain more rural than urban in 2010. The trends taken in perspective also underscore earlier observations that the critical issue

Table 2.1
Level of Urbanization and Annual Change
(percentages)

Subregion/Country	Level of Urbanization				Average Annual Change		
	1950	1970	1990	2010	1950–1970	1970–1990	1990–2010
East Asia	**11.6**	**19.3**	**29.1**	**44.7**	**2.6**	**2.1**	**2.2**
China, People's Rep. of	11.0	17.5	26.2	43.0	2.3	2.1	2.5
Hong Kong	82.5	87.7	94.1	96.6	0.3	0.4	0.1
Korea, Rep. of	21.4	40.7	72.1	86.3	3.3	2.9	0.9
Mongolia	18.9	45.1	57.9	69.4	4.4	1.3	0.9
Taipei,China	...	59.1	78.8	...	...	1.4	...
Southeast Asia	**14.6**	**19.9**	**29.2**	**42.6**	**1.5**	**1.9**	**1.9**
Cambodia	10.2	11.7	11.6	19.7	0.7	≈0.0	2.7
Indonesia	12.4	17.1	28.8	44.5	1.6	2.6	2.2
Lao PDR	7.2	9.6	18.6	32.6	1.4	3.4	2.8
Malaysia	20.4	27.0	43.0	58.4	1.4	2.4	1.5
Philippines	27.1	33.0	42.7	55.7	1.0	1.3	1.3
Singapore	100.0	100.0	100.0	100.0	0.0	0.0	0.0
Thailand	10.5	13.3	22.2	36.6	1.2	2.6	2.5
Viet Nam	11.6	18.3	19.9	27.4	2.3	0.4	1.6
South Asia	**15.8**	**19.0**	**24.9**	**34.6**	**0.9**	**1.4**	**1.6**
Bangladesh	4.2	7.6	16.4	30.3	3.0	3.9	3.1
Bhutan	2.0	3.1	5.3	11.4	2.2	2.7	3.9
India	17.3	19.8	25.5	33.8	0.7	1.3	1.4
Myanmar	16.2	22.8	24.8	35.4	1.7	0.4	1.8
Nepal	2.3	3.9	10.9	23.2	2.7	5.3	3.8
Pakistan	17.5	24.9	32.0	45.4	1.8	1.3	1.8
Sri Lanka	14.4	21.9	21.4	30.7	2.1	≈0.1	1.8
Pacific Islands	**4.3**	**14.2**	**19.5**	**29.5**	**6.2**	**1.6**	**2.1**
Fiji	24.2	34.8	39.3	48.7	1.8	0.6	1.1
Papua New Guinea	0.7	9.8	15.8	26.7	14.2	2.4	2.6
Asia	13.6	19.3	27.4	39.8	1.7	1.8	1.9
World Total	**29.3**	**36.6**	**43.1**	**52.8**	**1.1**	**0.8**	**1.0**
More Developed Regions	54.3	66.6	72.7	79.1	1.0	0.4	0.4
Less Developed Regions	17.0	24.7	34.3	46.8	1.9	1.7	1.6

... means data are not available.
Note: The figure for Asia excludes West Asia.
Sources: United Nations 1992b; Asian Development Bank 1989, 1992.

has not been so much rapid urbanization per se as high overall population growth rates occurring in both rural and urban areas (Davis 1965, 1972; Pernia 1977; Fuchs et al. 1987). A key related problem, of course, has been slow economic growth and structural change, particularly prior to the mid-1980s, in many Asian countries including the large ones.

Urban Population Growth

Urban population growth in developing Asia as a whole was at a sustained high annual rate of about 4.0 per cent—3.25 times rural population growth—in the 1980s[4] but appears to be beginning to slow in the 1990s. Growth was even higher in East Asia at just under 5 per cent, owing mainly to the exceedingly high rate of 6.7 per cent in the PRC (see Table 2.2 for longer time intervals and Appendix Table 2.1 for rural population growth).

In Southeast Asia, urban growth was at its peak of about 4.3 per cent per annum in the 1980s, with rates for Indonesia and other large countries close to or exceeding 5 per cent. Urban growth deceleration is also apparent in the 1990s for these countries and the subregion as a whole. On the other hand, South Asia absorbed urban growth of around 4 per cent in the 1980s and will sustain this rate in the 1990s before experiencing the beginnings of a slowdown. Urban growth in Bangladesh and Nepal was well over 6 per cent in the 1980s and will stay at above 5 per cent beyond the turn of the century. Pakistan's rate was about 5 per cent in the 1980s, dropping somewhat in the 1990s. In India, the urban growth rate was slightly below 4 per cent in the 1980s; this will be maintained through the year 2005 before decelerating.

Despite slowing urban population growth in most Asian countries in the 1990s or thereafter, huge population bases mean that large additional numbers of population in urban areas will persist for some time to come. Accordingly, greater efforts and more substantial resources will need to be devoted to such nagging problems as poverty, unemployment and underemployment, inadequate infrastructure and social services, and environmental degradation.

Internal migration plays an increasing role in urban population growth in the process of economic development. Broadly, in the more developed countries, the share of migration and reclassification of places in urban growth has been around 60 per cent, with the balance being accounted for by natural increase; in the less developed countries the situation has been the reverse. This pattern also applies to

Table 2.2
Urban Population and Annual Growth Rates

Subregion/Country	Urban Population (thousands)				Growth Rate (per cent)		
	1950	1970	1990	2010	1950–1970	1970–1990	1990–2010
East Asia	**67,144**	**170,645**	**356,178**	**657,080**	**4.8**	**3.7**	**3.1**
China,							
People's Rep of	61,024	144,953	302,209	605,995	4.4	3.7	3.5
Hong Kong	1,629	3,458	5,374	6,125	3.8	2.2	0.7
Korea, Rep. of	4,347	12,995	31,288	42,500	5.6	4.5	1.5
Mongolia	144	566	1,269	2,460	7.1	4.1	3.4
Taipei,China	...	8,673	16,038	...	...	3.1	...
Southeast Asia	**23,978**	**51,560**	**117,290**	**233,249**	**3.9**	**4.2**	**3.5**
Cambodia	443	812	970	2557	3.1	0.9	5.0
Indonesia	9,863	20,534	53,060	109,107	3.7	4.9	3.7
Lao PDR	127	261	782	2,320	3.7	5.6	5.6
Malaysia	1,244	2,929	7,701	15,268	4.4	5.0	3.5
Philippines	5,695	12,380	26,661	49,800	4.0	3.9	3.2
Singapore	1,022	2,075	2,710	3,158	3.6	1.3	0.8
Thailand	2,097	4,749	12,148	24,459	4.2	4.8	3.6
Viet Nam	3,487	7,820	13,258	26,580	4.1	2.7	3.5
South Asia	**74,581**	**140,450**	**288,834**	**581,203**	**3.2**	**3.7**	**3.6**
Bangladesh	1,774	5,074	18,691	53,757	5.4	6.7	5.4
Bhutan	15	32	82	281	3.9	4.8	6.4
India	61,695	109,616	216,081	401,717	2.9	3.5	3.1
Myanmar	2,881	6,188	10,353	21,798	3.9	2.6	3.8
Nepal	187	450	2,139	7,193	4.5	8.1	6.3
Pakistan	6,923	16,354	37,809	89,830	4.4	4.3	4.4
Sri Lanka	1,106	2,736	3,679	6,627	4.6	1.5	3.0
Pacific Islands	**81**	**418**	**898**	**2,038**	**8.6**	**3.9**	**4.2**
Fiji	70	181	285	431	4.9	2.3	2.1
Papua New Guinea	11	237	613	1,607	16.6	4.9	4.9
Asia	165,784	363,073	763,200	1,473,570	4.0	3.8	3.3
World Total	**737,495**	**1,352,143**	**2,282,367**	**3,778,494**	**3.1**	**2.7**	**2.6**
More Developed Regions	452,081	698,438	880,947	1,060,729	2.2	1.2	0.9
Less Developed Regions	285,414	653,705	1,401,420	2,717,765	4.2	3.9	3.4

... means data are not available.
Sources: United Nations 1992b; Asian Development Bank 1989, 1992.

Asian countries (United Nations 1984). Additionally, to the extent that economic growth is accompanied by fertility transition, the share of migration steadily expands relative to that of natural increase. In fact, this has been happening in countries that have undergone or are undergoing rapid economic growth and structural transformation, such as two of the newly industrializing economies (NIEs) (Republic of Korea and Taipei,China) and the near-NIEs (Thailand, Malaysia, and Indonesia). This pattern can be expected to apply to other Asian countries as well, following in the path of structural reforms leading to improved economic performance.

To the degree that these economic reforms are complemented by more effective population policy, as in the NIEs and near-NIEs, economic growth can be more sustained, with the side effect of natural increase playing a lesser role in the urban growth balance. In terms of policies and approaches to deal with urban growth, there would in principle be an advantage if such growth were due more to an increase in migrants belonging to the labor force than to an increase in dependent children. This is because in the former case, cities would be relatively less burdened by expenditures for basic social services. On the other hand, employment would be a critical issue in the short run.

CHARACTERISTICS OF URBAN SYSTEMS

Urban Primacy and Dispersal Trends

A salient characteristic of urban systems in developing countries, not least those in Asia, has been the concentration of population and economic activity in one or a few large cities. This is commonly referred to as urban primacy and the primate city is typically the national capital. A convenient and useful measure of urban primacy is the percentage of a country's urban population (or total population) residing in the largest urban agglomeration, which is also known as its primate city. Urban primacy is perceived to be a manifestation of agglomeration and scale economies needed for economic efficiency and growth. Its degree is often associated with, inter alia, a country's historical factors, geography and physical size, stage of development, system of government, and policies.

The data indicate broadly varying trends in urban primacy among developing countries in Asia (Table 2.3). In East Asia, the Republic of Korea, with 23.5 per cent of urban population residing in Seoul, had the highest spatial concentration in 1950. Urban primacy peaked at about 41 per cent in 1970, thereafter diminishing gradually to about 36 per cent in 1990, and is expected to slide further to 34 per cent at the turn of the century. This reflects some dispersal of Seoul's (actual and potential growth in) population and economic activity to the satellite cities of Inchon and Taejon. At the same time, Taegu has served as an intermediate magnet in the corridor between Seoul and Pusan. Nonetheless, the share of total population in Seoul rose steadily from 5 per cent in 1950 to 26 per cent in 1990, and is expected to rise to more than 27 per cent by the year 2000 (Appendix Table 2.2).

Urban primacy in Taipei,China had been far less pronounced than in the Republic of Korea. This has been attributed by observers to a development strategy that put sufficient and early emphasis on the development of agriculture and small-scale industries. Kaohsiung city (just half the size of Taipei) in the south and other intermediate urban centers such as Taichung and Tainan have contributed to a more balanced regional development.

In contrast to the Korean case is the PRC's urban primacy which has been low and declining from about 9 per cent concentration in Shanghai in 1950 to 3.5 per cent in 1990. The share of urban population in Beijing, the capital and second largest city, was even smaller and also declining over time. The PRC's relative lack of spatial concentration is most likely related to its geographic size and political system. It has several secondary or intermediate urban centers, foremost among which are Tianjin, Shenyang, Wuhan, and Guangzhou.

In Southeast Asia, Thailand stands out as having the highest spatial concentration (in all Asia, in fact), with 57 per cent of the urban population located in Bangkok as of 1990, followed by the Philippines (32 per cent), Viet Nam (22 per cent), Malaysia (22 per cent), and Indonesia (16 per cent). Bangkok's primacy is probably attributable to its geography, especially the lack of other adequate harbors in coastal areas to service the economy. However, this urban concentration appears to have been easing slowly from its high of 65.5 per cent in 1970 to a projected 55 per cent by 2000, likely reflecting agglomeration diseconomies and dispersal policies (such as the development of the eastern seaboard).

Similar signs of primacy reversal have also been apparent in Indonesia beginning in the 1960s, and in the Philippines and Viet Nam in the 1980s. Jakarta's urban population share, which was relatively low to begin with, was down to about 16 per cent in 1990. Even such secondary cities as Bandung and Surabaya have been showing diminishing urban population shares, suggesting that smaller cities

Table 2.3
Urban Primacy
Percentage of Urban Population Residing in Urban Agglomerations
(with 1 million + residents in 1990)

Subregion/City/Country	1950	1960	1970	1980	1990	2000
East Asia						
Beijing, PRC	6.4	5.0	5.6	4.6	2.8	2.3
Shanghai, PRC	8.8	7.1	7.7	6.0	3.5	2.8
Seoul, Rep. of Korea	23.5	34.1	40.9	38.2	35.7	33.6
Taipei,China	...	...	20.4	...	17.0	...
Southeast Asia						
Jakarta, Indonesia	19.9	19.8	19.1	17.9	16.4	15.9
Kuala Lumpur, Malaysia	16.7	16.7	15.4	19.4	22.2	23.4
Manila, Philippines	27.1	27.2	28.6	33.0	31.9	31.2
Bangkok, Thailand	64.9	65.1	65.5	58.7	56.8	54.7
Ho Chi Minh City, Viet Nam	24.9	25.9	25.6	26.4	22.2	18.3
South Asia						
Dhaka, Bangladesh	23.7	24.5	29.6	33.0	35.0	35.2
Calcutta, India	7.2	6.9	6.3	5.7	5.1	4.7
Delhi, India	2.3	2.9	3.2	3.5	3.8	3.9
Yangon, Myanmar	23.2	23.3	23.1	27.3	32.0	32.0
Karachi, Pakistan	14.9	16.7	19.1	20.7	19.6	19.0

... means data are not available.
Sources: United Nations 1990; Asian Development Bank 1989, 1992; *Statistical Year-book of the Republic of China* 1991.

and towns in this large country have been absorbing population shifts. However, unlike cities in the PRC and India, Jakarta continues to clearly dominate the country's urban system. Moreover, Jakarta's share of total population doubled to 5 per cent between 1950 and 1990, and is still increasing (Appendix Table 2.2). In Kuala Lumpur, urban population concentration has continued to rise slowly, and is expected to reach more than 23 per cent in 2000. The relatively low primacy of Kuala Lumpur can be ascribed to Malaysia's effective rural development program and its Bumiputra policy (Lim et al. 1992).

In South Asia, urban population concentration is highest in Bangladesh at 35 per cent, followed by Myanmar at 32 per cent, and Pakistan at 20 per cent. As expected, India has the lowest primacy with about 5 per cent and less than 4 per cent of its urban population, respectively, in Calcutta and Delhi (the capital). In Bangladesh, Chittagong and Dhaka switched roles as principal and secondary cities in the early 1960s, with the former experiencing a monotonic reduction in its urban population share and the latter showing the reverse. On the other hand, Karachi's primacy peaked in 1980 and has since been on a downward trend.

In a situation similar to that in cities in the PRC and Indonesia, Calcutta's urban primacy has been declining monotonically while Delhi, though remaining only the third largest city, has been absorbing a continuously larger share of urban population. India's other large cities, such as Bombay and Madras, have also been on a relative decline, while the intermediate cities of Bangalore, Patna, and Surat have been on the upswing. Still other medium-sized urban centers, such as Ahmedabad and Poona, have shown relative stability.

Spatial Dispersal Policies

The foregoing patterns of spatial concentration indicate that the large countries in the region, i.e., the PRC and India, have had comparatively balanced urban structures, as would be expected a priori. The other countries exhibit (as of 1990) wide-ranging degrees of primacy, from a low of 16 per cent in Indonesia (also a relatively large country) to a high of 57 per cent in Thailand.

Owing to official or popular dissatisfaction with spatial imbalances, governments have for some time formulated and implemented, in one way or another and with varying degrees of success, different kinds of explicit population distribution policies (Fuchs and Demko 1981; Fuchs 1983; United Nations 1992). Most notable due to their efficacy are the policies that have been adopted by the PRC. These include policies to contain the growth of large cities and foster the development of intermediate cities and small towns via an array of instruments, such as controls for internal migration and family size, land-use planning, development of coastal cities and special economic zones, service provision and employment generation in small towns. In the Republic of Korea, policies have been directed at controlling the growth of Seoul, reducing the imbalance in the urban structure and stemming rural depopulation, by employing such measures as the "green belt" project, installing legislation which regulates industrial location, providing fiscal incentives and disincentives, constructing satellite cities, promoting regional growth poles, and encouraging rural development through Saemaul Undong.

In Indonesia, the Government has aimed to lessen the imbalance between Java and the outer islands, as well as reduce primacy and uneven urban growth through its transmigration program, rural and urban development in the outer islands, restraints on Jakarta's growth, and industrial dispersal. More recently, the transmigration program has been curtailed owing to budget constraints; accordingly, private sector financing is being sought. In Malaysia, the goal has been to equalize regional development and the distribution of economic benefits among ethnic groups, giving special attention to ethnic Malays (Bumiputra policy), and to develop new townships through rural urbanization (infrastructure and credit and extension services), colonization and resettlement (Federal Land Development Authority [FELDA]), industrial location incentives in low-income states, and urban development and renewal.

In the Philippines, the objective has been to stem urban concentration in Manila and foster balanced regional development via integrated rural development and the promotion of regional growth centers and medium-sized cities and, more recently, through the agrarian reform program. The Government of Thailand continues to regard limiting the growth of Bangkok as a priority and has employed such measures as land-use and zoning regulations, taxation, industrial dispersal, promotion of regional growth centers and, more recently, development of the eastern seaboard to achieve that goal. In Viet Nam, the Government has aimed to slow the pace of urbanization, especially the growth of Ho Chi Minh City, through the establishment of new economic zones and the opening up of land for cultivation in the south, designed to result in large-scale population redistribution.

The thrust of India's five-year development plans has been to improve infrastructure and social services in medium-sized urban centers and small towns to function as service centers for the countryside. In Nepal, spatial policy has attempted to promote rural growth centers and resettlement areas to curtail migration from the Hills to the Terai. Pakistan also aims to modify internal migration patterns through rural development programs such as electrification of villages, provision of health care centers and farm-to-market roads, and through the distribution of land to landless households. Sri Lanka has attempted to curtail metropolitan growth and rural-urban migration through resettlement schemes, and by establishing industries outside Colombo, effecting welfare and income transfers, and providing social services to address rural-urban disparities. Similarly, the Government of Myanmar is building a new capital city in the forest south of Yangon for a target population of four million.

A common theme runs through the above spatial policy goals and instruments. This is to slow or reverse urban concentration by means of programs to spur the development of alternate urban centers, intermediate cities and small towns, as well as to energize rural areas to discourage rural out-migration. Apart from the PRC (which in many ways is a special case), Malaysia and Sri Lanka are noted for having contained spatial concentration through effective rural development strategies (Lim et al. 1992; Abeysekera 1981). A number of countries have more recently begun to show signs of primacy reversal, as discussed in the preceding section, including Indonesia, Republic of Korea, Philippines, Thailand, and Viet Nam. By contrast, other countries, notably Bangladesh and Myanmar, are manifesting either persisting or further increasing concentration. To what extent the apparent primacy reversals are attributable to lagged effects of explicit spatial policies, to natural forces of agglomeration diseconomies, or to macroeconomic policy reforms is an empirical question for each country to investigate.

Megacities

Many primate cities in Asia have grown to become megacities, and others are rapidly increasing in size to assume such status by the end of the century[5] (Table 2.4). This is a remarkable phenomenon fraught with various implications, favorable and unfavorable. In 1960, there were only two megacities in the region, namely, Tokyo and Shanghai. In 1970, Beijing was added, and Asia had three of the ten megacities in the world, or two of the five in the developing world. By 1980, Bombay, Calcutta, Osaka, and Seoul had assumed similar status, and Asia had seven of the world's 15 megacities. In 1990, with Tianjin, Jakarta, Delhi, and Manila becoming megacities, developing Asia contained nine of the 14 megacities in the less developed regions. In the year 2000, four more Asian cities are expected to reach megacity status for a total of 13 of the 22 in the developing world. By contrast, there are still only six in the more developed regions, a number which has remained unchanged since 1980.

The present megacities in East Asia (including Japan) experienced their peak growth in the 1950s, long before they became megacities; their growth rates ranged from 4.1 per cent per annum for Osaka to 8.4 per cent for Seoul (Table 2.5). In the 1990s, the annual growth rates are expected to be as low as 0.1 per cent for Osaka and 3.1 per cent for Tianjin.

In Southeast Asia, Manila and Bangkok grew fastest in the 1970s when they were in the 3.0–3.5 million range, while Jakarta's expansion rate peaked in the 1980s, also prior to its having achieved megacity status. All three cities continue to expand at a fairly brisk annual rate of 3.5–4.0 per cent.

Four of the six emerging megacities in South Asia are in India. Among the largest in developing Asia, their annual growth rates have remained at the 2.7–5.5 per cent range. Dhaka has been the fastest growing (6–7 per cent per annum in 1980–2000) among both actual and potential megacities in Asia. Meanwhile, Karachi is expanding at an annual rate of over 4 per cent.

The general slowdown in the growth of the largest urban agglomerations in Asia has been closely related with the process of spatial deconcentration and the emergence of regional growth centers and secondary cities in the various countries. While these trends may be heartening to policymakers and planners concerned with promoting

Table 2.4
Population Size of Urban Agglomerations in Asia
(with 8 million + residents in 2000)
(millions)

Agglomeration	Country	1950	1970	1990	2000
East Asia					
Beijing	PRC	3.9	8.1	10.8	14.0
Shanghai	PRC	5.3	11.2	13.4	17.0
Tianjin	PRC	2.4	5.2	9.4	12.7
Seoul	Rep. of Korea	1.0	5.3	11.0	12.7
Southeast Asia					
Jakarta	Indonesia	2.0	3.9	9.3	13.7
Manila	Philippines	1.5	3.5	8.5	11.8
Bangkok	Thailand	1.4	3.1	7.2	10.3
South Asia					
Dhaka	Bangladesh	0.4	1.5	6.6	12.2
Bangalore	India	0.8	1.6	5.0	8.2
Bombay	India	2.9	5.8	11.2	15.4
Calcutta	India	4.4	6.9	11.8	15.7
Delhi	India	1.4	3.5	8.8	13.2
Karachi	Pakistan	1.0	3.1	7.7	11.7

Source: United Nations 1991.

regional development or preoccupied with the familiar problems of big cities, the momentum of growth will push these urban agglomerations to higher levels before stabilization is achieved and regional development becomes self-sustaining. National urbanization policy must understand the key trends and underlying forces in each country, so that suitable instruments can be adopted to help bring about the objectives of regional development. Also, such policy must recognize the important function of the megacity in the system of supra-national cities, especially in the dynamic Asian region (Lo and Yeung 1994). Prudent and efficient urban management can enhance both   the national and supra-national roles of the megacity, while dealing with typical big-city problems.

FACTORS ASSOCIATED WITH URBANIZATION

Income Level, Sectoral Growth, and Population Growth

The relationship of urbanization with economic development is well recognized. If data on levels of urbanization are plotted against the logarithms of per capita incomes, the result is an upward-sloping curve (Figure 2.1).[6] Evidently countries at higher economic levels also tend to be more highly urbanized. However, the level of income alone does not suffice to explain the pattern of urbanization across countries. Besides historical and geographical parameters, internal and international market forces, macroeconomic and sectoral policies, and explicit spatial and urban policies, among others, have direct or indirect influences on the nature and pace of urbanization. As the effects of these various factors tend to be peculiar to each country's spatial development, an analysis of urbanization should be a country-specific exercise. Various country studies do allude to the aforementioned factors as the principal explanatory variables with respect to urbanization and population distribution (e.g., Pernia 1977; Mills and Song 1979; Abeysekera 1980; Mohan 1984; Becker et al. 1992).

A number of cross-national studies show consistent results. For instance, data on 66 low-income and middle-income countries were analyzed to determine the relative significance of specified factors in explaining the variation in level of urbanization, pace of urbanization, and degree of urban concentration (Tolley and Thomas 1987). The hypothesized explanatory variables included the per capita income rank of a country, the growth rate of per capita income, the growth

Table 2.5
Average Annual Rate of Change of Urban Agglomerations
(with 8 million + residents in 2000)
(per cent)

Subregion/ Agglomeration	Country	1950– 1960	1960– 1970	1970– 1980	1980– 1990	1990– 2000
East Asia						
Beijing	PRC	4.7	2.5	1.1	1.8	2.6
Shanghai	PRC	5.1	2.3	0.5	1.3	2.4
Tianjin	PRC	4.2	3.7	3.3	2.5	3.1
Seoul	Korea, Rep. of	8.4	8.1	4.4	2.8	1.5
Southeast Asia						
Jakarta	Indonesia	3.4	3.4	4.2	4.4	4
Manila	Philippines	3.9	4.4	5.2	3.5	3.3
Bangkok	Thailand	4.6	3.7	4.2	4.1	3.6
South Asia						
Dhaka	Bangladesh	4.3	8.4	7.8	7.0	6
Bangalore	India	4.3	3.2	5.5	5.7	5
Calcutta	India	2.1	2.3	2.7	2.7	2.8
Delhi	India	5.0	4.4	4.5	4.6	4.1
Bombay	India	3.4	3.6	3.3	3.3	3.2
Karachi	Pakistan	5.9	5.2	4.6	4.4	4.1

Source: United Nations 1991.

rate of total population, and dummy variables denoting the region in which a country is located.

The results showed the highest degree of correlation ($R^2 = 0.77$) for the level of urbanization function, with income rank being the most significant independent variable. Total population growth had a significant negative effect, attributable to the negative association between income and population growth. The growth of per capita income exhibited a negative, though less significant marginal effect. This is because countries with high levels of income and urbanization usually have relatively low per capita income growth rates, while those experiencing the most rapid per capita income increases are at intermediate stages of economic development and urbanization. Further, the regional dummy variables indicated that individual country circumstances also account for intercountry differences in urbanization levels.

Figure 2.1
Level of Urbanization and GNP Per Capita, 1990

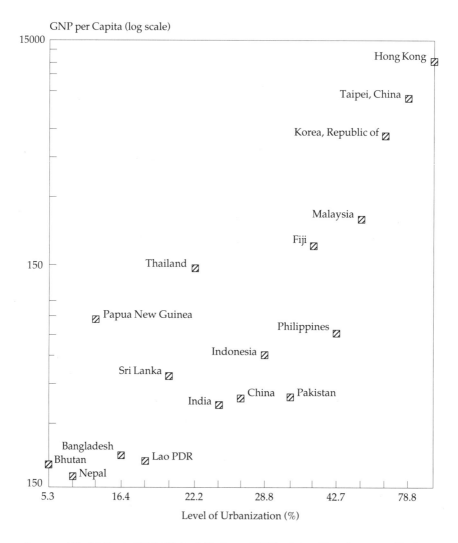

Sources: World Bank 1992; United Nations 1992b; Asian Development Bank
        1989, 1992.

Another study using a similar approach and focusing on Asian
developing countries yielded consistent and complementary results
(Pernia 1982). These showed that: (i) degree of industrialization had
a significant positive effect on the level of urbanization, while

agricultural growth had a negative effect; (ii) growth in manufacturing had a positive though not a significant effect, while total population growth had a significant negative effect on the level of urbanization; (iii) initial level of industrialization had a negative effect on the pace of urbanization, implying that urbanization tends to slow down at higher industrialization (or income) levels; (iv) agricultural growth continued to exert a potent negative effect on the speed of urbanization, while manufacturing had a strong positive effect; (v) total population growth also had a potent negative effect on the pace of urbanization; (vi) manufacturing had a significant positive impact, while population growth had a weak negative effect on spatial concentration (urban primacy); and (vii) the degree of openness of the economy exerted a potent positive effect on spatial concentration.[7]

In sum, while manufacturing growth influences urbanization in a positive way, population growth and agricultural development appear to exert the opposite effect. Population growth tends to dampen the rise in the level of urbanization, though not urban population growth itself. Agricultural growth also seems to retard urbanization in that it allows for greater labor absorption in the rural sector. This may reflect the effect of agricultural growth at low levels of economic development. It is likely that at higher levels, agricultural development would have the reverse result, as in the experience of the industrial countries.

The observed negative relationship between agricultural growth and urbanization appears to support the view that a buoyant agriculture sector can slow migration to the cities. This is an alternative interpretation to the more conventional notion that agricultural development leads to urban migration. The crux would seem to be the prevailing technology used in agriculture, whether labor-using or labor-displacing, besides the more general issue of rural development, including the availability of basic infrastructure and social services in rural areas.[8]

It can be inferred from the foregoing analysis that rapid industrialization and manufacturing growth, coupled with agricultural modernization and overall fertility decline, provided a powerful impetus to urbanization in the two Asian NIEs (Republic of Korea and Taipei,China) and the two near-NIEs (Malaysia and Thailand). These processes also appear to contribute to a quicker transition beyond the peak of urban primacy towards a more balanced urban structure. In comparison, slow economic growth and weak structural transformation, combined with continuing high fertility in South Asian and other similarly-performing economies have resulted in a generally slower pace of urbanization but faster growth in both urban and rural populations. Rapid urban population growth, stemming from relatively high urban fertility as well as voluminous rural out-migration have resulted in concentration in the emerging megacities.

It appears that in the NIEs and near-NIEs, migration has functioned as a relatively effective mechanism in allocating labor between sectors and in alleviating pressure and reducing poverty in the rural areas. In the other countries, however, migration has tended to compound problems in the cities and has done little to ease the burden in the countryside. In many cases, migration from the countryside has been a reaction to natural resource depletion, farm density, natural calamities, and civil conflicts. All in all, the preceding processes reflect the interrelationships among a country's economic growth, structural economic change, demographic transition, population movements, and spatial development.

Implicit and Explicit Spatial Policies

Besides the above factors and processes which underlie urbanization, evidence from research also indicates that government policies are important in one way or another (e.g., Alonso 1970; Renaud 1981; Pernia et al. 1983; Fuchs, et al. 1987). Urbanization and spatial concentration appears to have been partly an unintended consequence of macroeconomic and sectoral policies embodied in the import-substitution industrialization strategies of many Asian countries in the post-war period.

Indications are that concentration of population and industrial activity in a country's capital city has been a rational response to the need to be near the international gateway and the national agencies that furnish the required industrial licenses, foreign exchange allocations, credit, tax privileges, and other incentives. Also, trade policy in industrial countries and price policy in developing countries have strong influences on urban trends and patterns (Kelley and Williamson 1984). Further, excessive regulation and centralization of functions by the national government contribute to spatial concentration (Mills 1992).[9] On the demand side, import substitutes find their main market among urban residents of the capital city.

Infrastructure policy has also often favored the national capital while agricultural policy has tended to effectively penalize the rural sector and subsidize urban consumers (David 1983; Solon 1992). To these implicit spatial policies may be added the national capital's long-established advantage as the center of education and culture,

communications, and modern facilities and services that further enhance its strength and attractiveness.

In reaction to urban primacy and uneven spatial development,
several countries in Asia began to adopt explicit spatial policies, as
discussed above, in the latter part of the 1960s. Policy measures to
pursue decentralization and balanced regional development have
generally included investment incentives for lagging regions, controls
on industrial location in and migration into the metropolitan region,
integrated area development, export processing zones, and regional
growth centers. However, indications are that these measures have
been largely ineffective in countering the deep-seated and more potent
spatial biases of the implicit policies. Moreover, evaluations of the
explicit spatial policy instruments suggest that controls on location
were fundamentally unsound and investment incentives ill-conceived.
Further, the choice of location for export processing zones was based
more on political rather than economic considerations; integrated area
development projects take more time than anticipated to have a
perceptible impact, and sufficient resources may not have been allocated to the designated regional growth centers (Fuchs et al. 1987;
Herrin and Pernia 1987; Pernia 1988).

Policy effectiveness varies among countries, and it is possible that
the incipient or advanced primacy reversals that have become apparent more recently in a number of countries are partly attributable to
the lagged effects of policies.[10] These deconcentration trends may also
be ascribable to successful economic policy reforms having the side
effect of removing the inherent spatial biases of previous policies:
cases in point are Republic of Korea, Taipei,China, Thailand and Malaysia.

CONCLUSION AND POLICY IMPLICATIONS

Asia in the aggregate is, by standards of the other world regions, not
yet highly urbanized. However, within this vast and heterogeneous
region, the trends and patterns of population distribution and spatial
development vary immensely. Even within subregions the variation
across countries is enormous, rendering attempts at generalization
difficult and perhaps not altogether meaningful.

To some extent and in a somewhat loose way, the degree and pace
of urbanization can be predicted from the level of economic development and the rate of economic growth. Thus, the more progressive
economies in East Asia, as well as those in Southeast Asia, have

urbanized rapidly and appear to be in a transition not only to a slowdown in urban population growth but also to a diffusion of urban primacy.

A problem in the less developed Asian economies has been rapid urban population growth, especially in terms of absolute increases on top of already large urban demographic bases, not to mention the growth momentum inherent in young populations. Another critical issue concerns the excessive spatial concentration in the primate cities that have become or are fast emerging as megacities. This is a visible issue because it manifests itself in terms of the highly charged problems of poverty, unemployment and underemployment, inadequate infrastructure and housing, deficient social services, and environmental degradation.[11]

These persistent urban ills indicate that the urban population is growing faster than the economic absorptive capacity of cities. In all likelihood, this continuing gap between urban growth and capacity largely stems from market failure that is further compounded by policy failure. While the majority of governments in the region have expressed the need for policy intervention on urbanization or spatial distribution of population, difficulties remain in clarifying the specific nature, extent and timing of intervention.

Population distribution and urbanization policy is obviously a country-specific matter, and a broad cross-country analysis can at best only suggest some general policy considerations. First, urbanization policy should be formulated and implemented as a functional part of national development strategy, such that conflicts with other policies are minimized, and complementarities optimized. Second, the implicit spatial biases of economywide and sectoral policies, such as fiscal and monetary, trade, industrial, and agricultural policies, should be sufficiently understood. Policy reforms for economic restructuring towards labor-intensive export industries, as well as for deregulation and decentralization, may have the beneficial side effect of reducing the large-city bias.

Third, explicit dispersal policies should be thoroughly re-evaluated for their relevance, timeliness, and overall effectiveness. Research and experience show that locational controls and fiscal incentives have generally not been effective. They are also costly. Access to markets, adequate power and water supply, and communication facilities are more important considerations in determining the location of industries. Any new spatial policy schemes should be formulated in consonance with the government's broader economic and other development policies. Fourth, urban management policy tools that directly address such problems as congestion, pollution, transport, housing, and basic social services are strongly recommended as part of the solution to the overall urbanization problem.

Equally important is a determined policy to improve basic infrastructure and services in towns and rural areas towards raising economic efficiency and living standards. Otherwise, national development strategy will continue to address merely the symptoms of a broader malaise that is partly manifested in urban ills. Furthermore, given the important role played by the demographic factor, an effective policy for slowing population growth, especially in the less developed Asian developing countries, should form part of the policy package.

Appendix Table 2.1
Rural Population and Annual Growth Rates

Subregion/Country	Amount (thousands)				Growth (per cent)		
	1950	1970	1990	2010	1950–1970	1970–1990	1990–2010
East Asia	**510,708**	**711,827**	**868,920**	**812,017**	**1.7**	**1.0**	**−0.3**
China, People's Rep. of	493,736	685,722	851,261	803,951	1.7	1.1	−0.3
Hong Kong	345	484	335	216	1.7	−1.8	−2.2
Korea, Rep. of	16,010	18,928	12,089	6,767	0.8	−2.2	−2.9
Mongolia	617	690	920	1,083	0.6	1.4	0.8
Taipei,China	...	6,003	4,315	...	...	−1.6	...
Southeast Asia	**139,745**	**207,314**	**283,936**	**314,584**	**2.0**	**1.6**	**0.5**
Cambodia	3,903	6,126	7,367	10,403	2.3	0.9	1.7
Indonesia	69,675	99,746	131,223	136,180	1.8	1.4	0.2
Lao PDR	1,628	2,452	3,420	4,799	2.1	1.7	1.7
Malaysia	4,866	7,924	10,191	10,870	2.5	1.3	0.3
Philippines	15,293	25,160	35,776	39,537	2.5	1.8	0.5
Singapore	0	0	0	0	...	...	...
Thailand	17,913	30,996	42,529	42,278	2.8	1.6	−0.0
Viet Nam	26,467	34,910	53,430	70,517	1.4	2.2	1.4
South Asia	**398,701**	**598,964**	**869,319**	**1,100,092**	**2.1**	**1.9**	**1.2**
Bangladesh	40,009	61,597	94,993	123,734	2.2	2.2	1.3
Bhutan	718	989	1,457	2,184	1.6	2.0	2.0
India	295,866	445,295	630,111	787,679	2.1	1.8	1.1
Myanmar	14,951	20,914	31,472	39,833	1.7	2.1	1.2
Nepal	7,995	11,039	17,433	23,855	1.6	2.3	1.6
Pakistan	32,590	49,352	80,314	107,842	2.1	2.5	1.5
Sri Lanka	6,572	9,778	13,539	14,965	2.0	1.6	0.5
Pacific Islands	**1,821**	**2,524**	**3,703**	**4,870**	**1.6**	**1.9**	**1.4**
Fiji	219	339	441	454	2.2	1.3	0.1
Papua New Guinea	1,602	2,185	3,262	4,416	1.6	2.0	1.5
Asia	1,050,975	1,520.629	2,025,878	2,231,563	1.9	1.4	0.5
World Total	**1,778,695**	**2,344,864**	**3,012,933**	**3,371,035**	**1.4**	**1.3**	**0.6**
More Developed Regions	380,344	350,468	330,191	279,803	−0.4	−0.3	−0.8
Less Developed Regions	1,398,359	1,994,395	2,682,742	3,091,233	1.8	1.5	0.7

... means data are not available.
Sources: United Nations 1992b; Asian Development Bank 1989, 1992.

Appendix Table 2.2
Percentage of Total Population Residing in Urban Agglomerations
(with 1 million + residents in 1990)

Subregion/City/Country	1950	1960	1970	1980	1990	2000
East Asia						
Beijing, China, People's Rep. of	0.7	1.0	1.0	0.9	1.0	1.1
Shanghai, China, People's Rep. of	1.0	1.3	1.3	1.2	1.2	1.3
Seoul, Rep. of Korea	5.0	9.4	16.6	21.7	25.7	27.4
Taipei,China	...	...	12.1	...	13.4	...
Southeast Asia						
Jakarta, Indonesia	2.5	2.9	3.3	4.0	5.0	6.3
Kuala Lumpur, Malaysia	3.4	4.2	4.2	6.7	9.6	12.0
Manila, Philippines	7.4	8.3	9.4	12.3	13.6	15.2
Bangkok, Thailand	6.8	8.2	8.7	10.2	12.9	16.1
Ho Chi Minh City, Viet Nam	2.9	3.8	4.7	5.1	4.9	5.0
South Asia						
Dhaka, Bangladesh	1.0	1.3	2.3	3.7	5.8	8.1
Calcutta, India	1.2	1.2	1.3	1.3	1.4	1.5
Delhi, India	0.4	0.5	0.6	0.8	1.0	1.3
Yangon, Myanmar	3.8	4.5	5.3	6.6	7.9	9.1
Karachi, Pakistan	2.6	3.7	4.8	5.8	6.3	7.2

... means data are not available.
Sources: United Nations 1991; Asian Development Bank 1989, 1992; *Statistical Yearbook of the Republic of China* 1991.

Acknowledgements

An earlier version of this chapter appeared as EDRC Report Series
Number 58, which benefited from comments by J.M. Dowling, W.T.C.
Ho, J.S. Lee and P. Blok. Able research assistance was provided by
Emma M. Banaria with secretarial support by Helen K. Buencamino.

Notes

1. The related terminology used in this chapter is as follows: *level*
    of urbanization refers to the proportion (percentage) of the
    population that is urban at a point in time, while *rate* of urbani-
    zation is the pace of change in the level over time. The latter is
    also to be distinguished from rate of urban growth which refers

to the change in the number of people living in urban places relative to the number at the start of a given interval.

2. This average includes West Asia which is the most urbanized among the Asian subregions; without this subregion, the Asian regional average is only 27 per cent.

3. The 50 per cent level roughly marks the inflection point of the logistic urbanization curve, with the 40–60 per cent range representing the phase of fastest urbanization (see Figure 2.1).

4. This 4.0 per cent annual rate of urban population growth also meant that Asia had the fastest urbanization tempo among the world's regions.

5. A megacity is defined by the United Nations as an urban agglomeration with eight million or more inhabitants.

6. Similar scattergrams show curves that approximate a logistic function, as, e.g., in Renaud (1981) and Pernia (1988).

7. A related analysis of urban trends based on a computable general equilibrium model shows that terms of trade between agricultural and manufactured goods, productivity changes, and technical progress (economywide total factor productivity growth) are important determinants (Kelley and Williamson 1984). Unbalanced sectoral productivity increases seem to be the most potent factor. Furthermore, urban growth appears to be sensitive to employment conditions and rents in urban squatter housing, with higher rents tending to dampen urban growth.

8. Various types of agricultural development policy instruments appear to have different spatial effects. Farm mechanization, for example, by raising the marginal productivity of labor, results in labor displacement (Squire 1981). In contrast, by raising both land productivity and average and marginal labor productivities, irrigation tends to retain labor. Hence, for a given increment in output, irrigation would retain a larger work force in agriculture than would mechanization (Preston as referred to in Cho and Bauer 1987).

9. Location in the metropolis has been considered even more important for foreign investment (Fuchs and Pernia 1987; Herrin and Pernia 1987).

10. There is some evidence that some regional growth centers in the Philippines are reducing the dominance of Manila in terms of such global factors as foreign direct investment and exports (Solon 1992).

11.   Some of these problems and corresponding approaches are discussed at length in Asian Development Bank (1987, 1991); Pernia (1992); and Yeung (1992).

References

Abeysekera, Dayalal. 1980. "Urbanization and the Growth of Small Towns in Sri Lanka, 1901–71." Papers of the East-West Population Institute, no. 67. Honolulu.

_____ . 1981. "Regional Patterns of Intercensal and Lifetime Migration in Sri Lanka." Papers of the East-West Population Institute, no. 75. Honolulu.

Alonso, William. 1970. "The Question of City Size and National Policy." Institute of Urban and Regional Development Working Paper, no. 125. Berkeley, California.

Asian Development Bank. 1987. *Urban Policy Issues*. Proceedings of the Regional Seminar on Major National Urban Policy Issues. Manila.

_____ . 1989. *Key Indicators of Developing Asian and Pacific Countries*. Manila: Asian Development Bank.

_____ . 1992. *Key Indicators of Developing Asian and Pacific Countries*. Manila: Asian Development Bank.

Asian Development Bank, and Economic Development Institute. 1991. *The Urban Poor and Basic Infrastructure Services in Asia and the Pacific*. Manila.

Becker, C.M., J.G. Williamson, and E.S. Mills. 1992. *Indian Urbanization and Economic Growth Since 1960*. Baltimore: The Johns Hopkins University Press.

Cho, Lee-Jay, and J.G. Bauer. 1987. "Population Growth and Urbanization: What Does the Future Hold?" In *Urbanization and Urban Policies in Pacific Asia*, edited by R.J. Fuchs, G.W. Jones and E.M. Pernia, pp. 15–37. Boulder and London: Westview Press.

David, Cristina C. 1983. "Economic Policies and Philippine Agriculture." Philippine Institute for Development Studies (PIDS) Working Paper, series no. 83–02. Manila.

Davis, Kingley. 1965. "The Urbanization of the Human Population." *Scientific American* (New York), vol. 213 (September), pp. 28–40.

_____ . 1972. *World Urbanization 1950-70.* 2 vols. Population Monograph, series 4 and 9. Berkeley: University of California Press.

Fuchs, Roland J. 1983. "Population Distribution Policies in Asia and the Pacific: Current Status and Future Prospects." Papers of the East-West Population Institute, no. 83. Honolulu.

Fuchs, Roland J., and G.J. Demko. 1981. "Population Distribution Measures and the Redistribution Mechanism." In *Population Distribution Policies in Development Planning,* edited by Demko and Fuchs, pp. 7–84. New York: UN Population Division.

Fuchs, Roland J., G.W. Jones, and E.M. Pernia, eds. 1987. *Urbanization and Urban Policies in Pacific Asia.* Boulder and London: Westview Press.

Fuchs, Roland J., and E.M. Pernia. 1987. "External Economic Forces and National Spatial Development: Japanese Direct Investment in Pacific Asia." In *Urbanization and Urban Policies in Pacific Asia,* edited by R.J. Fuchs, G.W. Jones and E.M. Pernia, pp. 88–111. Boulder and London: Westview Press.

Herrin, A.N., and E.M. Pernia. 1987. "Factors Influencing the Choice of Location: Local and Foreign Firms in the Philippines." *Regional Studies,* vol. 21, no. 6, pp. 531–541.

Kelley, Allen C., and J.G. Williamson. 1984. *What Drives Third World City Growth? A Dynamic General Equilibrium Approach.* Princeton: Princeton University Press.

Lim, Lin Lean, N. Ogawa, and R.W. Hodge. 1992. "The Impact of an Integrated Agricultural Development Program on Migration in Malaysia." NUPRI Research Paper Series, no. 61. Tokyo.

Lo, Fu-chen, and Yue-man Yeung, eds. 1994. *Emerging World Cities in Pacific Asia: Growth and Adjustment to Global Restructuring.* United Nations University. Forthcoming.

Mills, E.S. 1992. "Urban Efficiency, Productivity, and Economic Development." In *Proceedings of the World Bank Annual Conference on Development Economics,* pp. 221–235. Washington, DC.

Mills, E.S., and B.N. Song. 1979. *Korea's Urbanization and Urban Problems.* Cambridge: Harvard University Press.

Mohan, Rakesh. 1984. "The Effect of Population Growth, the Pattern of Demand and of Technology on the Process of Urbanization." *Journal of Urban Economics,* vol. 15, no. 2 (March).

Pernia, Ernesto M. 1976. "Urbanization in the Philippines: Historical and Comparative Perspectives." Papers of the EWPI, no. 40. Honolulu.

_____ . 1977. *Urbanization, Population Growth and Economic Development in the Philippines.* Westport and London: Greenwood Press.

_____ . 1982. "Asian Urbanization and Development: A Comparative View." *Philippine Review of Economics and Business,* vol. 19, pp. 383–403.

_____ . 1988. "Urbanization and Spatial Development in the Asian and Pacific Region." *Asian Development Review,* vol. 6, no. 1, pp. 86–105.

_____ . 1992. "Southeast Asia." In *Sustainable Cities: Urbanization and the Environment in International Perspective,* edited by R. Stren, R. White and J. Whitney. Boulder: Westview Press.

Pernia, Ernesto M., C. Paderanga, V. Hermoso, and Associates. 1983. *The Spatial and Urban Dimensions of Development in the Philippines.* Manila: Philippine Institute for Development Studies.

Renaud, Bertrand. 1981. *National Urbanization Policy in Developing Countries.* New York: Oxford University Press.

Solon, Orville. 1994. "Global Influences on Recent Urbanization Trends in the Philippines." In *World Cities in Pacific Asia: Growth and Adjustment to Global Restructuring*, edited by Fu-chen Lo and Yue-man Yeung. Forthcoming.

Squire, Lyn. 1981. *Employment Policy in Developing Countries: A Survey of Issues and Evidence*. New York: Oxford University Press.

Statistical Yearbook of the Republic of China. 1991. Republic of China: Directorate General of Budget Accounting and Statistics, Executive Yuan.

Tolley, George S., and Vinod Thomas, eds. 1987. *The Economics of Urbanization and Urban Policies in Developing Countries*. A World Bank Symposium. Washington, DC.

United Nations. 1984. "Population Distribution, Migration and Development." Proceedings of the Expert Group on Population Distribution, Migration and Development, Hammamet, Tunisia, 21–25 March 1983.

_____ . 1991. *World Urbanization Prospects 1990*. Department of Economic and Social Information and Policy Analysis. New York: UN Publications.

_____ . 1992a. *World Population Monitoring 1991*. Department of International Economic and Social Affairs. Sales No. E.92.XIII.2.

_____ . 1992b. *World Urbanization Prospects 1992*. Department of Economic and Social Information and Policy Analysis. New York: UN Publications.

World Bank. 1992. *World Development Report 1992: Development and the Environment*. New York: Oxford University Press.

Yeung, Yue-man. 1992. "China and Hong Kong." In *Sustainable Cities*, edited by Stren, White, and Whitney.

Chapter Three

Urban Poverty and Labor Markets

Dipak Mazumdar

The growth of population in urban areas in Asia, as in other developing countries, has been heavily dependent on rural-urban migration. Therefore, the first topic in an analysis of how the working of labor markets affects urban poverty must be the efficiency of the process of internal migration flows in reducing disparities between regions. This chapter addresses that process, beginning with a review of the literature on rural-urban migration. Does migration lead to economic gains, thereby relieving poverty in both rural and urban areas, or is it a nonrational process exacerbating the incidence of unemployment and low incomes in urban areas? The discussion of that issue leads directly to an analysis of the nature of urban labor markets, and in particular, to the question of the segmentation of these markets into subsectors with widely differing wage levels. This chapter exposes the theory of segmented labor markets and reviews the empirical material related to that theory. It also presents an eclectic framework for understanding intra-urban wage differences in developing countries and outlines the consequent policy implications for poverty reduction.

PROCESS OF RURAL-URBAN MIGRATION
AND URBAN POVERTY

The relationship between rural and urban poverty depends crucially on the nature of migration of the population from rural to urban areas in the economy concerned. At one extreme is the People's Republic of China (PRC) where migration into urban areas is controlled by a system of residential permits. Since there is a large disparity in per capita income between the rural and urban areas in the PRC, the incidence of poverty, by any criterion, is much less in the urban sector. The poor remain in the villages. In most developing countries, however, there is little administrative control on internal migration. Thus, how much of rural poverty will translate into urban poverty depends on the magnitude as well as the determinants, economic or otherwise, of rural to urban migration.

Scale of Migration and Overurbanization Thesis

There is a popular presumption that developing countries, at least since World War II, have experienced urban growth much more rapidly than has been known in the history of economic development of the now developed economies. The presumption has included the Asian countries.

The hypothesis of overurbanization, which appears both explicitly and implicitly in the literature on urban migration, draws its support from two presumptions: factors which tend to "push" people out of rural areas, and factors which "pull" people towards the cities. The first is based on the assumption that the pressure of population has nearly exhausted both the external and internal margins of living, while the pull factor emphasizes the draw of the "city lights" and the rural-urban wage gap. The latter has been highlighted in models of urban migration by Harris and Todaro. Migrants are attracted by the gamble of being absorbed in high wage employment, and are willing to be openly unemployed or to accept very low earnings in the urban labor market for a period of time in the expectation of achieving a high lifetime income.

Some broad data on the pace of urbanization may have relevance here. The most common measure of the rate of urbanization is the annual change in the percentage of the population living in urban areas. Between 1875 and 1900 the percentage urban of the now developed countries grew from 17.2 to 26.1 (Preston, footnote 5). Table 3.1 presents recent data on the scale of urbanization in different groups of countries in the last 25 years. For the low-income and middle-income countries, the increase in the share of urban population is double the increase that occurred for the now developed countries in the last quarter of the nineteenth century. However, there are important differences in the experience of subgroups of the less developed countries. In particular, within Asia, a marked difference is evident between South Asia and East Asia and the Pacific. While South Asian urbanization has been no greater than the nineteenth century experience referred to above, the East Asian pace has been much more accelerated. A comparison of the different rates of growth of the urban population in the two periods 1965–1980 and 1980–1990 shows that the rate of growth of the urban population in the latter period was no higher for any country subgroup with low to middle-income, except for the East Asian subgroup. In fact, remarkably, the near doubling of the rate of growth of the urban population in the countries with low and middle-incomes is due entirely to the quadrupling of the rate of growth for East Asia.

This observation has some implications for the pessimistic view of overurbanization. Since East Asia has experienced one of the fastest rates of growth recorded in history in the last decade, the accelerated pace of urbanization is most likely related to rising incomes. South Asia, with a much more stagnant record of growth, has not changed its pace of urbanization in the 1980s relative to the earlier decade. The implied sensitivity of urban growth to economic growth would seem to undercut the more extreme hypothesis of overurbanization.

The relationship between urbanization and per capita income has been a topic of continuing interest to researchers who have examined levels of urbanization on either an international cross-sectional or

Table 3.1
Urbanization in Different Regions

	Urban Population				Population in Capital City as percentage of		Population in City of >1m as percentage of	
	As a percentage of total population		Average annual growth rate (per cent)					
					Urban	Total	Urban	Total
Country Group	1965	1990	1965– 1980	1980– 1990	1990	1990	1965	1990
Low and middle- income countries	24	44	3.7	6.6	15	6	41	33
Sub-Saharan Africa	14	29	5.8	5.9	32	9	30	29
East Asia and Pacific	19	50	3.0	12.0	9	3	48	30
South Asia	18	26	3.9	3.9	8	2	35	34
Europe	40	60	2.7	2.6	15	10	31	27
Middle East and North Africa	35	51	4.6	4.4	27	13	42	42
Latin America and Caribbean	53	71	3.9	3.0	23	16	44	45
High-income countries	72	77	1.3	0.8	12	9	38	37

Source: World Bank 1992.

time-series basis. The hypothesis is that the functional form connecting the two is logistic, shown by an equation of the type:

$$U^{-1}=a+be^{g(y)}$$

where u is the percentage of population urban; g is a function of y, the per capita GNP; e is the base of natural logarithms; and a and b are parameters to be estimated.

The key characteristics of the logistic function is that the urban share responds slowly to economic development at low levels of per capita income, then accelerates, but again slows down at higher levels.

Mills and Becker (1986) recently estimated a variant of the above equation (1) with an international data set spanning the years 1960 to 1980. Apart from using several versions of per capita GNP, they included two other explanatory variables in their regression model: the share of agricultural employment (A) and time (t).

First, they argued that "economic base theory shows that since industrial output is mostly sold outside the urban area in which it is produced, it influences but is not influenced by the population of the urban area. That makes it a desirable independent variable in our regressions." At the same time, an unknown part of services production is consumed outside the urban area (e.g., agricultural education extension and research services). Thus, there is a case for including the share of manufacturing and service industries together among the explanatory variables. Alternatively, the share of agricultural employment could be used: this is equivalent to including the sum of manufacturing and services employment since the three categories sum to unity.[1]

Second, if the hypothesis that developing countries urbanize faster than is justified by their pace of economic development proves true, then time should be correlated with urbanization. Mills and Becker therefore added time to their set of explanatory variables to test the overurbanization hypothesis.

After some experimentation they found that the best estimate of the logistic equation performed as well as the simpler parabolic form of the functional relationship between urban share and per capita GNP. The following is an example of their set of best equations:

$$U_{it}=73.0286 - 0.7157\ A_{it} + 13.3706Y_{it} - 6.6886Y^2_{\ i} + 1.0338t$$
$$(15.19) \qquad (1.67) \qquad (1.58) \qquad (1.30)$$

$R^2=0.799$; $N=105$, consisting of various countries i and years t (t values are given in parentheses).

A and Y were correlated (about -0.35 in the sample), so that only one tended to be significant in the same regression. The inclusion of A^2 added little to the regressions, but the deletion of Y^2 made most regressions somewhat less satisfactory.

It is seen from the coefficient of t in the equation that urbanization increases as time passes, but the significance level of the coefficient of t is not high and the value is also small. The urban share increases only one percentage point per decade as a result of the passage of time. "The conclusion is that urbanization occurs independently of economic development to only a negligible extent" (Mills and Becker 1986, 20).

The predictions from the above equation for urban shares in different groups of countries are compared to the actual levels shown in Table 3.2.

Table 3.2
Predicted and Actual Values of U, 1980

	Country Type		
	Average Low-Income	Average Middle-Income	Average Industrial
Actual	17	50	77
Predicted	24.6	46.1	77.5

Source: Mills and Becker 1986.

The predicted urban share is not as close to the actual value for low-income countries as for the average industrial country. However, the actual urban share for the low-income countries is lower than what would be expected on the basis of the experience of the industrial countries. From this evidence and alternative equations, Mills and Becker concluded that there is nothing in their estimated models to suggest that present day developing countries are urbanizing too greatly or at too high a rate.

This does not imply, however, that the problem of urban agglomeration today is any less serious than it was in the late nineteenth century. Indeed, there are two major differences today from the earlier experience of the now developed countries. First, the growth rates of urban and rural populations in the developing countries today are much higher simply because the growth rate of the population is higher. Second, Asian urbanization, as in several other parts of the developing world, is characterized by a large concentration of the urban population in the largest or a few very large cities. Both create severe pressures on the developing country's infrastructure. The phenomenon of urban concentration and, in particular, its labor market aspects will be examined in a later section. Before that, the economic causes and consequences of internal migration are summarized from research on individual countries or areas.

Economics of Rural-Urban Migration

Does migration respond to economic incentives? Does it lead to a significant equalization of incomes between origin and destination areas? It is clear that an affirmative to the first question does not imply the same to the second. Even if internal migration is sensitive to economic considerations, the flows might be too small to achieve substantial equalization of income per earner or per capita. Furthermore, the process of migration might be accompanied by certain types of nonequilibrating factors which might prevent the erosion of income differences. The selective survey of migration studies in this section will focus on these two related but separate questions.

Studies on migration which have sought to evaluate the importance of economic factors in migration flows are of two types. One set of studies examined if migration pays for the migrant, and sought to answer this question either by comparing the real income of migrants in urban areas with the income of those of similar groups in rural areas, or by comparing the earnings of migrants with those of natives in the urban sector. Clearly in both cases comparison of gross earnings will not suffice. Factors such as differences in human capital attributes of the samples concerned must be controlled. Earnings functions are generally used for this purpose. Mazumdar, using three cities in Peninsular Malaysia (1981, Chapter 11), found that the experience-earnings profile for male migrants, after controlling for education and race, lay significantly above that for the native population, more so in the metropolis than in the smaller towns. Similar results have been obtained for urban areas in many countries, thus confirming that the private gains from migration are substantial in that migrants seem to do even better than what the observed rural-urban earnings gap would suggest.

There are clearly limitations to this approach to measuring the private gains to migration. Migration produces changes over a prolonged period in a person's life, but the difficulty and expense of collecting longitudinal data sets impede recurring empirical work on the life-cycle effects of migration. As in other fields of economics, inferences about lifetime effects derived from cross-sectional material can sometimes be misleading.

A second set of studies attempts to understand the determinants of migration flows by estimating econometrically macro migration functions. The starting point of these functions is the well-known gravity model. Based somewhat dubiously on nineteenth century physics, this model hypothesizes that the gross migration flow between two areas is directly proportional to the size of the two regions and inversely proportional to the distance between them (Zipf 1946). This formulation leads to an equation such as:[2]

$$M_{ij} = \log K + a_i \ \log P_i + a^2 \log P_j - a_3 \log D_{ij},$$

where

M_{ij} is gross migration from area i to area j,
(generally normalized by dividing the gross
flow by the area of origin population):
P_i, P_j are the population of i and j respectively;
D_{ij} is the distance between i and j;
and K is a constant.

Although some attempts have been made to give behavioral content to this mechanical model,[3] generally it is expanded to include economic variables. These have included income (or wages) in the origin and destination areas; employment rates (or variants to provide an index of labor market tightness); as well as some "push" factors.

If these economic variables are added to the gravity model in multiplicative forms representing ratios of variables in destination and origin areas, an expanded double logarithmic equation is obtained in which M_{ij} of equation (1) is in logarithms, and there are terms added to the right-hand side giving economic characteristics of areas i and j.

Studies of this type have generally achieved results which suggest that the economic factors affecting migration flows are significant, and often strong. Thus the influence of the destination wage on the rate of migration is generally quite substantial. Sabot, for example, found that, *ceteris paribus*, the wage elasticity of the migration rate was 2.0 for urban wages in Tanzania.[4] In some studies, employment conditions or the growth rate of employment in the destination area significantly influence the migration rate in addition to destination wage. Barnum and Sabot (1981) found that in Tanzania the expected wage (as adjusted for the probability of being employed) explained a larger proportion of the variance. As far as push factors in the area of origin are concerned, some studies, though not all, have provided evidence suggesting that such factors have an additional effect on migration flows. Arnold and Cochrane (1980) found that in Thailand, the greater the proportion of land farmed in a *changwat*, the greater the outflow of migration. In a study of India, Banerjee and Kanbur (1981) found that, *ceteris paribus*, the more unequal is the distribution of land, the higher is the rate of migration.

These results from econometric migration functions are consistent with the observations reported earlier, i.e., that generally significant private gains are associated with migration. Migration function studies, however, have also yielded results which suggest that there are significant factors which impede the equilibrating effect of migration. The following is a review of the major factors which enable inter-area wage differences to persist despite migration responding to such differentials.

First, as indicated above, even when economic variables are added to equations of the type (1), the density and population variables continue to be significant determinants of migration flows along with the economic variables. Density is the most pervasive of all variables in estimated migration functions, resulting in a strong negative coefficient for distance between the areas of origin and destination. This result is as true of studies on developed countries as of those on developing countries. Observers have often expressed surprise at the strength of this variable because the economic cost of transportation from one area to another is generally estimated to be quite small. After all, the gains from migration extend into the lifetime of the migrant. From what is known about the hierarchy of wage structures in urban areas ranked by size, it is extremely unlikely that, in an economy, the potential gain from migration will not be increased by traveling a further distance for a large majority of migrants.

Psychic costs and the availability of information about labor markets are the most likely factors involved in the deterrent effect of distance. Such noneconomic barriers to migration lead to the widely observed pattern that migration to a particular urban area which is not too large is usually fed by migrants from the surrounding rural areas. If a town is located in a relatively prosperous rural area, it will rarely draw migrants from more impoverished rural areas beyond its hinterland. Thus the economic gains from migration, even if they are large, may not lead to greater equality in the distribution of income for the country or the economy as a whole.

When large primate cities play a significant role in the distribution of the urban population, short distance migration may not be the dominant form of rural-urban movements. The surrounding rural areas are no longer sufficient to meet the demand for labor in the urban conglomerates; however, it is not always apparent that the areas supplying migrants are concentrically distributed in terms of distance. Large cities typically develop their individual catchment areas and the lines of migration are maintained over long periods of time. Such catchment areas are not necessarily the areas of particularly low income in the country either. There are many reasons why a particular area or set of villages might develop into a major source of migrants for a particular conglomerate; low income is only one of many variables which determine this role.

The reason why the lines of migration tend to persist, sometimes for decades, is because the risks of migration are perceived to be considerable by the typical migrant, and the presence of previous migrants connecting the same areas of origin and destination reduce considerably the psychological costs of migration. Migrants from the same area hope to find and do get essential support in the transitional period from family and friends. This "family and friends" effect appears in econometric migration functions as the variable which measures the stock of previous migrants and is a significant explanatory factor. It is the basic reason for the significance of "the population at destination" variable being high in gravity models of the type described in the above equation.

The consequence of this persistent effect is that the role of migration of labor in ironing out wage differences between areas is considerably weakened. It also suggests a reason for the continued growth of large urban conglomerates.

Although past migration patterns do determine the present patterns significantly, this argument cannot be carried to its logical conclusion; if so, ever increasing concentrations of population would be in evidence. Eventually areas of large population (or in-migration) must begin to repel migrants, at least relative to other areas. However, most importantly, the cumulative nature of migration flows works against the redistributive effects of population transfer over long periods in most countries.

The policy implication follows that there is a strong case for government action in promoting "growth poles" as alternative points for attracting migrants, particularly in low-income areas. This point will be discussed at some length later in this chapter.

A second important result found in many econometric migration functions is that although income variables are generally significant in explaining migration flows, there is an observed asymmetry between conditions at destination and origin. Most migration functions have found, both in the United States and in developing countries, that destination wage is much more important in determining the migration rate than the wage at the place of origin. One explanation might be that personal characteristics dominate the decision of whether or not to migrate, whereas income levels at the destination influence the decision as to where to migrate. Another hypothesis is based on the idea that capital market imperfections significantly affect mobility. While low origin income means low opportunity cost of migration, it also implies limited ability to finance migration. The latter may dominate the migration decision up to a point. The two effects working against each other weaken the origin income variable.

Banerjee and Kanbur (1981) used this concept to derive a function of net benefit from rural-urban migration which is nonlinear in relation to rural income. Their estimate of interstate, rural-urban migration rates[5] in India in 1961 yielded a significant positive coefficient for rural income, and a negative coefficient for the square of term. The hypothesis of a nonmonotonic relationship between migration propensity and rural income was further supported by the result that an index of poverty in the origin (rural) area which was also included in the model had a significant negative coefficient. This "runs counter to the idea of rural push necessarily leading to more migration. Rather, poverty appears to hinder out-migration in the Indian case, perhaps because the ability to finance migration expenditures is lowest for the poorest of the poor" (Banerjee and Kanbur 1981, 21).

The implications of such results for the nonequilibrating aspect of labor migration is clear. The process of migration works in such a way that although individual migrants improve their conditions, the process does not unambiguously help either families or areas at the low end of the income distribution.

More traditional demographic factors in migration selectivity (which are well represented in the literature) also work in a way that increases private gain but exacerbates rural inequality. These selectivity factors refer particularly to age and education.

Age. In all countries, migration is concentrated in the 15–year to 30–year age group, with a substantial portion in the 15–year to 24–year subgroup. The economic explanation, i.e., that lifetime income gains are larger for the young, has been stressed for many years (e.g., Sjaastad 1962). Since the proportion of out-migration from this age group is seldom very large in any single rural community, probably the adverse effect on rural productivity and growth is not by itself significant. However, when combined with the fact that a substantial number of these young people come from middle-income families, and that such migrants are likely to be more permanently absent, out-migration has implications for the rural society. These migrants are potential leaders in an economic as well as political sense, and their absence removes the possibility of the most likely challenge for village gerontocracy.

Education. Although in terms of sheer numbers, migrants are not dominated by higher educational groups (reflecting the education distribution in the rural areas of less-developed countries), evidence from most countries in Asia shows that the propensity to migrate is generally higher for the more educated. This is not merely due to the age selectivity noted earlier, and the fact that the young tend to be more educated. In fact, controlling for age, migration rates increase with education.[6]

The higher migration rate of the educated may be due to a combination of three factors, each of varying importance: (i) wage differentials, regional or rural-urban, may be larger for the more educated; (ii) the responsiveness of individuals to wage incentives may be larger for the educated; and (iii) the role of growth of new vacancies may increase with education relatively more in the urban labor market.

The location of a large part of the market for educated labor in the urban economy is a feature of the recent economic development of less developed countries. This concentration is encouraged by the content of school courses. As Caldwell (1969) wrote about Ghana: "Almost inevitably that which has been taught has hardly ever been about traditional society and has never sought to encourage a firmer establishment in that society. Rather, it has been about a foreign way of life, most closely approximated in the towns, or about aspects of society only found in the modernized sector of the economy which is identified to a considerable degree with the towns."

The higher rate of demand relative to supply of educated job seekers is then a factor of importance in the education selectivity of rural-urban migrants. Formalized selection for vacancies, e.g., through employment exchanges, is much more common for educated labor. Hence, physical presence in the urban labor market for job search as per the Harris-Todaro model is more logical for the educated.

This does not mean that informal contacts and kinship ties are not also important for the more educated rural-urban migrants. However, preparation and financing of the job search is as important as the direct recruitment to the high-wage sector. Both factors in the migration process lead to unequalizing distribution. The cost of acquiring education for migration is high, as is the cost of waiting in the employment queue when necessary. Migrants who have succeeded in reaching the higher-income curve are more able to bear these costs and also to reduce the costs of acquiring information for succeeding migrants. The resultant chain migration favors wealthier families and wealthier villages.

Urbanization and Pattern of Employment Growth

Urbanization is associated with economic development, and more specifically with the growth of employment outside the rural agriculture sector. Historically, the growth of modern industry has been the moving force behind urbanization. The experience of developing countries in recent decades has been quite different from the traditional pattern. Differences in the rate of industrial growth or in the shares of industrial output in gross domestic product (GDP) are not sufficient to explain differences in the degrees of urbanization in the sample of developing countries today. This is because of the deviation of the pattern of employment growth in developing countries from the pattern postulated in classical hypotheses such as that of Clark-Fisher. Based on the historical data of the now developed countries, the Clark-Fisher theory postulated that as per capita income increased, the sectoral composition of employment changed in a predictable way. Up to a certain level of economic growth, the proportion employed in manufacturing increases at the expense of agriculture. Only after income levels have reached a certain level does the share of employment in the tertiary sector begin to increase at the expense of the other two sectors. These shifts follow changes in the composition of demand with increasing per capita income, as dictated by the varying income elasticities of demand for the products of the three sectors. Besides European countries in the nineteenth century,

Japan in the twentieth century recorded a pattern of employment growth consistent with this model.

The record of change in the composition of employment in developing countries since World War II has been quite different. As the role of agriculture in providing employment to the growing labor force has weakened over time, it is the tertiary rather than the manufacturing sector which has taken the lead in the absorption of labor. This is as true of economies in Asia which have stagnated as of economies which have experienced rapid growth. For example, in Indonesia, between 1975 and 1985, the share of agriculture in total employment declined by 8.2 percentage points; practically the whole of this decline was absorbed by the tertiary sector. In the rapidly growing economy of the Republic of Korea, on the other hand, the decline in the share of agriculture was much higher at 21 percentage points. Manufacturing accounted for just 5.4 points of this decline, with the tertiary sector absorbing the remaining 15.6 points.

There are many reasons for this pattern of employment growth in the recent experience of developing countries. While a full discussion of this important topic is outside the scope of this chapter, there are forces operating both on the supply and demand sides of the equation which must be noted. On the supply side, there is a much more rapid rate of growth of the labor force pressing on a limited land area. On the demand side, there are technological as well as institutional factors which tend to reduce the elasticity of employment with respect to output in modern industry compared to earlier periods of economic development. The growth and spread of cost-saving, capital-intensive technology is probably much more rapid. Furthermore, developments in factor markets (for example, the increase in wages in the modern sector, and the low value of interest rates on capital borrowed by this sector) have induced firms to employ less labor-intensive technology in the feasible spectrum.

The implications of these developments for the urban labor markets of developing countries are profound. A substantial portion of employment created in the tertiary sector of the urban economy is in small-scale or even one-person enterprises. They coexist with large establishments found both in the tertiary and manufacturing sectors. Together with small-scale manufacturing enterprises they constitute the so-called informal sector of the urban labor market which contrasts with the large-scale subsector. The implications of this heterogeneity for urban poverty, and the factors strengthening it, are discussed in more depth below.

LABOR MARKET SEGMENTATION AND URBAN POVERTY

The division of the urban labor market between the large-scale sector, which is growing very slowly, if at all, and the small-scale sector to which much of the new labor force (fed either by natural growth or urban migration) is employed, coincides roughly with the distinction made in the literature between the "formal" and "informal" sectors. The split has been presented as a central feature of urban poverty. Most discussions assume there are widely different levels of earnings in the two sectors, unrelated to differences of human capital attributes of labor found in the two. In the formal sector, through a combination of economic and institutional factors, wages (and employment) are protected in the sense that they are not available to job-seekers unless they somehow manage to cross the barrier to entry. In the informal sector, entry is reasonably free so that labor is absorbed at a wage which approximates the low supply price of labor. Most urban poverty is found in this unprotected sector.

Harris-Todaro Model

The Harris-Todaro model, which has been a dominant paradigm of the urban labor market for a number of years, adds some further elements to the above scenario. Apart from the formal-informal sector dichotomy and the wage gap between the two, the Harris-Todaro model incorporates a migration function which explains rural-urban migrants' responsiveness to the expected rather than the actual wage in the urban labor market. In deciding to migrate to the urban areas, the migrant takes into account (i) the certainty of a low wage in the informal sector and (ii) the probability of obtaining a high-wage, formal sector job at some point. If the latter is not too low, the expected wage would be higher than the wage actually obtained in the informal sector. Thus, the migrant may initially be willing to accept very low wages. Harris-Todaro migrants could thus add to the problem of low earnings and poverty in the urban economy. As already mentioned, the net rate of expansion of employment in the formal sector is typically very low. Thus, the Harris-Todaro hypothesis depends crucially on there being a reasonable rate of turnover of labor in this sector, so that at least the gross rate of new employment (including replacement) is reasonably high. If this does not occur, no matter how high the relative wage in the formal sector, the expected wage in this sector faced by a fresh migrant (the product of the wage and the probability of employment in the sector) would be small and play a minor role in the calculations.

Besides the above, the Harris-Todaro model rests on three additional crucial assumptions relating to the nature of the urban informal sector, the recruitment of labor by formal sector firms, and the economics of rural-urban migration. Much empirical research in recent years has cast serious doubt on these assumptions.

Nature of the Urban Informal Sector. The view that the informal sector is predominantly a transition stop for migrants moving from rural areas to the formal sector is not supported by empirical evidence. As noted earlier, the informal sector is extremely heterogeneous. Although transitory migrants are an important part of the sector, many are circulatory migrants who divide their time between town and country, and many others are in the informal sector to stay. Many also perform specialized tasks not generally undertaken in the formal sector, such as domestic service. Self-employed persons in the informal sector tend to show a steep rise in earnings as they grow older and become more experienced. Furthermore, the informal sector contains small-scale enterprises that produce the same product lines as large firms, but their output is generally at the low end of the quality spectrum and they use different technology and different factor proportions. The empirical evidence on mobility of labor between the two sectors of the urban labor market indicates that, overall, labor is as likely to move in the direction of the informal sector and require capital investment. Thus, factory workers in the high-wage sector often raise the required capital from their savings and establish themselves as independent entrepreneurs in their middle years.

Recruitment to the Formal Sector. The Harris-Todaro view that the path to a formal sector job is predominantly through the informal sector is also not supported by empirical evidence. Banerjee (1983), for example, compared the probability of a migrant from the rural areas moving to Delhi and finding a formal sector job directly in a particular year with the probability of landing a formal sector job within a few years of first entering the informal sector. He found that the former was nearly six times as high as the latter. Studies in Bombay (Mazumdar 1984) and Ahmedabad (Poppola 1977) also suggest that recruitment to formal sector jobs occurs directly from the rural areas and much more often than it does through the urban informal sector. Both labor market supply and demand account for this. On the supply side, circular migration and low wages have a sustained impact on the potential efficiency of a worker seeking entry into the formal sector. Employers tend to choose fresh entrants into the labor market who have not been exposed to the different work patterns of the informal sector. On the demand side, because employers attach great value to social solidarity, they often rely on existing employees and supervisors to find new applicants for vacancies. Studies in India and Africa have repeatedly noted the importance of kinship ties in the recruitment process, what Poppola (1977, 153) calls "a de facto closed-door system."

Economics of Rural-Urban Migration. The Harris-Todaro model assumes that the typical migrant is a gambler who hopes to take advantage of an expected high wage in the urban labor market. The research on internal migration reviewed earlier, however, suggests that the risks of migration have been underestimated by this characterization of the rural-urban migrant. There is no evidence to substantiate urban job search as a gambling process. In fact, several studies have shown that migrants usually get their first job after a short waiting period.

One fourth of the workers surveyed in the Bombay study said that they had migrated after securing a job or a firm offer of one; one third said they suffered no unemployment before obtaining their first job; and nearly one half said they needed no support from their families because they did not have to wait long to get a job. Data collected on worker unemployment before they obtained their first job showed that only about 15 per cent of the migrants in the factory sector were unemployed six months or more (Mazumdar 1984, 179).

Theory of Segmented Labor Markets

Although the Harris-Todaro model has pessimistic implications for overurbanization, it postulates relatively easy movement of workers from the informal to the formal sector after a period of waiting. However, the literature presents an alternative view, which hypothesizes that the urban labor market is segmented in the sense that, although new workers may find it relatively easy to enter the informal sector, their further progress into the formal sector is difficult or limited. This hypothesis, if true, has serious implications for the distribution of income in the urban labor market. The large difference in earnings between the two sectors along with limited entry into the high-wage sector creates a "labor aristocracy" in the urban labor market. A relatively small proportion of the labor force employed in the sector shares in the high income generated in the modern economy, whereas a large number of workers are left more or less permanently in the low-wage, low-productivity sector.

In examining the conceptual and empirical basis of the hypothesis of labor market segmentation, it is important to consider the long-term trends in the shares of the two sectors in total urban employment, as well as the response to recent cyclical shocks.

Labor movement into the high-wage formal sector may be restricted, owing to institutional factors such as the closed-shop practices of unions. However, it is unusual for such restrictions to exist in formal collective bargaining agreements. If employers are found to depend heavily on union representatives to fill vacancies, there must be strong economic reasons for that dependence. As already noted, employers attach great importance to the social solidarity of the work force in large establishments. Where unions are strong, union leaders and management both tend to want to achieve a socially integrated and motivated work force. Managers might well depend on unions to introduce new recruits. Nonetheless, a closed shop might also operate without unions. If employers attach more importance to the productivity-augmenting effects of a cohesive work force than to getting new workers at the lowest wage possible, they will depend on the foremen and senior workers to assist in recruitment. As a result, the field of new recruits may be restricted to those with close kinship or community ties to those already employed.

A second factor inhibiting mobility from the informal to the formal sector is the operation of internal labor markets in large establishments. Firms that encourage a lifetime commitment from their workers typically recruit young employees who are at a relatively low point on the career structure. Vacancies higher up the structure are filled through internal promotions rather than through outside recruitment. Thus, the opportunity to move into a formal sector job decreases significantly with the number of years spent in the informal sector.

The foregoing factors represent the demand side of the labor market. Segmentation can also occur when labor with different attributes is offered to the market. When these attributes are used as labels in the hiring of employees, the labor market may split into noncompeting groups. The most important of these supply-side attributes are sex and education.

Because of the traditional concentration of women in the service sector, especially in domestic service, a disproportionate number of women work in the informal sector (see Mazumdar 1976). Even when female workers are employed in the large-scale manufacturing sector, they are usually concentrated in certain occupations or industries. Young unmarried females in Japan, for example, tend to be employed in textile industries, while in India's textile industry, women workers are employed only in specific occupations labeled *magi* (female) jobs. Further, the proportion of women in industrial employment in the formal sector has been small and has declined over time.

When jobs are labeled in this way, female job seekers are crowded into certain occupations. Occupational crowding drives down the supply price of women throughout the economy, so that even the relatively small number who manage to get jobs in other parts of the labor market have lower earnings than men in the same occupation.

In sum, the informal sector contains a heterogeneous collection of workers with different degrees of entrepreneurial skills and capital. Those who are selling their labor power with little entrepreneurial assets find substantial barriers to movement to the high-wage segment, while entry into the self-employed sector showing high returns to enterprise is limited by the need for prior acquisition of a minimum amount of human and financial capital.

EMPIRICAL EVIDENCE ON INTRA-URBAN EARNING DIFFERENTIALS

This section presents some evidence on the magnitude and nature of differences in the earnings of comparable workers in different segments of the market. It also discusses possible trends in these differences.

Empirically, the informal sector is identified as consisting of the self-employed and wage workers in establishments below a certain size, a demarcation which is, of course, not perfect. Some self-employed belong to professions whose earnings are protected, often by highly organized trade unions, and should, by any reasonable criterion, belong to the formal sector of the labor market. Sometimes, as in the Economic Commission for Latin America (ECLA) studies, researchers have accounted for this discrepancy by limiting the category of informal sector self-employed to those without post-secondary education. In defining the category for wage employees, the variable must distinguish the small-scale or informal from the formal enterprises; traditionally, size in terms of employees has been favored for this. However, with changing technology, particularly in the new industrial sectors, this criterion has become less clear. Highly sophisticated technology is sometimes employed by firms with very few employees but high value of capital equipment per worker. The workers in such establishments might develop the usual characteristics of the formal sector, i.e., high degree of organization, formal working conditions and a protected wage structure, because of the high value of the equipment for which they are responsible. Such considerations must be taken into account when defining the criterion for the informal sector in a particular economy. However, when comparing intersectoral wage differentials across countries, and the reference for this comparison is limited to secondary published sources rather than specially-designed surveys, employment size is the preferred criterion. It is, thus, the criterion used in the following discussion.

Evidence on Intra-Urban Earning Differentials in India

Data on India for labor markets in the cities of Ahmedabad, Bombay, Calcutta, Coimbatore, and Madras have been summarized by Harris (1989).

Notably, the data show that the picture of the dual labor market with its suggestion of a two-peak earning distribution which corresponds to the formal and informal sectors is a simplified one. There are, in fact, several compartments to the labor market, each with widely different earning levels. At the very least, five segments can be distinguished: the self-employed; casual laborers who are typically employed by a multiplicity of employers on daily contracts; wage laborers on longer contracts within small-scale enterprises; a high-wage formal sector whose boundary is defined partly by enterprise size and partly by ownership characteristic; and the public sector in which wages are determined administratively. The self-employed are a heterogeneous group whose earnings are a bundle of mixed income, representing returns to labor, capital, and entrepreneurship. A wide distribution of earnings which straddles the wage level (or band of wages) in the formal sector can be observed. The wage-labor market is easier to differentiate, partly because it is easier to control for the heterogeneity of labor by taking into account standard human capital attributes of the workers.

The Bombay Labor Market study (Deshpande 1979; Mazumdar 1984, 1989, Appendix A) found that in a multiple regression analysis of the monthly earnings of male manual earnings, the labor market segment (i.e., casual labor and enterprise size) was the most important determinant of the level of earnings. In industrial countries, age and education, and possibly seniority of the worker in the firm, are the most important explanatory factors in a model such as that used in the Bombay study.

In the same study, casual workers were at the bottom of the hierarchy of earnings, with a level of earnings half those found in the largest (more than 1,000 workers) factories.

Differences in the level of earnings did not adhere to strict institutional demarcations. Factories in the sample were institutionally distinguished from small enterprises insofar as the former came under the coverage of industrial and labor legislation. However, earnings, after controlling for human capital factors, although higher in the factories than in small enterprises, continued to increase within the factory sector as the units were distinguished by employment size categories. The critical point within the factory sector seemed to be when employment size reached 100–499 employees. The net difference in earnings in the three size classes above 100 workers was not large.

The fact that wages did not coincide with institutional boundaries underlines the point that wage differences within the urban labor market are not crucially dependent on institutional factors such as labor legislation or trade unions. This conclusion is reinforced by historical studies of the Bombay labor market which show that significant wage differentials by types of enterprises existed in earlier years when labor legislation and trade union organization were rudimentary. The post-World War II spate of labor laws and the strengthening of trade union organization in India have increased the wage differential somewhat.

Other Indian labor market studies, although not as detailed as the Bombay study, point to similar large wage differences between segments of the market. In particular, "the divide between what is described as casual work and protected wage work—a divide which we have seen as almost unbridgeable for the worker—is very defined in all the studies offering evidence" (Harris 1989, 253).

Labor Market Segmentation and Urban Poverty in India

Harris (1989, Table 10.18, 254) provides a summary of wages per day (in rice equivalents) for the Indian studies surveyed in the unprotected sector. The table shows "a variety of unprotected work, in different places and years, a clustering of wages between the equivalent of 2 and 5 kg of rice per day. Data such as those presented for Coimbatore show that wage levels in this range must push many families near to, if not below, a nutritionally-defined poverty line" (Harris 1989, 253).

There is some evidence to suggest that workers in the high-wage sector have larger household sizes (and a higher burden of dependency) than workers in the casual and small-scale sectors (Mazumdar 1984, 194–5). Income per adult equivalent unit in the households of workers in the different subsectors vary less than earnings per worker. This is due, in part, to the greater prevalence of lone, circulatory migrants in the unprotected sectors. It would be incorrect to interpret this difference as a life cycle phenomenon, and the evidence on the very limited degree of graduation from the informal to the formal sector has already been discussed. The Bombay study revealed another significant point: although the mean wage of workers in the casual sector was lower than in the small-scale sector, and the latter lower than that of factory workers, migrant casual workers were generally older and more likely to be married at the time of migration. The lower household size of casual workers in the city merely reflected a way of their coping with low incomes. The incidence of poverty in this group could be minimized by the casual worker leaving much of his family behind in the villages, and the principal earner dividing his time between the rural and the urban areas during his working life. The factory workers, by contrast, and to a lesser extent the workers in the small-scale sector, had a high enough level of earnings to be settled with most of their family in town.

The discussion thus far has been limited to the nature of intra-urban wage differences at a given point of time. Equally important for the understanding of the trends in the inequality of earnings and the incidence of urban poverty over time, is the evidence on the changes in the shares of employment in different sectors of the urban market, and in the magnitude of wage differentials. Such evidence as exists for India suggests somewhat different trends in the wage labor and the self-employed sectors of the urban economy in the last two decades.

(i) Employment growth in the high-wage formal sector stagnated in the 1980s. The organized manufacturing industry in India has not been a significant creator of jobs for a long time, absorbing just 2.1 per cent of the growth of the labor force between 1960 and the mid-1980s. The World Bank (1989) documented the dramatic change that occurred between the 1970s and the 1980s, noting that the rate of growth of value added in this sector more than doubled from 4.5 to 9.4 per cent per annum, but the growth in employment, which was 4.3 per cent between 1973–1974 and 1980–1981, was negative (at –0.2 per cent) between 1980–1981 and 1984–1985 (World Bank 1989, Table 4.1,

107). Pakistan and Bangladesh, and even some countries of Southeast Asia share this experience of very low employment elasticity with respect to output in large-scale manufacturing (Amjad 1990, 134). At the same time, the already bloated public sector is no longer able to make as large a contribution to employment growth in the formal sector as in the past.

(ii) Some evidence suggests that while wages in real terms have increased in the formal sector, they have stagnated or even fallen somewhat in the informal sector (Little et al. 1987, 265; Harris 1989, 254–5).

(iii) There is evidence that "informalization" of labor occurred as employers in the public sector and large enterprises found it advantageous to employ labor in such a way as to avoid the laws which protect workers (Harris 1989, 248–251).

(iv) There is also evidence of rapid employment growth (5.7 per cent per annum in the 1970s) in the mainly urban-based non-household, non-large factory sector. Observers have linked the growth in urbanization that occurred in the 1970s to the sustained growth of employment in small workshops (World Bank 1989, para 2.78, 75).[7]

(v) What happens to the inequality of income in the urban economy depends on the dynamism of the small-scale business and self-employment sector, not just in terms of the numbers employed but also in terms of the income generated. Analysis of the National Sample Survey data on the distribution of household expenditure for different dates does suggest a decline in the incidence of poverty between 1970 and 1988, somewhat more so in the urban than in the rural areas (World Bank 1989, Annex Tables 6A and 6B, 175–6). There is strong reason to believe that the growth of unregulated enterprises was critical in this process.

Evidence on Intra-Urban Earning Differentials in Other Asian Countries

Intra-urban wage differentials vary markedly from one economy to another. They are influenced by the varying rates and patterns of growth in the formal sector, and by the nature of rural-urban labor migration. An example of such differentials is the contrast between intra-urban wages in Indonesia and Malaysia. Differences in wages in Indonesia by the size of employment group in manufacturing are as wide as, if not wider than what has been observed for India. Wages in large capital-intensive firms were two-and-a half times those in nonmechanized firms for comparable labor. The situation in Malaysia differs. An analysis similar to that of the 1978–1979 Bombay study was undertaken for three cities in urban Malaysia. The size of the firm was a significant determinant of the earnings of unskilled labor, but wages for enterprises of one to nine workers were only 32 per cent lower than in enterprises of 100 or more workers (Mazumdar 1981, Table 9.6, 162).

A major explanation for the difference between the two econo-mies, although not the sole cause, is the difference in rural-urban migration patterns. In Indonesia, circulatory migrants divide their time between urban and rural areas, and this has a significant impact on the urban labor market. In a survey of fourteen villages from as early as 1973, Hugo (1977, 59) found that no less than two thirds of his sample of migrants were non-permanent (i.e., did not meet the census criterion of being absent for six months or more). As mentioned earlier in this chapter, such migrants are predominant in the informal sector, and with their low supply price, they keep wages down. By contrast, the incidence of temporary migration is much lower in urban Malaysia (Mazumdar 1981, 202–04, 221–23). The importance of stage migration, i.e., migrants stopping at smaller, intermediate urban areas before reaching the larger cities, suggests a more permanent urban drift and a different pattern of adjustment to the urban economy.

Factors other than the nature of rural-urban migration undoubt-edly play a role in determining the extent of intra-urban wage differentials. Some of the more important factors are those relating to differences in technologies (for example, the relative importance of highly capital-intensive enterprises); ownership patterns (such as the prevalence of foreign firms); capital market imperfections; and the degree of protection given to the large-scale sector. The latter two factors tend to increase the "rent" accruing to large firms either by lowering the supply price of capital in the formal finance sector or by enabling such firms to raise product prices above competitive levels. Organized firm-specific labor in these enterprises shares in the rent created and enjoys high wage levels.

Systematic and detailed studies on the extent of intra-urban wage differentials in Asian countries have not yet been done. Some data on employment, labor productivity, and wages by size of firms have been

Table 3.3
Small Manufacturing Enterprises in Southeast Asia

Country/Class	(number of workers)	Employment (per cent)			Value added (per cent)			Productivity differential (Small=100)		
		Mid–1970s	Late 1970s	Mid–1980s	Mid–1970s	Late 1970s	Mid–1980s	Mid–1970s	Late 1970s	Mid–1980s
Hong Kong										
Cottage	(1–9)	12.0	13.2	14.1	...	...	...	...	...	84.2
Small	(10–19)	9.2	9.9	10.7	...	...	...	...	...	100.0
Medium	(20–99)	30.8	34.0	34.5	...	...	...	...	...	124.0
Large	(>100)	48.0	42.9	40.7	...	...	...	...	...	154.4
Total		100.0	100.0	100.0	...	...	...	...	...	130.4
Indonesia										
Cottage	(<5)	79.5	62.2	52.4	13.5	13.6	11.0	13.7	46.0	45.9
Small	(5–19)	7.0	18.4	14.9	8.7	8.8	6.8	100.0	100.0	100.0
Medium/large	(>20)	13.5	19.4	32.7	77.9	77.6	82.2	466.6	842.6	549.0
Total		100.0	100.0	100.0	100.0	100.0	100.0	80.8	210.3	218.4
Japan										
Cottage	(1–9)[a]	19.1	19.6	13.7	9.6	9.6	7.5	67.3	64.6	77.3
Small	(10–49)	25.5	26.9	29.0	19.1	20.3	20.6	100.0	100.0	100.0
Medium	(50–99)	11.1	11.4	12.6	9.4	9.7	10.7	113.2	112.5	119.3
Large	(>100)	44.4	42.1	44.8	61.8	60.5	61.2	185.7	190.4	192.1
Total		100.0	100.0	100.0	100.0	100.0	100.0	133.2	132.5	140.6
Republic of Korea										
Small	(5–19)	10.5	8.0	10.3	4.9	4.5	4.7	100.0	100.0	100.0
Medium	(20–99)	16.0	19.4	26.8	11.5	13.6	16.5	153.5	125.1	136.5
Large	(>100)	73.4	72.6	62.8	83.6	81.9	78.9	243.0	200.7	279.0
Total		100.0	100.0	100.0	100.0	100.0	100.0	213.6	178.0	222.3

[a] in 1946, 4–9 workers; [b] in 1984, 1–49 workers.

... means data are not available.

Note: Periods covered: Hong Kong (1975, 1978, and 1982); Indonesia (1974/5, 1979, and 1986); Japan (1975, 1980, and 1986); Republic of Korea (1974, 1979, and 1986); Malaysia (1973, 1978, and 1984); Philippines (1973, 1980, and 1986); Singapore (1973, 1978, and 1983); Thailand (1975, 1979, and 1984).

Table 3.3 (continued)
Small Manufacturing Enterprises in Southeast Asia

Country/Class	(number of workers)	Employment (per cent)			Value added (per cent)			Productivity differential (Small=100)		
		Mid–1970s	Late 1970s	Mid–1980s	Mid–1970s	Late 1970s	Mid–1980s	Mid–1970s	Late 1970s	Mid–1980s
Malaysia										
Cottage	(1–4)	3.9	18.9	...	1.3	6.7	...	48.9	39.1	...
Small	(5–49)	26.0	32.4	16.2	17.0	29.3	9.5	100.0	100.0	100.0
Medium	(50–99)	26.7	21.7	31.7	30.7	32.3	26.9	176.1	164.0	144.4
Large	(>200)	43.4	26.9	52.2	51.0	31.7	63.6	179.4	130.2	207.8
Total		100.0	100.0	100.0	100.0	100.0	100.0	152.7	110.5	170.3
Philippines										
Small	(10–99)[b]	46.6	18.4	18.1	17.2	7.5	5.0	100.0	100.0	100.0
Medium/large	(>100)	5	153.5	125.1	136.5					
Large	(>100)	73.4	72.6	62.8	83.6	81.9	78.9	243.0	200.7	279.0
Total		100.0	100.0	100.0	100.0	100.0	100.0	213.6	178.0	222.3
Singapore										
Cottage	(1–9)	4.3	3.5	5.1	1.8	1.5	2.1	52.2	58.1	58.2
Small	(10–49)	14.8	17.5	18.4	11.9	12.9	13.1	100.0	100.0	100.0
Medium	(50–99)	9.9	10.7	11.6	9.2	8.8	11.3	117.1	111.8	136.5
Large	(>100)	71.4	68.3	64.8	77.1	76.9	73.4	134.7	153.5	158.9
Total		100.0	100.0	100.0	100.0	100.0	100.0	125.1	136.4	140.3
Thailand										
Small	(10–19)	4.1	4.4	3.4	1.5	2.0	1.2	100.0	100.0	100.0
Medium/large	(>20)	95.9	95.6	95.6	98.5	98.0	98.8	274.7	220.8	296.1
Total		100.0	100.0	100.0	100.0	100.0	100.0	267.5	215.5	289.5

Sources: *Hong Kong Annual Digest of Statistics* (Hong Kong); *Statistik Indoenesia* (Indonesia); *Japan Statistical Yearbook* (Japan); *Korea Statistical Yearbook* (Republic of Korea); *Census of Manufacturing Industries* (Peninsular Malaysia), James and Akrasanee (1986), and Lim and Ali (1989) (Malaysia); Anderson and Khambata (1981), Bruch and Hiemenz (1985), and National Statistics Office (the Philippines); Lee Soon (1984) (Singapore); and *Report of Industrial Census* (Thailand).

Table 3.4
Wage Differentials by Employment and Establishment Size:
Selected Southeast Asian Countries

Hong Kong		Japan			Republic of Korea			Philippines		Thailand	
Size	1982	Size	1975	1986[a]	Size	1975	1986	Size	1964	Size	1964
	72.3	5–9	62.5	83.0	5–9	82.8	85.2			1–9	62.6
10–19	100.0	10–19	100.0	100.0	10–19	100.0	100.0	10–19	100.0	10–19	100.0
29–49	193.3	20–29	110.7	101.8	20–49	110.1	111.2	20–49	166.8	20–49	115.3
50–99	105.3	30–49	109.1	107.6	50–99	124.2	120.9	50–99	205.5	50–99	131.7
100–199	105.9	50–99	109.7	110.6	100–199	133.1	127.9	100–199	251.5	100+	203.4
200–499	110.0	100–199	114.3	120.6	200–299	128.8	137.1	200–499	282.6		
500–999	112.4	200–299	127.3	133.8	300–499	141.7	143.8	500+	303.1		
1000+	111.9	300–499	140.8	148.2	500+	158.8	161.6				
		500–999	152.8	161.4							
		1000+	158.2	190.6							
20+	107.2	20+	140.9	135.3	20+	143.2	139.6	20+	281.4	20+	166.3

[a] 1986 data for 4–9 workers.
Sources: Hong Kong Annual Digest of Statistics; Japan Statistical Yearbook; Korea Statistical Yearbook; National Statistics Office (Philippines and Thailand), various years for all.

compiled for a number of Asian countries and are reproduced in Tables 3.3 and 3.4.

The data are not ideal. Because they are derived from widely different published sources, standardization for identical groups according to size is not possible. Also, the coverage of unregistered manufacturing establishments varies from country to country. Nevertheless, some comparisons can be made.

In general, countries differ greatly in the extent of the difference in labor productivity (value added per worker) between small and large firms. The relative difference in wage levels by firm size follows closely the productivity differentials, but are somewhat smaller than the latter. Generally, it can be expected that economies that have a relatively high productivity and wage differential in favor of the large firms, will suffer from a higher incidence of urban poverty. This is particularly true if the share of labor in the small-scale sector is large. Because of the low employment elasticity in the large-scale manufacturing sector, it would be unrealistic to expect that the growth rate of output in large-scale manufacturing will be high enough to absorb the low productivity labor in the urban economy.

For the sample of countries represented in Tables 3.3 and 3.4, roughly three different levels of wage differentials between the large and small firms can be discerned. Small productivity and wage differentials are in evidence in the city-states of Hong Kong and Singapore, while Indonesia and the Philippines have productivity differentials of 4:1 or higher. The East Asian countries, Japan and the Republic of Korea, are in between with productivity differentials of between 2:1 and 3:1.

Hong Kong. Hong Kong comes closest among the Asian countries to a free-market model of development. Beng (1988, 58) observes that "within the proclaimed *laissez-faire* environment in Hong Kong the government does not seem to have a policy towards manufacturing not to mention any policy towards the SSIs [small-scale industries]." In this noninterventionist atmosphere, the small-scale producers seem to have achieved relatively high levels of productivity and wages compared to the larger units. At the same time, the small-scale sector has remained dynamic over the entire period of industrial growth. As can be seen from Table 3.3, nearly 60 per cent of the manufacturing employment is in enterprises of less than 100 workers and this proportion increased during the 1970s. The greater ability of small firms to adapt to changing international market conditions contributed to this success (Beng 1988, 32).

Singapore. Singapore, in contrast to Hong Kong, did have significant paternalistic interventions from the state in industrial policy. One of the more important measures was a mandated wage increase in the early 1980s over three consecutive years, which was designed to force firms to rely extensively on low-wage labor; the Government believed intervention would encourage a break from the low-wage syndrome which had been encouraged by the import of foreign workers. This restructuring phase did raise the capital/labor ratio dramatically (Beng 1988, 20). While employment and output grew dramatically in all size categories, large establishments achieved a much higher share of total employment and value added than was evidenced in Hong Kong. However, the interventionist policies did not create dualism, thus small firms achieved productivity and wage levels near to those achieved by the larger firms.

Given the high rate of growth of employment in manufacturing and the absence of dualism, it seems fairly clear that within the city-states, labor markets have worked in a way to achieve equitable growth, at least for manual workers.

Philippines. The inferior performance of the Philippine economy relative to that achieved in the other countries of the region, especially striking since the 1970s, is reflected in the evolution of the manufacturing sector (UNIDO 1988). Total manufacturing employment grew at about 2.1 per cent per annum between 1956 and 1985, compared with a rate of 3.0 per cent for total employment; by 1985, the manufacturing share had fallen to 9.7 per cent. As of 1967, most manufacturing workers were still in the household sector, and only about a quarter were in establishments of 20 or more workers; over half were located in rural areas. Between 1967 and 1983, there was a striking employment increase of 91 per cent in establishments of over 100 workers, pushing their share of employment up from 22 per cent to 31 per cent. Employment in middle-size establishments of 10–99 workers remained small compared to other countries of the region and to countries at the Philippines' stage of development, accounting for just 6.3 per cent of manufacturing employment in 1967 and 6.1 per cent in 1983.

In the 1980s, a sharp employment decline occurred in the 20–99 worker category, probably accompanied by a significant increase in the household sector, some of it taking the form of production under subcontract. In his study of subcontracting, Hill (1985) concluded that government programs to foster small industry, through the establishment of subcontracting networks with large industry, had met with limited success, and that this reflected, *inter alia*, the early stage of industrialization and a policy environment unconducive to efficient subcontracting.

The labor productivity differential by firm size is large at around 5 between establishments of 200 workers and up, and those with 10–19 workers, as of 1986 and 1987. The wage differential is, as expected, somewhat smaller, at about 2.6–2.7 in 1986–1987; the two appear to have widened since 1956, as wages held roughly constant in the large-scale sector and fell markedly in the smallest categories.

Indonesia. Manufacturing has until quite recently been relatively unimportant in the Indonesian economy, accounting for just 7–8 per cent of total employment in 1971 and 9–10 per cent in 1985. Because of the predominantly rural location of the population (84 per cent in 1965 and 75 per cent in 1985), most manufacturing employment was found there (Manning 1988, 62). Labor productivity was relatively low. As of 1986, approximately 55–60 per cent of manufacturing employment was located in the household sector, and about 30 per cent was in the medium and large-scale sector, defined as including establishments with 20 or more workers (Hill 1990, Table 7.12). Although manufacturing output rose quickly during the heart of the oil boom period (14 per cent over 1973–1981), much of it was judged to be inefficient and internationally uncompetitive. However, effective macroeconomic management and increasingly decisive microeconomic reform resulted in strong non-oil export growth after 1985. Many of the large firms have been and remain state owned.

Labor productivity in Indonesia varies widely by establishment size: in 1985, the average for firms of 1,000 or more workers was 4.4 times as high as that in firms of 5–19 workers (Hill 1990, Table 19). These gaps appear to be comparable to those of the Philippines, which are large, and greater than those of the other countries of the region.

Although systematic research on this point remains to be done, several important conclusions can be drawn from the record of Indonesian economic growth. First, agricultural growth was strong due to the state-supported seed-fertilizer revolution partly financed by oil revenue. Second, agricultural growth as well as widespread public spending on infrastructure led to strong increases in employment in the tertiary sector. Earnings in the services and transport sector were quite high, at least relative to agricultural wages. An increasing number of commuters and circular migrants, often from distant rural locations, entered these activities (Hugo 1978). The typical Indonesian household engaged in multiple occupations with family members dividing their time between farm and off-farm activities, in varying proportions at different times of the year. In sum, it is the development of tertiary activities rather than full-time manufacturing jobs in the informal sector which led to the growth in earnings. The observed low wages in informal manufacturing may indeed be due to the predominance of part-time work in this subsector.

Republic of Korea. Similar to Japan, the Republic of Korea pursued industrialization through a policy of selective support leading to the expansion of large firms. However, unlike in Japan and Taipei,China small and medium-scale enterprises did not play a major role, although small-scale manufacturing remains significant in Korean employment. Among the Asian countries, the Republic of Korea (along with Taipei,China and the two city-states) have had a respectable record of employment growth in the formal manufacturing sector. Between 1973 and 1983, for example, employment in manufacturing firms of more than 50 workers increased by an amount which accounted for a fifth of the growth in the labor force. Nevertheless, the increase in the share of large firms in total manufacturing employment seems to have reversed itself in the mid-1970s (Nugent 1989, Table 10). The productivity and wage differentials between large and small firms were in between the levels of the city-states and those of the Philippines. There was a cyclical movement in the wage differential between large-scale and small-scale enterprises, which increased in the 1960s and fell in the 1970s, but widened again in the 1980s (Mazumdar 1991b, 30). However, the differential in 1986 was only slightly above that in the early 1960s. Thus, for the period as a whole, the small-scale sector seemed to have shared in the strong real wage growth at a trend rate of nearly 6 per cent per annum over 25 years.

THEORIES OF INTRA-URBAN EARNING DIFFERENTIALS

As has been shown in the preceding discussion, not all or even most of the intra-urban wage differentials can be ascribed to institutional factors. Such differences were observed in the years before government intervention or strong trade unions, and are also found in economies where paternalistic governments have succeeded in suppressing aggressive workers' movements. Hence, Mazumdar (1983) has proposed an eclectic framework to describe such wage differences, which includes important determining elements. These elements are:

(i) differences in the supply prices of temporary and permanent migrants to the urban labor market, and the associated difference in the demand prices for stable and "floating" labor;

(ii) formation of firm-specific labor in large enterprises followed by forces which tend to put upward pressure on the wage level of such workers, including the wage-efficiency relationship and internal labor markets; and

(iii) unionization of firm-specific labor, perhaps supported by governments in the interests of political stability. High labor productivity in the large firms enables unions to claim a share of the profit or rent created; the size of the surplus determines an upper limit to the wage level.

If the above elements are generally true, then some important implications for policy can be postulated.

First, if wage differences are partly due to the wage-efficiency relationship, then the observed difference in wage per worker is much greater than the wage cost per standard unit of labor in small and large enterprises.

Second, if the difference in labor productivity both enables and sets a limit to wage differentials, then the causes of the differences in capital-labor ratios between small and large firms must be examined, since the latter is the major reason for differences in inter-firm labor productivity.

Finally, there is a fairly regular positive relationship in most economies between firm size and capital/labor ratio, particularly when firms are aggregated by groups of value of capital used rather than by number of employees (Little et al. 1987). It is, however, inappropriate to ascribe the increase in capital intensity to higher wage levels prevailing in large firms. The capital/labor ratio is determined by the firm's response to the ratio of the prices of labor and capital (the wage/rental ratio) facing it. The higher capital/rental ratio observed in large firms could be due as much to the higher relative wage facing these firms as to the lower price of capital they have to pay, or some combination of the efficiency unit labor between small and large firms is likely to be significantly less than the observed difference in wage per worker. Institutional factors causing capital market segmentation are, however, very important in most economies, making the availability of capital the reason that the role of segmented capital markets is more important than that of labor markets in causing the observed increase in capital/labor ratio by firm size.

If this line of argument is continued, it is possible to draw a conclusion which, although extreme, could be applicable in some important subsectors of the economy. In some lines of production, modern technology may be economically dominant, i.e., it uses less capital per unit of output produced as well as less labor. If this is the case, firms would tend to use modern technology with a high capital/labor ratio at any wage/rental ratio, provided they have access to the lump-sum capital needed. Small firms, however, continue to use older or household (nonmechanical) technology simply because they have no access to the capital needed at any price. In other words, the price of capital is a small positive number for large firms, but infinite for small firms or household enterprises.

In this scenario, the line of causation might indeed be from high capital/labor ratio to high wage, rather than the opposite direction. The large firm with a dominant modern technology has a high capital/labor ratio and high labor productivity. There is a large surplus to be shared between owners of capital and labor. Unions, perhaps supported by government, will successfully stake a claim to a share. Employers in their turn will tend to reduce their wage bill by increasing wages as well as the efficiency of a small number of select workers, particularly in situations where the cost of managing the work force increases sharply with the number of workers.

It is appropriate at this point to introduce the idea of product heterogeneity and product differentiation which provides an additional reason for the coexistence of small and large firms. Even when firms of different sizes produce ostensibly the same product (for example, washing soap), the bundle of attributes which are contained in different brands of soap will differ markedly. Small firms generally cater to the low-income groups and will, therefore, tend to concentrate on a brand which emphasizes cleaning ability over the cosmetic properties, such as scent. Simple technologies could be more appropriate in the production of the basic attributes answering to the needs of low-income consumers. Small firms, and even micro-enterprises, may be able to use such technologies successfully with low capital/labor ratios, while larger capital-intensive firms which cater to the high-income segment of the market may use more mechanized technologies to produce the attributes demanded by their wealthier consumers. Elements in the market structure, such as monopoly pricing, advertising, and barriers to entry, accentuate product market segmentation which increases the economic distance between large and small firms.[8] It is possible that in many lines of production, this type of product market segmentation helps to perpetuate industrial dualism, although the process is no doubt encouraged by capital market segmentation as well.

How important the above scenario is in a particular economy is a matter of empirical investigation. More generally, it is appropriate to conclude that the causes of the coexistence of small and large firms, with widely different wages, capital-intensity, and labor productivity, are to be found more in capital and product market segmentation than in the labor market.

POLICY IMPLICATIONS FOR POVERTY REDUCTION

Promotion of Small-Scale Enterprises

The factor-price distortion discussion above suggests that if the problem of capital market segmentation favoring large firms cannot be addressed directly, there is a case for policies which encourage smaller enterprises on the grounds of economic efficiency alone.

Another area to be considered is that of income distribution. It is widely, but often implicitly, assumed that an economy with a larger share of production in small-scale industry will have a more equal income distribution. It seems fairly clear that the capital share of manufacturing value added will increase with a shift towards large establishments, both because these large establishments tend to be capital intensive and because they more often operate under oligopolistic market conditions which tend to permit a higher above cost mark-up.

The expectation of a more equal distribution of entrepreneurial income is also fairly straightforward. The typically large wage difference between the small-scale industry and the large establishment implies that when the former have a larger share in total output, more of the income accruing to labor goes to the lower wage groups. This favorable effect on the distribution of labor earnings may indeed be a more compelling argument for policies to promote the growth of small-scale enterprises (SSEs) than the efficiency argument based on distortions in the labor market, since, as noted above, the efficiency wage difference between the small and large enterprise may not be that substantial.

In an attempt to confront this issue empirically, Nugent (1989) examined the possible income distribution effect of the large shift away from SSEs in Korean manufacturing during the country's rapid growth in the 1960s and 1970s. While acknowledging that the "hypothesized relationship between a structural indicator pertaining to one particular sector (i.e., size shares in manufacturing) and the overall distribution of income would not be expected to be very strong," (Nugent 1989, 10) he found that all of the available measures of income inequality, either among all households or among nonagricultural or urban households, peaked in 1976 or 1977, the very years in which the shares of large establishments in manufacturing employment and value added were at their zenith (Nugent 1989, 11).

Although promotion of efficient SSEs both raises output and improves the distribution of income, an attempt to improve that distribution which results in the promotion of inefficient enterprises may create a conflict with the equally important objective of maximizing output or increasing the rate of growth. This would be the case, for instance, when labor-intensive technology uses both more labor and more capital per unit of output.

There are other means of making the distribution of income less unequal, or of providing transfer to the marginal workers with little or no income. To pursue these objectives through the promotion of SSEs, without exploring such other measures, could be costly for the economy.[9]

Flexibility. An advantage of SSEs which has been cited more frequently in the last few years is that small firms are better able to adapt to changing (and sometimes disruptive) economic circumstances. Indeed, the 1970s and 1980s did produce several shocks which demanded a flexible response from industrial firms, and according to some authors, traditional mass production units were less successful in absorbing those shocks than were small establishments, a conclusion they base on a modern version of the craft principle that "flexible tasks and machines augment the craftsmen's skills and ability to produce ever more varied products" (Schmitz 1982, 4).

The most influential work embodying these ideas is that by Piore and Sable (1984). Their paradigm of successful flexible adjustment comes from the recent appearance in Germany, Italy, and Japan of a "new" type of industrial unit: flexible, small, and better able to respond to the challenges of the last two decades than the giant plants of the older industrial countries, e.g., the United States.

Particularly impressive is the development of a vast network of very small enterprises, spread through the villages and small cities of central and northern Italy. These shops range across the entire spectrum of modern industry, from shoes, ceramics, textiles, and garments to motorcycles, agricultural equipment, automotive parts, and machine tasks. "The firms perform an enormous variety of the operations associated with mass production, excluding only the kind of final assembly involved in the automobile production line" (Piore and Sable 1984, 392–3).

Average size varies by industry, but is generally extremely small, with shops of ten workers or less not uncommon. The flexibility which has been viewed as a hallmark of small firms in Taipei,China certainly seems to fit this pattern (Levy 1991). Although there is considerable anecdotal evidence from other countries to support this theory, organized information remains limited; this could be an important area for future research.

Contribution to Export Potential. Chen (1986, 3–4) concludes that the experiences of Hong Kong, Japan, the Republic of Korea, Singapore, and Taipei,China suggest that a strong and viable small industrial sector is necessary for successful export-oriented growth. Small-scale industry can play a significant role in the early stages of manufactured export growth because products are labor intensive, there are rapid changes in demand (due in part to world economic fluctuations), and output growth is demand driven. Small firms have the advantage of low overheads and the capacity to respond quickly to changing conditions. In the 1973–1975 recession, while large manufacturing firms in Singapore retrenched 20,000 workers, the small ones absorbed an additional 5,000 (Lau 1984, 28–9, in Beng 1988, 36). There is a growing international preference for high-quality personalized items, often skill-intensive, in place of mass-produced ones. The production of the former requires flexibility, which often places the advantage on the smaller firm.

According to Beng (1988, 37), a reliable support sector has been important in attracting high technology foreign investment to Singapore. In the absence of support services, foreign firms would either hire their own subcontractors or import foreign workers; neither option is agreeable to the Government. In Japan, and more recently in Hong Kong, Singapore, Taipei,China, and elsewhere, subcontracting with small producers has allowed the export sector to keep costs down and flexibility high. Small firms' absorptive capacity can also be an important determinant of technology transfer; in Singapore, for instance, a major channel involves skilled personnel, previously trained by a multinational company, who then take up employment in smaller local firms or start their own firm (Beng 1988, 38).

Other Economic and Social Advantages. Small-scale industry is also expected to perform better than larger firms in two other areas: contribution to decentralization and the fostering of entrepreneurship.

Support for the development of small-scale industry has often been based on the hope of reducing the excessive infrastructural and social costs associated with large assembly plants and large urban agglomerations. Ho (1979, 1980) contrasted the regional dispersion of industry in Taipei,China (with its prominent small-scale industry sector) with the Republic of Korea (with its dominant large firms). In general it appears that very small (mainly household) enterprises are much more widely dispersed, including a fairly high density in rural areas, than are small-scale to medium-scale plants (World Bank 1978).

Another major objective of those supporting SSE development has been the promotion of a widely based class of small entrepreneurs. For example, at the outset of the period of export-led industrialization in Taipei,China, Japanese trading companies promoted subcontracting and exporting through a network of small and medium manufacturers and export traders.

Government Policies to Promote Small-Scale Enterprises

Though some programs are in place, government policies have not yet made advances on reducing the skewed size distribution of enterprises. Worse, there is evidence to suggest that policies have been implicitly biased towards large firms. India is an exception to this. However, because of the manner in which India's policy of protecting the SSE was conceived and implemented, it is doubtful if its declared objectives have been achieved (Little et al. 1987; Mazumdar 1991).

Macroeconomic policies have been generally inimical to SSE growth. Perhaps the most important, in terms of their impact, have been differential rates of tariff protection and/or subsidies in favor of industries in which large enterprises predominate. A second set of policies favoring the large-scale sector are administrative interventions, such as licensing of scarce inputs. Large enterprises have a financial and political advantage over SSEs in obtaining allocations of such inputs from the authorities controlling and rationing their use. A third example is overvaluation of currencies which artificially depresses the price of imported capital equipment and implicitly favors large capital-intensive units.

As mentioned earlier, a major factor helping the large enterprises is capital market segmentation. Governments often help to intensify the degree of segmentation by encouraging the link between the formal banking system and large enterprises. While the experience in the Republic of Korea is well known, that in Taipei,China is equally instructive. The experience in the latter suggests that this type of policy of favoring the large-scale enterprise is not essential for rapid, even export-oriented growth. The initial conditions were clearly different in the Republic of Korea and Taipei,China; government policies built on these differences (Levy 1991).

In most countries, however, government policies to counter capital market segmentation have been weak. When governments have instituted credit policies to help the SSEs, the general experience has been that the policies have been too small and too costly. Effective policies are particularly difficult when capital market segmentation is caused by ethnic differences in the ownership of finance capital.

Policies to extend technology and marketing support to the SSEs to promote SSE growth are similar in importance to credit policies. However, it is difficult to devise schemes which deliver consistent success, as is evidenced by the diverse country experiences with respect to subcontracting. For example, the reputedly successful Japanese experience has been so closely tied to its industrial and cultural evolution that it is doubtful if it is an exportable model.

An important constraint on the potential expansion of the SSE sector is that of markets. Export markets are notoriously difficult to maneuver unless the SSE is tied to or led by larger national or multinational units. At the same time, the domestic market is often limited by the low income of the typical customer of SSE products. It is at this point that the link between policies to reduce income inequality and the promotion of SSEs assumes importance. With more equal distribution, the markets for products of SSEs would be larger. There is a virtuous circle in which SSE growth and increasing income equality sustain each other.

Increasing Employment Growth in the Formal Sector

As mentioned earlier, many Asian countries have experienced slow growth in employment in the formal wage sector. An important solution, albeit partial, to the problem of employment growth in the formal sector was provided in the 1960s and 1970s by the rapid expansion of the public sector. The changed economic climate of recent years has meant that this avenue of job creation is likely to shrink rapidly in the coming decade. In fact, a substantial shrinking of the public sector is the prerequisite of required structural adjustment in several Asian economies. It is in this context that policies which might have an impact on employment growth in the large-scale manufacturing sector assume importance.

Employment lag seems to be a particularly serious problem in South Asia. In Pakistan during the 1960s and 1970s, large-scale manufacturing accounted for around 23 per cent of total investment in the economy, but absorbed only 3 per cent of the increase in the labor force in the first period and 2.6 per cent during the latter. In the 1980s, despite an impressive output growth of over 8 per cent, employment hardly increased at all in large-scale manufacturing. In Bangladesh, between 1973-1974 and 1981-1982, this sector absorbed only 2.6 per cent of the labor force. As already shown, this is also the order of magnitude of the contribution of this sector to employment growth in India in recent decades.

World Bank (1989) found that the dramatic decline in employment elasticity which occurred in India in the 1980s compared to the 1970s was not due to a composition-of-industry effect. If the labor value-added coefficient had remained unchanged, employment growth would have matched the accelerated output growth of the later period. The across-the-board decrease in the use of labor per unit of output suggests some pervasive factor affecting a range of industries. World Bank concluded that the factor responsible was to be found in the labor market. While the product wage reflecting the real cost of labor to employers (nominal wages deflated by the wholesale manufacturing price index) fell by 1 per cent per annum in 1973/74–1979/80, it rose by as much as 7.2 per cent per annum in 1979/80–1984/85. In part, this reflected a not uncommon trend during inflationary processes in which the ratio of consumer price indices to producer price indices drifts upwards. But it also partly reflected the development that real wages (i.e., deflated by consumer price indices) increased by a higher rate in the latter period, up from 1.7 per cent per annum to 3.4 per cent per annum. Labor demand functions were estimated from pooled cross-section and time-series data. The coefficient of real labor cost was highly significant along with real value added (World Bank 1989, 109). The estimated long-run elasticities of real labor cost clustered around –0.8, implying that the annual increase in the real cost of labor of 7.2 per cent in the 1980s reduced the annual growth of employment by 5.7 per cent.

A major element in the employment policies of the Government of India, as in other South Asian countries for a long time, has been the protection of workers who have found employment in the formal sector. While the employers try to circumvent the problem by increasingly resorting to the employment of "temporary" workers, this is an inefficient solution. The low productivity of nontenurial or casual workers is bound to reduce competitiveness, and dampen long-term growth of output and employment. Meanwhile, the difficulty of laying off workers increases the effective cost of labor from the point of view of the employer and leads to a low labor/output ratio.

Changing the Sectoral Composition of Public Investment

A continuing concern in the literature on urbanization in developing countries has been the problem of overexpansion of large urban conglomerations and megacities. Even with the spiraling costs of rent and wage costs which such developments entail, external economies enjoyed by firms locating in these areas encourage continued concentration of private capital and investment. As was highlighted in the first part of this chapter, excessive rural-urban migration or an uncontrolled trek of people in response to "city lights" is not the basic problem. Rather, it is the distribution of three factors of production between the rural and urban areas, and between urban areas of different sizes which influences rural-urban migration, namely: private capital, public capital, and labor.

The distribution of public capital in most developing countries plays an autonomous role, and the marginal rates of return to capital as well as labor are determined by the way public capital is allocated among different geographical subsectors. Even if the distribution of labor and private capital equalizes individual marginal rates of return in the different subsectors, it would be far-fetched to assume that public capital is allocated in a way that achieves Pareto efficiency.

First, much of the public investment in infrastructure or in areas such as education or health does not necessarily have a clearly recognized rate of return. Second, and perhaps more importantly, the efficiency of public investment cannot be divorced from the welfare of specified classes in society whose interests such investment tends to promote, i.e., public investment cannot be meaningfully disentangled from considerations of income distribution. For example, the welfare of the middle or upper classes in most developing countries may be served most efficiently by concentrating public investment in large urban metropolises, whereas policies designed to promote the well-being of the mass of low-income people might be better served by a more widely dispersed pattern of public investment. The economic and social costs of growth of megacities cannot then be separated from the income distribution goals and the political economy of the state.

CONCLUSIONS AND SUGGESTIONS FOR RESEARCH

This chapter has examined labor market segmentation and the division of the urban labor markets into sectors with widely different levels of earnings. Rural-urban migration has been shown to be largely profitable for the individual migrant in terms of improvement of economic conditions. However, various basic characteristics of the process of migration prevent it from being an equilibrating one, and the social effects of rural-urban migration could indeed be less beneficial than its private gains. Few migrants reach the high-wage formal sector of the urban market. Kinship ties in the process of recruitment ensure that these fortunate few are not the migrants from the poorer rural families. A low degree of intersectoral mobility ensures that a large majority of those starting in the low wage sector fail to make it to the high wage sector within a reasonable period. Thus, rural poverty translates itself into urban poverty despite higher incomes in the urban sector.

As was also shown in this chapter, the heterogeneity of earnings in the informal sector suggests that there is considerable dynamism within this sector and the acquisition of skill and entrepreneurial activity by the workers in this sector offer perhaps the best prospects for reducing urban poverty. This is particularly true because of the low elasticity of employment with respect to output growth in the formal sector in recent economic history. While some data on differentials in earnings between small and large firms and their changes over time were presented for a number of countries, this chapter was unable to document the course of development of the informal sector on a comparative basis, mainly because of the lack of information on earnings over a specific period in the self-employed sector. This topic must remain a priority item in the agenda for research. In particular, the differences in the experience of the faster-growing economies from those of the slower-growing ones within Asia would be an important area of research. The question also has to be asked if intra-urban mobility is significantly greater in the economies with high growth. In this connection, the question of inter-generational mobility assumes importance. It is possible to hypothesize that the new entrants to the informal sector may not be able to graduate to the formal sector within their lifetime, but the human capital accumulation which they are able to induce in their children may indeed be instrumental in the next or succeeding generation obtaining access to the high-wage sector. Again, the question should be addressed as to whether this phenomenon is more marked in the faster-growing economies.

Another important group of topics which have not been discussed because of the nonavailability of adequate data is the impact of international contacts on the formal-informal wage differential in the urban economy. There are two different ways in which the international economy has impinged on the urban labor market in recent years. First, international migration has been an important enough flow to affect wages in critical segments of the market, for example, female service workers in the Philippines, or the market for construction labor in the Republic of Korea. Secondly, the subcontracting activities of multinationals have had a significant effect on some parts of the labor market, perhaps more so on female workers in the informal sector. Systematic research on this topic could highlight the changes in urban labor markets and urban poverty brought about by international economic contacts.

Notes

1. "It is by no means true that inclusion of agriculture's share makes the relationship with the urban shares definitional. In both developed and developing countries, large amounts of nonagricultural employment are located in rural areas" (Mills and Becker 1986, Chapter 3).
2. These models often seek to explain several different migration flows of which rural-urban migration is only a part. On the other hand, some studies have specifically distinguished rural-urban flows, e.g., Barnum and Sabot (1981); Banerjee and Kanbur (1981).
3. See also Barnum and Sabot (1981)
4. Results from four studies are compared in Yap (1975).
5. Data apply only to male migration in the year prior to the census
6. For more on the increase of migration rates with education see, for example, Barnum and Sabot (1981, Table 1, 17) and Caldwell (1969), Table 3.5, 65, for Tanzania and Ghana, respectively.
7. Reliable evidence for the 1980s awaits more detailed analysis of the 1991 Census.
8. See the extended discussion of this point in Little, Mazumdar and Page (1987, Chapter 12). The author is indebted to Nasreen Khundker for insisting on the critical importance of this point.
9. Reference may be made to the Indian policy of reserving part of the weaving industry for the small-scale sector (Mazumdar 1991a), and to the protection of handlooms in Indonesia during the Sukarno regime.

References

Amjad, Rashid. 1990. "Urban Planning and Employment Generation in the Asian Megalopolis." In *Employment Challenges for the 90s.* Geneva: International Labour Office. Chapter 5.

Arnold, F., and S. Cochrane. 1980. "Economic Motivation Versus City Lights: Testing Hypotheses About Interchangwat Migration in Thailand." World Bank Staff Working Paper. p. 416.

Balan, Jorge, H.L. Browning, and Elizabeth Jelin. 1973. *Men in a Developing Society.* Austin, TX: University of Texas Press.

Banerjee, Biswajit. 1983. "The Role of the Informal Sector in the Migration Process: A Test of Probabilistic Migration Models and Labor Market Segregation for India." *Oxford Economic Papers* 35(3):399–422.

Banerjee, B., and S.M. Kanbur. 1981. "On the Specification and Estimation of Rural-Urban Migration Functions." *Oxford Bulletin of Economics and Statistics.* 43:7–28.

Barnum, H., and R.H. Sabot. 1981. "Education, Employment Possibilities and Rural-Urban Migration in Tanzania." *Oxford Bulletin of Economics and Statistics.* 39.

Beng, Chew Soon. 1988. *Small Firms in Singapore.* Singapore: Oxford University Press.

Berry, Albert, and Dipak Mazumdar. 1991. "Small-Scale Industry in the Asian-Pacific Region." *Asian Pacific Economic Literature* 5(2):35–67.

Caldwell, J.C. 1969. *African Rural-Urban Migration: The Movement To Ghana's Towns.* Canberra: Australian National University Press.

Chen, Edward K.Y. 1986. "Small Industry in Export Oriented Growth." In *Small Industry in Asia's Export-Oriented Growth,* edited by E.K.Y. Chen. Tokyo: Asian Productivity Organization.

Deshpande, Lalit K. 1979. "The Bombay Labour Market." Bombay: University of Bombay, Department of Economics. Mimeo.

Harris, John. 1989. "Vulnerable Workers in the Indian Urban Labor Market." In *Urban Poverty and the Labor Market,* edited by Gerry Rogers. Geneva: International Labour Organisation.

Hill, Hal. 1985. "Subcontracting, Technological Diffusion and the Development of Small Enterprises in Philippine Manufacturing." *Journal of Developing Areas.* 19. January.

_____. 1990. "Indonesia's Industrial Transformation - Part I." *Bulletin of Indonesian Economic Studies.* 26(2). August.

Ho, Samuel. 1979. "Decentralized Industrialization and Rural Development: Evidence from Taiwan." *Economic Development and Cultural Change.* 28(1) October.

_____. 1980. "Small-scale Enterprise in Korea and Taiwan." World Bank Staff Working Paper 384. Washington, DC: The World Bank.

Hugo, Graeme. 1977. "Circular Migration." *Bulletin of Indonesian Economic Studies.* 13(3).

International Labour Organisation (ILO-ARTEP). 1990. *Employment Challenges for the 90s.* Geneva: International Labour Office.

Lau, Puay Choo. 1984. "The Role of Small Industries in Singapore's Restructuring." Honors Thesis, Department of Economics and Statistics, National University of Singapore.

Levy, Brian. 1991. "Transaction Costs, The Size of Firms and Industrial Policy." *Journal of Development Economics.* 34.

Little, Ian M.D., Dipak Mazumdar, and John Page. 1987. *Small Manufacturing Enterprises: A Comparative Study.* New York, NY: Oxford University Press.

Lluch, C., and D. Mazumdar. 1985. "Wages and Employment in Indonesia." Washington, DC: World Bank. A World Bank Country Study.

Manning, Chris. 1988. "Rural Employment Creation in Java; Lessons from the Green Revolution and Oil Boom." *Population and Development Review.* 14(1). March.

Mazumdar, Dipak. 1976. "The Urban Informal Sector." *World Development* 4(8):655–679.

_____. 1981. *The Urban Labor Market and Income Distribution: A Study of Malaysia.* New York, NY: Oxford University Press.

_____. 1983. "Segmented Labor Markets in LDCs." *American Economic Review* 73(2):254–59.

_____ . 1984. "The Rural-Urban Wage-Gap, Migration and the Working of Urban Labor Markets: An Interpretation Based on A Study of the Workers of Bombay City." *Indian Economic Review* 18(2):169–198; also in World Bank Reprint Series No. 300.

_____ . 1987. "Rural-Urban Migration in Developing Countries." In *Handbook of Regional and Urban Economics,* edited by Edwin S. Mills. Amsterdam: Elsevier. v.2, Chap. 28; also in World Bank Reprint Series, No. 422.

_____ . 1989. *Micro-Economic Issues of Labor Markets in Developing Countries: Analysis and Policy Implications.* Washington, DC: World Bank. Economic Development Institute Seminar Series No. 40.

_____ . 1990. "Korea's Labor Markets under Structural Adjustment." Policy, Research and External Affairs Working Papers, World Bank No. WPS 554.

_____ . 1991a. "Import Substituting, Industrialization and Protection of the Small-Scale." *World Development* 19(9):1197–1213; also in World Bank Reprint Series No. 467.

_____ . 1991b. "Malaysian Labor Markets Under Structural Adjustment." Policy, Research and External Affairs Working Papers, World Bank No. WPS 573.

Mills, E., and C. Becker. 1986. *Studies in Indian Urban Development.* New York: Oxford University Press.

Nugent, Jeffrey B. 1989. "Variations in the Size Distribution of Korean Manufacturing Establishments Across Sectors and Over Time." Korea Development Institute Working Paper 8932, Seoul, Korea.

Piore, M., and C. Sable. 1984. *The Second Industrial Divide: Possibilities for Prosperity.* New York: Basic Books.

Poppola, T.S. 1977. "The Ahmedabad Labor Market." In *Studies in Urban Labor Market Behavior in Developing Areas,* edited by Subbiah Kanappan. Geneva: International Institute of Labour Studies.

Schmitz, Hubert. 1982. "Growth Constraints on Small-Scale Manufacturing in Developing Countries: A Critical Review." *World Development*. 10(6), June.

Sjaastad, L. 1962. "The Costs and Returns of Human Migration." *Journal of Physical Economy*. 70, 80–93.

UNIDO. 1988. *The Philippines: Sustaining Industrial Recovery Through Privatization and Foreign Investment*. Vienna: Industrial Development Review Series, UNIDO.

World Bank. 1978. *Employment and Development of Small Enterprises*. Washington, DC: World Bank.

_____ . 1989. *India: Poverty, Employment and Social Services*. Washington, DC: World Bank. A World Bank Country Study.

_____ . 1992. *World Development Report 1992: Development and the Environment*. New York: Oxford University Press for the World Bank. Table 31, pp.278–279.

Yap, L. 1975. "Internal Migration in Less Developed Countries: A Survey of the Literature." *World Bank Staff Working Paper*. 215.

Zipf, G.K. 1946. "The P_1P_2/D Hypothesis: On the Intercity Movement of Persons." *American Sociological Review*. 11:677–86.

Chapter Four

Social Infrastructure and Urban Poverty

Paul J. Gertler and Omar Rahman

INTRODUCTION

Increased poverty associated with the rapid urbanization of many Asian countries is becoming a major public policy concern. Governments are grappling with how to structure poverty reduction policies targeted towards the urban poor. Unlike rural poverty reduction programs, it is not feasible to base urban programs on agricultural technical assistance. Moreover, because the urban poor are geographically integrated with the nonpoor, the feasibility of community-level interventions may be limited. One alternative is to promote investments in human capital: assist the children of the urban poor and thereby reduce the poverty of succeeding generations. This chapter explores the role of human capital in economic mobility and what governments can do to promote human capital investments.

Human capital measured in terms of health status and education are now regarded as key indicators of economic development. Health and education are considered critical measures of nonmonetary dimensions of welfare as well as important inputs into an individual's earning ability (Sen 1992). Indeed, most governments devote considerable resources to their health care and education systems. These systems tend to be universal in the sense that everyone is eligible and provision is at most at a nominal price. Government intervention is typically justified based on the following three reasons (Besley and Coate 1991):

(i) There may be social benefits or externalities that make public provision more efficient than private provision. For example, everyone benefits from living in a society of healthy well-educated people, and long-run macroeconomic growth objectives may be discounted away by individual households.

(ii) Individuals may undervalue the returns to health care and education, making these merit goods.

(iii) The public provision of health and education can help to redistribute income and reduce poverty measured both in economic and human capital terms.

This chapter evaluates the rationale and possible vehicles for governments to intervene in the delivery of health and education services in urban Asia. A striking observation is the lack of analyses on household data in urban areas and, more importantly, the lack of urban household data sets available for planning purposes. There is a relative paucity of data stratified by socio-demographic factors. Much of what is known about health and education in Asia is at the national level with little disaggregation by residence, gender, marital status, education, income, or other indicators of stratification. Thus, by necessity, much of the discussion that follows is limited to cross-national comparisons, although some figures on the urban situation are presented. Lack of data leads to the first recommendation from this research: baseline urban household level data should be collected and be part of any large donor projects in the delivery of social services in urban areas.

The first question addressed in this chapter is the degree of inequality in the current distribution of health and education. It is apparent from existing national level data sets that ill-health and low educational attainment are concentrated among lower-income groups. It is not surprising that economic poverty is correlated with human capital poverty. However, a somewhat surprising caveat is that the degree of inequality varies across national settings and that the poor are necessarily more worse off in less affluent countries. In some of the less wealthy countries, public policies are aimed towards improving the health status and educational attainment of the lower-income groups. These policies have served as a social safety net for the poor, suggesting a role for this type of government intervention in terms of income redistribution.

The chapter then examines the traditional motivation for government intervention, namely that health and education are productive inputs into an individual's earning capabilities and that households, both privately and socially, undervalue the returns to these human capital investments. Minimal discussion is devoted to this issue as it has been extensively reviewed elsewhere (e.g., Behrman 1990). However, recent methodological advancements in controlling for unobserved heterogeneity and important endogeneities have lead researchers to conclude that while the impact of human capital has a positive and statistically significant effect on economic productivity, the estimated returns are substantially lower than previously thought.

Several factors affect the returns to human capital investments. A critical factor is that the economic returns to health care and years of schooling depend heavily on the quality of those inputs. Moreover, the returns will vary among locations based on the supply and demand for a better educated and healthier work force, which will depend on the composition of economic output (e.g., industrial mix and technological sophistication) and on the supply of labor. Thus, economic returns to human capital must be investigated in each setting to determine if economic productivity is the best method for encouraging local economic growth, and if it serves as a justification for government intervention in the provision of social services. However, evaluation of the economic returns to human capital investments is still contingent on the availability of household level data.

The conclusion drawn from the first two sections of the chapter is that the poor are disadvantaged in terms of human capital measures and that improving their human capital will not only redress these inequalities but may also help reduce economic poverty. This begs the question as to what has been the impact of government interventions on the poor, a question which is addressed by examining the benefit-incidence of government health and education expenditures. The benefit-incidence methodology measures how much of government subsidies are consumed by households across income distributions, calculated as the utilization of the services times the government cost of delivering the service less the price charged users. In most countries, with some notable exceptions, benefit-incidence is regressive in that a disproportionate share of the benefits accrue to the nonpoor. This is because public schools and health care facilities tend to be located closer to the nonpoor and because, even when facing the same accessibility of services, the nonpoor use social services in higher proportions than do the poor due to income effects. The conclusion from this review is that government social service subsidies are not well targeted and, consequently, are currently not efficient at redistributing income.

A second aspect of government provision of social services is the productivity of government expenditures in improving health and educational outcomes. Possible government policies include opening new facilities closer to those households in need so as to reduce access costs, and increasing improvements in the quality of health care and schooling inputs, such as availability of drugs and teacher training.

The productivity of improving access to such facilities is addressed in this chapter. Recent research has shown both accessibility and the quality of inputs to be critical determinants of health status, health care utilization, school enrollment, and performance on tests of cognitive abilities. This research implies that well-targeted government social sector programs not only redistribute income, but can alter the distribution of human capital in terms of health and educational status.

Another means by which governments can induce increased investments in human capital is through family planning programs to help families limit the number of children. Because of the increased competition for scarce resources, children from large families are disadvantaged in terms of schooling, nutrition, and health opportunities. A reduction in the number of children increases available resources to the household; indeed, reducing the number of children is equivalent to an income effect. If children are normal goods, then the increase in income will be spent, in part, in investing in the quality of their lives, i.e., better schooling and health. Thus, this chapter reviews the effects of family size on human capital accumulation.

The first sections of this chapter establish the problem of inequitable distribution of human capital and discuss methods on how government intervention can redress the inequality. Government interventions include expanding social service infrastructure so as to reduce travel times, improve accessibility, and improve the quality of these services. However, such expansion requires additional resources. While some may be derived from general government allocations, most of the additional resources required must come from nongovernment sources (Jimenez 1987, 1989).

There are two general complementary approaches to mobilizing more resources into the social sectors. The first is to charge user fees for services rendered and the second is to better target existing subsidies to desired groups, especially the poor. While user fees have the potential to generate large amounts of additional revenue, there is a possibility that increased prices will reduce the use of social services by the poor. Empirical evidence supports this concern in that the demand of the poor for health and education is more price elastic than the demand of the nonpoor, and the nonpoor are willing to pay more than the poor for improvements in infrastructure (Alderman and Gertler 1989; Gertler et al. 1987; Gertler and van der Gaag 1990; Gertler and Glewwe 1990, 1992).

Concerns about imposing increased fees to finance social infrastructure improvements lead to an analysis of the critical role of mechanisms to protect the poor by better targeting government sub-sidies to them. Available methods for the latter typically include price discrimination by individual exemption, geographic targeting, and self-selection. These are discussed in this chapter, as is the alternative: to promote the expansion of a private sector that attracts the nonpoor out of the public sector. As the nonpoor move from the public sector into the private sector, public expenditure per poor person rises and public expenditure per nonpoor person falls. Public subsidies are thus better targeted to the poor, and administratively complicated price discrimination systems become less necessary.

DISTRIBUTION OF HUMAN CAPITAL

Health Status

However limited, the primary indicators of health status are infant mortality rates and life expectancy. As is shown in Table 4.1, there is wide variation in health status within Asia, with Bangladesh, India, Indonesia and Nepal having the highest infant mortality rates and the PRC, the Republic of Korea, Malaysia, and Sri Lanka having the lowest. Although, in general, countries with low per capita GNP have lower health status indicators than their wealthier counterparts, this is not always the case. The PRC, Myanmar, and Sri Lanka, for exam-ple, have much lower infant mortality rates and higher female life expectancies than one might expect on the basis of their per capita GNP (Figures 4.1 and 4.2). This suggests that sectoral policy decisions, for example focusing on maternal and child health, can help improve the health status of the population, particularly among historically disadvantaged groups, despite constraints on total economic resources (Griffin 1992).

Although data are relatively scarce, limited information does exist for selected countries about the distribution of child health outcomes by various socio-demographic indicators such as urban-rural resi-dence, mother's education, and marital status. As shown in Table 4.2, child mortality for urban residents is generally lower than for their rural counterparts, and children with mothers with no education are particularly disadvantaged relative to children with mothers with some education. In terms of urban-rural differentials, different countries exhibit different degrees of disparity; Sri Lanka, for example, is much more equitable than the Republic of Korea or the Philippines which have

Table 4.1
Health and Fertility Indicators in Selected Asian Countries, 1986

Country	Life Expectancy at Birth (years)			Infant Mortality Rate (per 1,000)	Child Mortality Rate (per 1,000)	Total Fertility Rate (children per woman)	Woman's Lifetime Chance of Death in Child-birth (per cent)
	F	M	F–M				
Bangladesh	50	51	−1	121	78	5.6	4.0
China, People's Rep. of	70	68	2	34	12	2.3	0.1
India	56	57	−1	86	55	4.4	2.6
Indonesia	58	55	3	87	46	3.6	3.4
Korea, Rep. of	73	66	7	25	7	2.2	0.1
Malaysia	71	67	4	27	9	3.5	0.3
Myanmar	61	58	3	64	24	4.4	0.7
Nepal	47	48	−1	130	78	5.9	5.9
Papua New Guinea	54	51	3	64	23	5.2	6.1
Philippines	65	62	3	46	29	4.6	0.4
Sri Lanka	72	68	4	29	10	2.9	0.3
Thailand	66	62	4	41	10	3.0	1.0
Country Average	62	59	3	63	32	4.0	2.1
Population-weighted	63	62	1	60	33	3.4	1.4

F = female, M = male.
Sources: World Bank 1988, and Ross et al. 1988.

similar levels of child mortality. This suggests once again that specific policy decisions can help correct maldistribution of health outcomes.

Data arranged by urban-rural residence mask significant variation within these strata, especially by different socio-demographic indicators such as gender, marital status, income, and education. For example, there is evidence from Bangladesh that health conditions among the urban poor are much worse than an overall urban classification might suggest. The infant mortality rate among slum dwellers in the capital city of Dhaka, who constitute roughly 50 per cent of the total population of 7 million, is over 150 per 1,000 live births compared to the national urban figure of 100.6 per 1,000 (International Centre for Diarrheal Disease Research, Bangladesh 1991; Statistical Pocketbook of Bangladesh 1987). The crude death rate among slum dwellers in Dhaka is five times higher than the overall figure for urban populations

Figure 4.1

Infant Mortality Rate and Per Capita GNP, Selected Asian Countries and World Trend, 1986

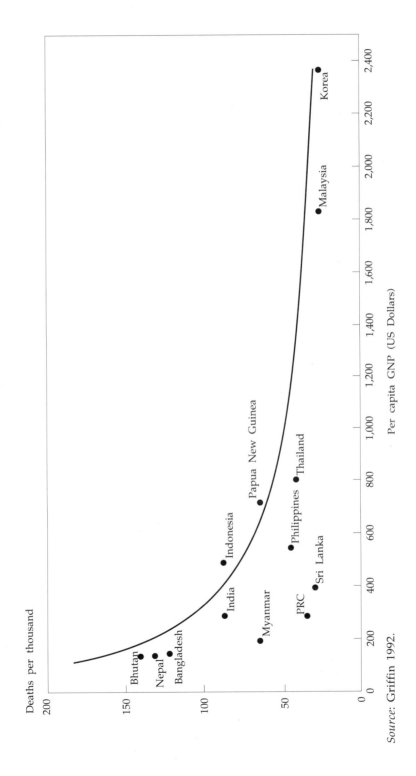

Source: Griffin 1992.

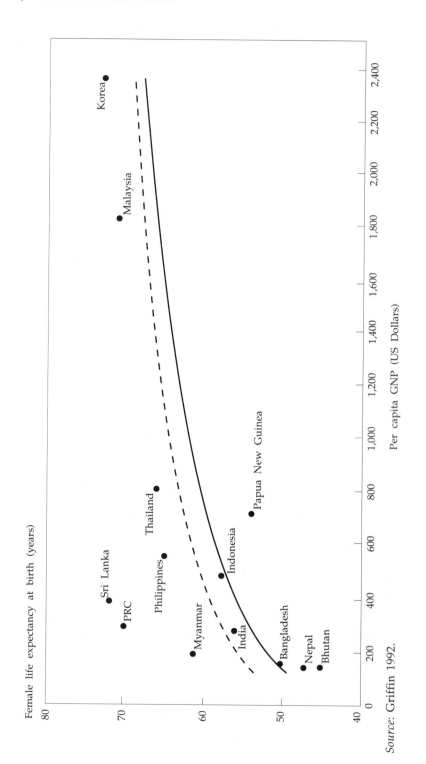

Figure 4.2

Female Life Expectancy at Birth and Per Capita GNP, Selected Asian Countries and World Trend, 1986

Source: Griffin 1992.

in Bangladesh. In the one year-old age group, the diarrhea rate exceeds 12 episodes per 100 child weeks of observation, a rate as high or higher than rates in rural Bangladesh or elsewhere in the developing world. The prevalence of xerophthalmia, or night blindness (most often caused by Vitamin A deficiency), is at least three times higher in urban slums than the maximum acceptable prevalence set by the World Health Organization. Besides diarrhea, slum communities are characterized by high prevalence of malnutrition, respiratory tract infections, reproductive tract infections, helminthiasis, gastritis, typhoid, measles, and tetanus (International Centre for Diarrheal Disease Research, Bangladesh 1991).

The majority of the data on health outcomes is concentrated on child health and child mortality in particular. Little information exists about adult health and even less about morbidity rather than mortality. This is a particularly important omission for a number of reasons. Adult health is becoming increasingly important as the proportion of adults in the population in Asian countries is expanding due to fertility declines and increases in life expectancy (Kinsella 1988). The health status of adults is important not only from the point of view of productivity losses (Over et al. 1992; World Bank 1991) but also due

Table 4.2
**Mortality of Children Under Five in Selected Asian Countries,
By Residence and Mother's Education, Early 1970s**
(deaths per thousand)

Country	All Children Under 5	Residence Metro-politan	Residence Other Urban	Residence Rural	None	Grade 1–3	Grade 4–6	Grade 7+
Bangladesh	215	180	188	218	222	198	186	122
Indonesia	180	143	137	188	193	194	143	77
Korea, Rep. of	83	63	87	90	107	94	74	56
Malaysia	61	42	46	68	67	64	56	18
Nepal	259	...	145	262	261	204	157	136
Philippines	90	57	77	98	130	118	94	53
Sri Lanka	84	71	74	87	104	97	80	55
Thailand	116	57	83	122	145	105	110	38

... means data are not available.
Source: Hobcraft et al. 1985.

to the indirect effect of adult health on child health (Strong 1992) and because ill health can place large demands on already overextended systems which are largely oriented towards taking care of the needs of children (Feachem et al. 1992). Information from Indonesia suggests that adult health is positively correlated with income.

Definite differences also exist with respect to within-household measures of socioeconomic status, such as gender and marriage. There are significant gender disparities in adult health, with women being uniformly worse off than men at all ages. These health status disparities between men and women persist even after appropriate corrections are made for the impact of (i) differential mortality selection by gender (whereby "unhealthy" men die at a faster rate than "unhealthy women," leaving behind a relatively robust group of older men and spuriously inflating gender differences in health at older ages) and (ii) socio-demographic factors such as age, education, income, and location of respondent. Data from Bangladesh (Rahman et al. 1992a) reported in Table 4.3 show that there are significant differences in adult mortality by marital status, with the currently married enjoying much higher survival than their nonmarried peers. This is especially true for older women, and may plausibly reflect differences in access to resources/services.

Health Care Utilization

Although there have been considerable improvements in the level of health services over the last two decades in Asia (Tables 4.4, 4.5, and 4.6), several countries, notably Bangladesh and Nepal, continue to have significant deficiencies in terms of immunization coverage, birth attendant coverage, contraceptive prevalence, and number and mix of health professionals (Griffin 1992). Moreover, utilization of services varies considerably within countries by socioeconomic factors, such as mother's education (Table 4.7) and urban-rural residence (Table 4.8). Not surprisingly, utilization increases with educational status and urban residence in the countries considered, but with different degrees of disparity for different countries. Also, the poor use lower quality providers than do the nonpoor. For example, of landholding households in Bangladesh using private providers, those with more than 2.5 acres use such providers substantially more often than do those with less than 0.5 acres (Figure 4.3).

Detailed analyses from Indonesia suggest that utilization rates are considerably lower for lower-income groups (Prescott 1993; van de

Table 4.3
Life Expectancy by Age, Gender, and Marital Status, Bangladesh

Exact Age (years)	e_x Widow (years)	e_x Married (years)	e_x Married– Widowed (years)
		Females	
45	23.61	27.89	4.3
50	19.44	23.93	4.5
55	15.78	19.73	3.9
60	12.27	16.01	3.7
65	9.48	12.91	3.4
70	7.10	9.70	2.6
75	5.18	9.09	3.9
80	4.32	6.73	2.4
85	3.10	3.50	0.4
		Males	
45	18.33	23.73	5.4
50	16.45	20.50	4.0
55	13.30	17.13	3.8
60	11.02	14.10	3.1
65	8.75	11.31	2.6
70	6.34	8.90	2.6
75	5.18	6.91	1.7
80	3.90	5.23	1.3
85	2.86	2.76	-0.1

Note: e_x = life expectancy at exact age x.
Source: Rahman et al. 1992a.

Walle 1992). Table 4.9 provides evidence, based on the 1987 SUSENAS (National Social and Economic Survey), of how individuals ranked into deciles of per capita household expenditures (with decile 1 being the poorest and 10 the wealthiest) responded to a health complaint. Health care utilization increases with income in both urban and rural settings. Indeed, the share of individuals who either took no medication, or were treated exclusively by themselves or their families, cuts across the income deciles. As incomes rise, individuals not only increase utilization, but consume higher quality care. The percentage of reported illnesses treated by higher quality providers (private doctors and hospitals) increases the fastest with income. However, visits to private doctors exceed those to hospitals for all groups, and also increase much more steeply across household expenditure quintiles. Primary health centers as a recourse for treatment drop

Figure 4.3
**Type of Health Care Used by Patients,
by Household Landholdings, Bangladesh, 1987**

Operational Landholdings

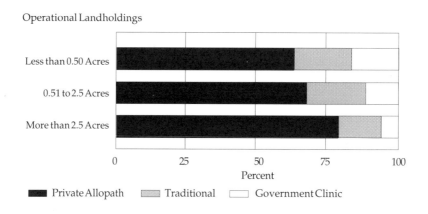

■ Private Allopath   ▨ Traditional   ☐ Government Clinic

systematically from the sixth decile on in urban areas, but are quite stable across rural deciles. Table 4.9 also indicates what proportion of those reporting an illness received in inpatient care and where. Again, the evidence suggests that the incidence of inpatient care is correlated with living standards.

Educational Attainment

As in the case of health, there is considerable variation in educational attainment within Asia. As shown in Table 4.10, educational attainment rates range from a low of 1.8 years of schooling for Bangladesh to a high of 8.4 years of schooling for the Republic of Korea (Tan and Mingat 1992). Typically, poorer countries have lower literacy rates and levels of educational attainment. However, both literacy and educational attainment have increased dramatically from 1970 to 1985. Table 4.11 shows that cross-country variation and general improvement have occurred at all levels of education in terms of coverage of the eligible population. Significant variations in entry and retention rates for different levels of education for various countries are indicated in Table 4.12 (Tan and Mingat 1992). On the whole, coverage of the eligible population at the primary level, except for Bangladesh,

Bhutan, and Nepal, is close to 100 per cent. However, although post-primary education coverage has increased considerably in Asia in the last twenty years, significant variations still exist in the secondary and post-secondary levels (shown in Table 4.11).

Attempts to investigate social selectivity in education are hampered, as in the case of health, by lack of data on specific subgroups. However, the fragmentary evidence that is available does show wide disparities in enrollment ratios as a function of parent's occupation in Asia (Tan and Mingat 1992). Table 4.13 indicates that children of white collar parents are overrepresented in all levels of education (Tan and Mingat 1992). Data on cohort survival rates from the Philippines (Table 4.14) and India (Table 4.15) confirm that children of rich, urban, white collar parents have a much higher likelihood of finishing school than their poor, rural, farm parent counterparts (Tan and Mingat 1992). Data from India (Table 4.15) also show that gender disparities are more muted in urban than rural areas.

Table 4.4
Health and Fertility Process Variables in Selected Asian Countries, 1986
(per cent)

Country	One-year Olds Immunized with Full DPT Cycle	Change in Coverage for Full DPT 1981–1986	Births Attended by Trained Personnel	Modern Contraceptive Prevalence Rate, Mid–1980s
Bangladesh	9	800	...	16
China, People's Rep. of	75	...	...	77
India	58	87	33	35
Indonesia	69	...	31	42
Korea, Rep. of	76	25	65	52
Malaysia	59	9	82	22
Myanmar	23	360	97	5 [a]
Nepal	46	188	10	14
Papua New Guinea	41	-18	34	4
Philippines	73	43	...	20
Sri Lanka	61	36	87	39
Thailand	80	54	33	66
Country Average	56	158	52	33
Population-weighted	65	155	37	53

... means data are not available.
[a] For all methods.
Sources: Ross et al. 1988.

Table 4.5
Population per Physician and Nurse in Selected Asian Countries, 1984

Country	Population per Physician 1984	Change in Population per Physician (per cent) 1965–1984	Population per Nurse 1984	Change in Population per Nurse (per cent) 1965–1984	Ratio of Nurses to Physicians 1984
Bangladesh	6,730	−17	8,980	...	0.7
China, People's Rep. of	1,000	−38	1,700	−44	0.6
India	2,520	−48	1,700	−74	1.5
Indonesia	9,460	−70	1,260	−87	5.4
Korea, Rep. of	1,170	−57	590	−80	2.0
Malaysia	1,930	−69	1,010	−24	2.0
Myanmar	3,740	−68	900	−92	4.2
Nepal	32,710	−29	4,680	−95	7.0
Papua New Guinea	6,160	−51	890	44	7.0
Philippines[a]	6,700	...	2,740	143	2.4
Sri Lanka	5,520	−5	1,290	−60	4.3
Thailand	6,290	−12	710	−86	8.9
Country Average	6,994	−43	2,204	−41	4.0
Population-weighted	2,937	−43	1,972	−56	1.8

... means data are not available.
[a] Government personnel only.
Source: World Bank 1989.

In Indonesia, enrollment rates increase with income regardless of urban or rural residence, with disparity growing as level of education increases (Prescott 1992; van de Walle 1992). The 1987 SUSENAS data indicate an overall school enrollment rate of 93 per cent among children of primary school age. For children in age groups corresponding to the junior secondary school level, the school enrollment rate is 75 per cent. The dropout rate is then quite rapid, with school enrollment falling to 49 per cent in the bracket corresponding to senior secondary school, and 12 per cent in the university age group. However, these aggregates conceal variations across consumption groups and regions. Table 4.16 presents the attendance rates stratified by subgroups defined by region of residence, schooling level, and by quintiles of per capita expenditures. Proportions in rural areas are consistently lower than those in urban areas. The proportion of children attending school increases as the per capita expenditure quintile increases. The exception is for the urban middle 40 per cent in Java who exceed the top

20 per cent at the junior and senior secondary age levels. However, the difference in attendance rates between different consumption groups becomes far more pronounced for age groups 16–18 and 19–25 than at the 13–15 age level. At the primary school level, the disparity is small.

Summary

There appears to be wide variation in health and educational outcome, expenditure, and service utilization both across different countries and within countries, stratified by socioeconomic status. Given the lack of data, it is difficult to draw firm conclusions about the status of health and education specific to the urban areas. However, it is likely that the urban situation mirrors the same patterns of strong variations by socioeconomic factors which have been described at the national level, as confirmed by the data on urban variations in Indonesia.

Table 4.6
Health and Fertility Indicators in Selected Asian Countries, 1986

Country	Nurses	Mid- wives	Health Assts.	Ratio of Midwives and Health Assts. to Physicians and Nurses	Ratio of Other Health Personnel to Physicians	Population per Health Professional
Bangladesh	0.4	0.7	0.7	1.0	1.8	2,414
China, People's Rep. of	0.8	0.8	1.9	1.5	3.6	246
India	0.6	1.4	0.0	0.9	2.1	842
Indonesia	1.1	7.4	3.2	5.0	11.7	765
Korea, Rep. of	2.0	2.0	0.1	0.7	4.0	229
Malaysia	2.9	2.9	0.5	0.9	6.4	338
Myanmar	0.8	1.6	0.4	1.1	2.7	985
Nepal	1.1	3.4	3.5	3.3	8.0	3,684
Papua New Guinea	14.6	14.6	1.1	1.0	30.4	415
Philippines	2.4	2.4	1.0	1.0	5.9	979
Sri Lanka	4.2	5.9	0.5	1.2	10.7	710
Thailand	6.7	7.8	1.1	1.1	15.5	388
Country Average	1.3	2.9	0.6	1.5	4.7	1,386
Population-weighted	1.6	2.7	1.1	1.1	6.2	738

Source: World Bank 1988; Ross et al. 1980.

Table 4.7
Mothers Using Various Health Inputs, By Educational Status,
Sri Lanka and Thailand, 1985

	No	P	S	>S	No	P	S	>S
Prenatal care (any visit)	87	96	98	99	48	78	94	100.0
Tetanus (1 or 2 doses)	80	79	84	86	...	...	...	...
Delivery (trained attendant)	80	92	96	99	44	64	94	99.0
Health card (child, ages 1–2)	66	79	85	87	16	34	58	58.0
DPT 3 (if health card)	90	87	95	99	...	82	83	94.0
At least one immunization	...	...	...	...	75	89	98	100.0

No = no education; P = primary education; S = secondary education; >S = higher than secondary; ... means data are not available.
Note: Tetanus toxoid coverage is not reported for Thailand. "At least one immunization" is not reported for Sri Lanka.
Sources: Chayovan et al. 1988; Institute for Resource Development, Westinghouse, and Sri Lanka 1988.

While much progress has been made in the last twenty years in improving the health and educational status of Asian populations, significant disparities persist, especially across income groups. This reflects not only different levels of national economic resources but also different allocative decisions by different countries. These variations suggest an important role of government in mitigating differences in health services utilization and educational attainment across subgroups in the population.

PRODUCTIVITY OF HUMAN CAPITAL

While the distribution of health status and educational attainment are in and of themselves measures of social welfare, their impact on worker productivity and consequently on income is another consideration in assessing the effect of social services on poverty. The evidence on the impact of improved health and education on poverty in terms of economic status is reviewed below. The findings suggest that when careful attention is paid to the problems of simultaneity bias and various levels of heterogeneity, the association between improved health and education and reductions in poverty is somewhat less strong than had been previously assumed, although it is still significant. Behrman (1990) provides a comprehensive review of the relationship between human capital and income.

Health

Although there is a considerable body of research which has investigated the association between health and labor productivity (income), much of it does not correct for simultaneity bias (i.e., does improved health/education lead to improved income or vice versa) and thus does not provide convincing evidence about the impact of improvements in health and nutrition on increased labor productivity and income. However, in recent years numerous studies have tried to control for simultaneity bias (Strauss 1986; Deolalikar 1988; Behrman and Deolalikar 1989; Sahn and Alderman 1988; Thomas and Strauss 1992). In general, these studies suggest that at least for poorer individuals in developing countries, improvements in health and nutrition do indeed have a positive effect on labor productivity and income (see Behrman 1990 for a comprehensive review).

The studies by Sahn and Alderman (1988) and Thomas and Strauss (1992) are among the few which examined urban labor productivity

Table 4.8
**Mothers Using Various Health Inputs, By Urban or Rural Residence,
in Three Provinces of the People's Republic of China, 1985**

| Health Care Input | Shaanxi (well-developed northwest province) | | Hebei (well-developed northern province) | | Shanghai (PRC's largest city) | |
	Urban (11 per cent)	Rural (79 per cent)	Urban (17 per cent)	Rural (83 per cent)	Urban (59 per cent)	Rural (41 per cent)
Prenatal care (any visit)	80	43	73	49	98	91
Delivery by trained attendant	70	20	50	36	100	96
Delivery in hospital or clinic	54	12	40	12	100	79
Some immunization in first six months	75	43	61	58	98	93
Infant mortality rate for province	49		33		15	

Note: Infant mortality is not reported by urban/rural classification. The survey was conducted during April 1985. "Delivery in hospital or clinic" is a subset of "delivery by trained attendant."
Source: China 1986.

Table 4.9
Utilization of Modern Health Providers, Indonesia, 1987
(annual rates per capita)

Deciles of Persons Ranked by Total Household Consumption Per Capita (1 the poorest, 10 the wealthiest)

	1	2	3	4	5	6	7	8	9	10	All
All Indonesia											
Total Visits	1.44	1.71	1.66	1.88	1.91	2.19	2.45	2.51	2.61	2.30	2.07
Doctor	0.06	0.08	0.11	0.17	0.23	0.31	0.45	0.52	0.76	0.98	0.37
Hospital	0.06	0.07	0.08	0.13	0.15	0.16	0.24	0.24	0.27	0.35	0.18
Primary Health Center	0.78	0.94	0.88	0.96	0.91	1.06	1.09	1.18	1.03	0.60	0.94
Polyclinic	0.10	0.09	0.06	0.13	0.12	0.08	0.08	0.12	0.13	0.09	0.10
Paramedic	0.44	0.52	0.53	0.48	0.50	0.59	0.58	0.45	0.43	0.27	0.48
Urban Indonesia											
Total Visits	1.76	2.50	2.16	2.39	2.06	2.16	2.25	2.10	1.95	2.17	2.15
Doctor	0.24	0.42	0.60	0.69	0.55	0.67	0.97	0.90	0.98	1.26	0.73
Hospital	0.22	0.22	0.27	0.40	0.40	0.28	0.26	0.37	0.42	0.42	0.33
Primary Health Center	0.85	1.09	0.92	0.93	0.88	1.00	0.74	0.61	0.44	0.30	0.77
Polyclinic	0.03	0.21	0.05	0.02	0.09	0.11	0.16	0.02	0.03	0.09	0.08
Paramedic	0.42	0.56	0.32	0.35	0.14	0.10	0.11	0.20	0.08	0.09	0.24
Rural Indonesia											
Total Visits	1.41	1.70	1.56	1.75	1.78	1.83	2.12	2.38	2.82	3.00	2.03
Doctor	0.05	0.06	0.07	0.11	0.14	0.20	0.22	0.30	0.49	0.69	0.23
Hospital	0.04	0.07	0.05	0.09	0.11	0.12	0.11	0.17	0.16	0.24	0.12
Primary Health Center	0.77	0.96	0.85	0.93	0.92	0.90	1.10	1.11	1.35	1.17	1.01
Polyclinic	0.10	0.09	0.09	0.07	0.13	0.10	0.07	0.11	0.14	0.15	0.11
Paramedic	0.44	0.51	0.50	0.55	0.47	0.51	0.62	0.68	0.67	0.74	0.57

Source: 1987 SUSENAS data tapes.

in the wage sector rather than farm productivity. Sahn and Alderman used data from urban Sri Lanka to estimate wages for men and women as a function of calorie intake, controlling for the simultaneity bias. They found significant positive coefficients of calorie intake on wages for both men and women. However these estimates are not very sensitive to changes in estimation technique. Strauss and Thomas used data from Brazil to estimate wages as a function of body mass, height, and nutritional intake. After controlling for the simultaneity bias, they found significant effects of the health measures on wages and earnings.

Education

As in the case of health, there have also been a wide variety of studies which have reported large economic returns to improvements in educational attainment (Psacharapoulos 1985; World Bank 1980). However, there has been considerable debate about whether these striking returns to education are purely a result of increased grade attainment or whether they represent correlated, unmeasured individual, household, and community characteristics, such as innate cognitive ability, family connections, and geographical aggregation bias. Recent studies which have attempted to control these unmeasured attributes report much lower social returns to investments in education (e.g., Behrman and Deolalikar 1988; Birdsall and Behrman 1984).

Other studies have also demonstrated that the returns to educational attainment depend on schooling quality (e.g., Alderman et al. 1992; Behrman and Birdsall 1983; Behrman and Sussangkarn 1989; Boissiere et al. 1985; King and Bellew 1988). When schooling quality indicators, such as test scores measuring cognitive achievement, are included in these models the returns to years of schooling drop substantially. However, the results indicate large returns to high quality schooling and small returns to low quality schooling.

Impact of Health on Education

Besides exploring the effect of improved health and education on increased earning power, there has been considerable interest in investigating the effect of improved schooling on increased health, particularly the impact of improvements in maternal education on infant and child health. Here again, once controls for mother's unobserved characteristics (such as endowments of ability, motivation,

Table 4.10
**Educational Attainment of Adults, Selected Asian Countries,
1970 and 1985**

Country	Literate Adults (per cent)			Average Years of Schooling, 1980		
	1970	1985	Increase	Males	Females	Overall
Bangladesh	23	33	43	2.6	1.0	1.8
Bhutan	...	15	...	...	...	...
China, People's Rep. of	...	69	...	6.1	3.8	5.0
India	34	43	26	...	...	...
Indonesia	54	74	37	4.9	4.3	4.6
Korea, Rep. of	88	92	5	9.5	7.3	8.4
Lao PDR	33	44	33	...	...	...
Malaysia	60	74	23	6.5	4.9	5.7
Myanmar	71	...	...	...	...	...
Nepal	14	26	86	...	...	...
Papua New Guinea	32	45	41	...	...	...
Philippines	82	86	5	7.0	6.9	6.9
Singapore	69	86	25	6.0	4.9	5.5
Sri Lanka	77	87	13	6.1	5.5	5.8
Thailand	79	91	15	4.6	3.8	4.2

... means data are not available.
Source: For all countries, data on literacy are from UNICEF 1988a, except data for
Lao PDR for 1985 which are from UNICEF 1987. Data on the average years
of schooling of adults are from Horn and Arriagada 1986.

habits, and tastes) are instituted, the magnitude of the impact diminishes considerably (Thomas et al. 1990; Wolfe and Behrman 1987).

INCIDENCE OF PUBLIC EXPENDITURES

As documented in this chapter thus far, significant disparities in health and education exist across socioeconomic groups at the national level in Asia, and for urban areas as well. An important underlying premise of public policies which attempt to deal with the issue of urban poverty is that government expenditures on infrastructure and services have a measurable impact on reducing disparities in health and education across income groups. While this is a plausible premise, until recently there was relatively little empirical documentation of this relationship. The discussion below explores the evidence on the distributional incidence of public investments in health and educational infrastructure in Asia. Benefit-incidence methodology is used in this discussion, in which estimated government unit subsidies are attributed to households, depending upon their rate of utilization of health/education facilities, all of whom are assumed to be of equal quality (Meerman 1979; Selowsky 1979). Benefit-incidence analysis measures the percentage of government subsidies captured by

Table 4.11
Gross Enrollment Ratios by Level of Education,
Selected Asian Countries, 1970 and 1985

Country	Primary		Secondary		Higher	
	1970	1985	1970	1985	1970	1985[a]
Bangladesh	54	60	...	18	...	5.2
Bhutan	6	25	1	4	...	0.1
China, People's Rep. of	89	118	24	39	0.6	1.7
India	73	92	26	41	8.6	9.0
Indonesia	80	118	16	42	2.4	6.6
Korea, Rep. of[b]	103	96	42	75	10.3	31.6
Lao PDR	53	94	3	19	...	1.5
Malaysia	87	99	34	53	2.8	6.0 (8.6)
Myanmar	83	107	21	23	2.1	5.4
Nepal[c]	22	82	10	25	2.3	4.6
Papua New Guinea	52	70	8	13	2.5	2.0
Philippines	108	106	46	65	18.4	38.0
Singapore	105	115	46	71	9.0	11.8
Sri Lanka	99	103	47	63	1.3	4.6 (5.1)
Thailand	83	97	17	30	3.4	19.6
Trend Average[d]	76	94	26	42	4.9	10.1

... means data are not available.

[a]   Figures in parentheses refer to the estimated enrollment ratio if students abroad are included. They are shown only for Malaysia and Sri Lanka, countries with sizable student populations abroad.

[b]   The data for secondary education in 1985 are lower than that reported in UNESCO 1987a because they include the average over both subcycles of secondary education. The UNESCO data refer only to the first subcycle.

[c]   The statistic for primary education for 1985 may be overestimated because of inaccuracies in official estimates of the relevant school-age population; see Smith 1988 for further details.

[d]   Excludes Bangladesh, Bhutan, and Lao PDR because data for these countries are incomplete. As a result of this exclusion, the averages for the region may differ slightly from the figures for Asia.

Table 4.12

Operational Characteristics of Educational Systems, Selected Asian Countries, Early to Mid-1980s

Country	Percentage of Population Entering Grade 1[a]	Percentage of First-Year Entrants Surviving to Last Year in Cycle[b]			Index of Extent of Intercycle Selection[c]	Percentage of Females in Total Enrollment		
		Primary	Lower Secondary	Upper Secondary		Primary	Secondary	Higher
Bangladesh	100	24	48	80	8	40	28	19
Bhutan	54	17	83	88	13	34	18	17
China, People's Rep. of	90	68	76	81	54	45	40	30
India	83	37	72	65	15	40	34	29
Indonesia	100	60	92	96	46	48	43	32
Korea, Rep. of	100	97	98	95	87	49	47	30
Lao PDR	100	40	65	68	21	45	41	36
Malaysia	100	97	90	965	79	49	49	45
Nepal	75	33	89	81	5	29	23	20
Papua New Guinea	74	67	63	95	57	44	36	23
Philippines	100	66	74	...	18	49	50	54
Singapore	100	100	100	97	99	47	50	42
Sri Lanka	100	85	75	100	58	48	53	40
Thailand	100	80	91	87	72	48	48	46
Regional Average	91	62	80	87	45	44	40	33

...　means data are not available.

a　There is a possible overestimation of entry rate for Bangladesh.

b　The denominator in each column is the number of entrants to the corresponding cycle.

c　Note that the larger the index, the more efficient the selection process in the education system.

households over the income distribution and measures the magnitude of transfer income. However, it understates the true benefit of public expenditures because it fails to measure the productivity effects in terms of improvements in health, educational attainment, and income.

Health

Health expenditures in Asia vary considerably along a number of different dimensions: the proportion of GNP, the source of resources (public versus private), the type of services (hospital versus nonhospital) and the mix of labor versus capital (Figure 4.4 and Table 4.17) (Griffin 1992). Health care spending varies from about 1.3 per cent of GNP in Nepal to over 5 per cent in the Republic of Korea. The public share of total health care spending varies from over 90 per cent in Papua New Guinea to less than 32 per cent in the Republic of Korea. Moreover, the allocation of public budgets to health care varies from 2.2 per cent in the Republic of Korea to 10 per cent in Papua New Guinea. There also appears to be significant within-country differences in the proportion of government health expenditure benefits

Figure 4.4
Health Expenditure by Source as a Percentage of GNP, in Selected Asian Countries, Most Recent Year

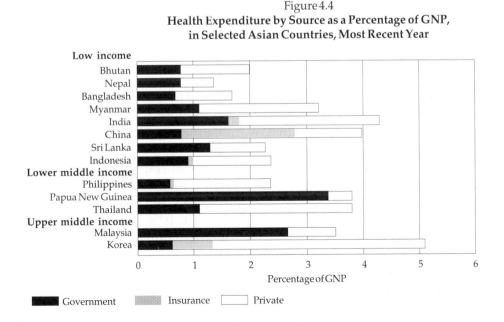

received by different subgroups (see, for example, Table 4.18 which shows a strong urban bias in public health care expenditures in India).

Results from detailed investigations of the Indonesian health sector (Deolalikar 1992; Prescott 1992; van de Walle 1992) show that benefits from government health expenditures are regressive. These studies examine the distributional effect of public spending on the two major health programs, hospitals and community health centers, which account for over three quarters of total government health care expenditure. Subsidies are measured by the difference between the government's current expenditures and revenues from prices charged to consumers. Judged in terms of per capita outlays, public spending on health does not appear effective in helping the poor (Figure 4.5). In 1987, the poorest decile benefited from a subsidy of only Rp101 per capita, with the next poorest group allocated Rp125 on average. Per capita outlays average Rp175 for all Indonesians, increasing to Rp235 in the ninth decile before falling away to Rp212 among the wealthiest groups.

The main factor behind this pattern of incidence is the pro-rich distribution of hospital spending. While most of the health subsidies which reach the poor are delivered through health subcenter programs, health center subsidies increase with income through the eighth decile before dropping away again with substitution of private providers (or public hospitals) by the rich. The mildly unequal distribution of health center subsidies is strongly reinforced by the use of public hospitals which deliver four times the subsides to the wealthiest group as to the poorest group. The pro-rich distribution of hospital subsidies is reinforced by the bias towards wealthier urban residents. Per capita outlays for public hospitals average three times as much in urban compared to rural areas. The pro-urban allocation of hospital subsidies overwhelms the modestly pro-rural distribution of health center spending, so that overall, urban residents receive over one-third more than the rural population.

In relative terms, health spending does not transfer a significant amount of income to the poor. In total, the relative income transfer amounts to about 1.2 per cent of income to the bottom quintile. Nevertheless, the incidence of the health subsidy is inequality-reducing, with the magnitude of relative transfers declining to 0.5 per cent among the rich. The modest benefits delivered to the poor through the main health sector programs reflect the inefficient targeting of public subsidies for health. The poor get a low share of the subsidy (13 per cent), while a disproportionately large share leaks to the rich whose

Figure 4.5
Health Subsidy Per Capita by Program, Indonesia, 1990
(Rp per month; by expenditure decile)

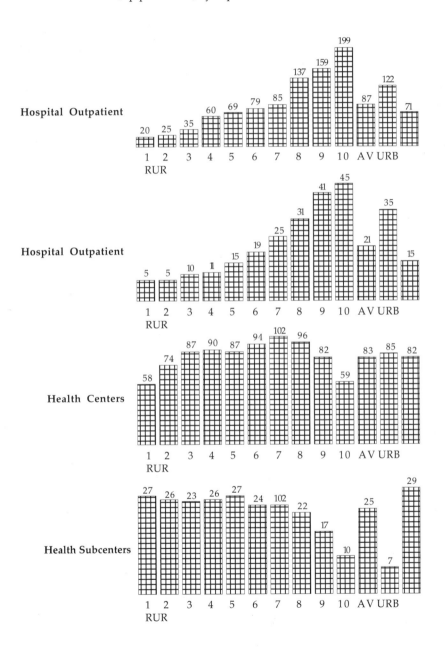

Table 4.13
**Composition of School and Reference Populations by Socioeconomic Groups,
Major World Regions, 1980s**
(per cent)

Region/Group	School Population at Each Level (percentage of total)			Reference Population[b]	School Population as Ratio of Reference Population[a]		
	Primary	Secondary	Higher		Primary	Secondary	Higher
Asia	100	100	100	100			
Farmers	53	25	19	58	0.91	0.43	0.33
Blue collar	34	43	38	32	1.06	1.34	1.19
White collar	13	32	43	10	1.30	3.20	4.30
Anglophone Africa	100	100	100	100			
Farmers	74	36	39	76	0.97	0.47	0.51
Blue collar	18	29	21	18	1.00	1.61	1.17
White collar	8	35	40	6	1.33	5.83	6.67
Francophone Africa	100	100	100	100			
Farmers	61	38	38	76	0.80	0.47	0.51
Blue collar	26	28	21	18	1.44	1.50	1.17
White collar	13	34	41	6	2.17	5.33	7.17
Latin America	100	100	100	100			
Farmers	31	12	10	36	0.86	0.33	0.28
Blue collar	52	54	45	49	1.06	1.10	1.17
White collar	17	34	45	15	1.13	2.27	3.00
Middle East and North Africa	100	100	100	100			
Farmers	37	15	22	42	0.79	0.36	0.52
Blue collar	49	57	31	48	0.90	1.19	0.65
White collar	14	28	47	10	1.20	2.80	4.70
OECD Countries	100	100	100	100			
Farmers	12	11	11	12	1.00	0.92	0.92
Blue collar	53	45	32	53	1.00	0.85	0.60
White collar	35	44	57	35	1.00	1.26	1.63

Note: Socioeconomic groups in the school and reference populations are defined to be the occupation of students' fathers. For each region, the column figures add up to 100 per cent.

[a] Derived by dividing the first three columns respectively by the fourth column.

[b] The reference population refers to the population of parents with school-age children.

share is twice that of the poor. The health sector is more efficient in transferring income to the rich than to the poor.

In contrast to Indonesia, the distribution of government health subsidies is decidedly pro-poor in Malaysia (Hammer et al. 1992). Households in the lowest income quintile constitute 25 per cent of outpatient and 24 per cent of inpatient visits to public health care facilities. The proportion of both outpatient and inpatient visits falls across income groups. Households in the wealthiest quintile of the income distribution account for only 16 per cent of inpatient and 15 per cent of outpatient visits. The reasons for this decidedly pro-poor incidence of public health care expenditures are that the placement of facilities is not biased against the poor, and the nonpoor obtain their medical care from private providers. The subsides measured in terms of income transfers are also substantially pro-poor. In 1989, health subsidies accounted for 17.8 per cent of per capita income in the lowest 20 per cent of the income distribution compared to 2.7 per cent on average. This subsidy led to a substantial reduction in income inequality in Malaysia.

Education

As in the case of health, countries that devote a smaller number and a smaller proportion of total resources to education generally do not fare as well as those spending more on education (Table 4.19). However, there are major differences in coverage between countries which reflect different priorities within the educational systems. For example, countries such as Bangladesh, India, Nepal, and Papua New Guinea have a distinct bias towards expenditures on higher education. This leads to a relatively low retention rate within primary and secondary levels of education (shown in Table 4.12), leading to low overall coverage at all levels of schooling (Tan and Mingat 1992).

The benefits of government expenditures on education in Asia are distributed asymmetrically among the population, with wide variation in the degree of asymmetry across various countries. Since government subsidies per pupil increase dramatically with increasing levels of education, those who manage to remain longest in the educational system receive a disproportionate amount of the public subsidies to education (Table 4.20). Educational attainment is highly correlated with income. For example, data from India, Indonesia and the Philippines show that educational attainment is dramatically higher for students from wealthier families (Tables 4.21 and 4.22). Increased

Figure 4.6
Education Subsidy Per Capita by Program, Indonesia, 1989
(Rp per month; by expenditure decile)

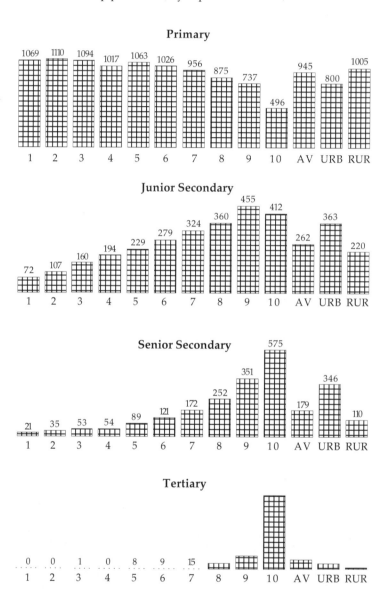

cohort survival rates of higher income groups also implies that, in general, the rich benefit more than the poor from public expenditures in education.

Prescott (1992) and van de Walle (1992) investigated the issue of who benefits from public spending in Indonesia on four major education programs which account for nearly all public spending on education: primary schools, junior and senior secondary education, and tertiary level education. The subsidy rates by source for each income quintile and urban-rural location are shown in Figure 4.6. Per capita spending on all education programs averages one-third higher in the wealthier urban areas, and across the income distribution, the overall education subsidy is decidedly pro-rich. Per capita subsidies average Rp1,520 for Indonesia as a whole, around 25 per cent more than the amounts received by the poor. The subsidies gradually

Table 4.14
Cohort Survival Rates in Elementary Education by Socioeconomic Groups, Philippines, 1982

Socioeconomic Group	Survival Rate (per cent)[a]
Family Income (pesos/year)	
<10,000	57
>30,000	89
Geographic Origin	
Rural	57
Urban	80
Father's Education	
No Schooling	19
Elementary	51
Secondary	69
College	92
Father's Occupation	
Farmer, Fisherman	53
Manual Worker	75
White Collar Worker	91

[a]   The cohort survival rate is defined as the proportion of entrants in grade 1 who survive to the end of a given cycle of education (here, elementary education).
Source: Tan and Mingat 1992.

increase up to Rp1,805 in the ninth decile, and then jump sharply to Rp2,469 among the richest 10 per cent of the population.

While the overall subsidy incidence is regressive, there is a pro-poor bias of primary education subsidies. Virtually all education subsidies reaching the poor in Indonesia are delivered through the primary education program, with the primary education subsidy accounting for about 90 per cent of all education subsidies captured by the poor. The distribution remains fairly flat through the fifth decile and then begins to taper off with a sharp decline for the wealthiest 10 per cent. The key factor driving this pro-poor bias of primary education is the variation in age composition of the population across deciles. Primary school-age children are twice as large a fraction of the population (21 per cent) in the poorest deciles than among the richest (11 per cent). Because primary education is targeted at young children, this is a particularly effective vehicle for channeling resources to the poor. The pro-poor bias of primary education is completely offset by the pro-rich bias of public spending at higher levels of education, which becomes more extreme the higher the level.

Table 4.15
Proportion of Grade 1 Entrants Surviving First 10 Grades of Schooling, India, 1980

Population	Percentage of Grade 1 Entrants Surviving to Various Levels		
	Grade 5	Grade 8	Grade 10
Overall Population			
Boys	39.5	25.0	15.9
Girls	32.1	16.9	9.7
Both Sexes	36.5	21.7	13.4
Urban Population			
Boys	60.7	54.0	40.3
Girls	55.7	42.2	27.4
Both Sexes	58.4	48.6	34.4
Rural Population			
Boys	34.9	18.8	10.1
Girls	25.5	9.9	4.8
Both Sexes	31.2	15.5	8.3

Source: Tan and Mingat 1992.

Viewed in relative terms, education spending in Indonesia succeeds in transferring a substantial amount of income to the poor. In total, education subsidies benefiting the poor are equivalent to 11.7 per cent of income, to which the primary education program alone contributes 10.6 per cent. Not surprisingly, the incidence of the subsidy appears progressive when expressed as a relative income transfer because of the unequal distribution of income itself. Thus, public subsidy is inequality-reducing relative to the distribution of private expenditures. Underlying this apparently progressive distribution, however, is a strongly regressive incidence of the subsidies for secondary and tertiary education. Here, the per capita amounts are so skewed to the rich that their relative income transfers are higher than those received by the poor, even taking into account their much higher income.

Although the education sector is relatively effective in transferring income to the poor, this outcome is not achieved very efficiently from a poverty reduction perspective. The fraction of education subsidies that reaches the poor is disproportionately low with the poorest 20 per cent receiving a share of about 15 per cent. The subsidy distribution is so heavily skewed towards the rich that the top two deciles capture twice as much as the poor (29 per cent). In other words, the education sector in Indonesia is far more effective in transferring resources to the rich than the poor. Even at the primary level, where the poor do benefit disproportionately with a 22 per cent share of the public subsidy, a sizeable fraction still leaks to the rich (14 per cent). At higher levels these leakages are much larger and strongly pro-rich. One third of the subsidy at junior secondary level is captured by the rich, rising to over one half of spending for senior secondary education, and nearly all of the tertiary education subsidy.

In contrast to Indonesia, Malaysia effectively targets both primary and secondary subsidies towards the poor (Hammer et al. 1992). However, similar to Indonesia, higher education subsidies are biased towards the nonpoor. Primary school enrollment is virtually universal and secondary rates have increased over 30 per cent in the last several years in Malaysia, an improvement which has come at a cost of over 15 per cent of public spending being devoted to education. In 1989, the poorest fifth of the population received 36 per cent of primary school subsidies, 52 per cent of secondary subsidies, and 10 per cent of higher education subsidies. The progressive nature of primary and secondary education subsidies are a result of poorer families having larger numbers of children and Malaysia's success in improving enrollment rates across the income distribution. While

Table 4.16

Proportion of Children in Different Age Groups Attending School, by Household Expenditure Quintiles, Area, and Region, Indonesia, 1987

Age Group	Household Expenditure Quintile (per cent)	Java			Other Islands			Indonesia		
		Urban	Rural	Total	Urban	Rural	Total	Urban	Rural	Total
Ages 7–12	Lower 40	93.3	89.2	90.4	93.8	89.2	90.0	93.4	89.1	90.2
	Mid 40	97.3	92.2	93.6	96.7	93.3	93.9	97.2	92.6	93.7
	Upper 20	97.9	94.8	95.6	97.7	96.2	96.5	97.8	95.7	96.2
	Total	95.5	91.2	92.4	95.5	91.9	92.5	95.5	91.5	92.5
Ages 13–15	Lower 40	81.7	54.8	63.2	89.2	71.4	75.4	84.1	61.3	67.6
	Mid 40	91.6	67.2	74.9	93.7	79.1	82.1	92.4	73.2	78.3
	Upper 20	88.9	81.8	84.1	94.2	88.0	89.3	90.4	85.2	86.7
	Total	86.9	64.5	71.6	91.7	77.5	80.5	88.5	70.3	75.3
Ages 16–18	Lower 40	52.9	18.0	30.6	71.0	35.7	45.0	58.8	25.0	35.9
	Mid 40	73.3	34.5	48.9	84.6	49.1	58.5	76.8	40.9	52.8
	Upper 20	72.2	55.4	61.2	87.7	64.6	70.0	76.9	60.2	65.3
	Total	65.7	33.5	45.1	80.0	47.6	56.0	70.2	39.6	49.4
Ages 19–25	Lower 40	9.0	2.0	4.6	17.6	5.6	8.6	11.4	3.1	5.8
	Mid 40	19.8	4.3	10.1	31.3	7.5	14.2	23.6	5.7	11.8
	Upper 20	38.3	13.4	22.6	39.8	12.3	19.2	38.6	13.3	21.5
	Total	20.8	5.8	11.4	29.2	8.2	13.7	23.3	6.7	12.2

Note: Individuals are ranked by per capita household expenditures and then divided into the lower 40 per cent, middle 40 per cent, and upper 20 per cent of the distribution.
Source: 1987 SUSENAS data tapes.

Malaysia and Indonesia have almost universal primary school coverage, Malaysia has substantially higher secondary coverage among the poor possibly because of the residential secondary school program which targeted lower-income children for more intensive academic preparation.

When the net effect of the subsidies are calculated for the system as a whole, the pro-poor primary and secondary subsidies are offset equally by the pro-rich higher education subsidies resulting in a flat subsidy income relationship in Malaysia. However, the magnitude of the subsidies relative to family income suggests that subsidies have benefited the poor substantially. In 1989, educational subsidies represented 26 per cent of household per capita income in the lowest fifth of the income distribution and less than 2 per cent in the top fifth of the income distribution.

PRODUCTIVITY OF GOVERNMENT INVESTMENTS

For governments to improve both the level and distribution of health and educational status, they must understand how public policy decisions affect household demand. In particular, they need to measure the impact of government health and education infrastructure on household health and education choices, controlling for other determinants such as household income, education, household structure, and residence. This approach has a number of advantages over the benefit-incidence methodology for calculating the benefits of social sector spending, including the following:

(i) It allows for a direct assessment of the contribution of public expenditures with measures of health care utilization and outcomes and educational outcomes.

(ii) Unlike the benefit-incidence methodology which essentially assumes equal quality for all infrastructure and services in the reduced form approach, this approach can account for variations in quality of health and education infrastructure and services in addition to quantity. This can be done explicitly if facility characteristics exist which can be matched to household characteristics or can be done implicitly by using measures such as per capita health/education expenditures by region which indirectly capture quality differentials.

Table 4.17
Government Spending on Health in Selected Asian Countries,
Most Recent Year

Country	Health Spending as Share of Total Government Spending (per cent)	Secondary and Tertiary Hospitals (per cent)	Clinics, Primary and Public Health (per cent)	Share in Health Budget, by Type of Expense		
				Salaries (per cent)	Nonsalary Expenses (per cent)	Capital Expenses (per cent)
Bangladesh	3.9	56	44	51	23	26
China, People's Rep. of	4.2	67	33	18	56	26
India	6.7	71	29	51	42	7
Indonesia	3.8	59	41	39	36	25
Korea, Rep. of	2.2	50	50	8	57	35
Malaysia	6.8	59	41	67	19	14
Myanmar	6.8	33	67	29	36	35
Nepal	4.3	50	50	53	37	10
Papua New Guinea	10.0	43	57	68	28	4
Philippines	3.3	58	42	43	51	6
Sri Lanka	4.5	70	30	44	44	12
Thailand	6.1	58	42	48	29	23
Mean	5.2	56	44	43	38	19
Median	4.4	58	42	43	37	19

(iii) It takes into account substitutions between public and private expenditures on health and education, an important omission in the benefit-incidence methodology.

(iv) Finally, it allows for explicit controls for household characteristics such as household income, education, and family size which are independently powerful determinants of health and educational outcomes and use of services.

Demand for Health

A number of studies have recently addressed the impact of public investments in health infrastructure on health outcomes in developing countries using the above reduced form demand approach. Public investments are measured in terms of accessibility (such as distance and waiting time) and quality of care in terms of the level of inputs (such as drugs and personnel).

Access to medical care seems to be a key determinant of health and health care utilization. Distance to health clinics has been shown to have a positive impact on child height in the Philippines (Barrera 1990) and on child survival in Indonesia (Frankenberg 1992). Also, according to Alderman and Gertler (1989), health care utilization in urban Pakistan is negatively related to travel and waiting time.[1]

Fewer studies have investigated the effect of quality of care on health and health care utilization. Thomas, Lavy and Strauss (1991), using detailed facility and household level data from Cote d'Ivoire, found that lower availability and quality of health care services as measured by variations in personnel, drugs, and availability of immunization services adversely affect child health (particularly height for age), controlling for household resources. With regard to the distributional impact of changes in health infrastructure and services, the authors found that the provision of basic health services such as immunizations and some simple drugs has a significant return for poor children in particular. This study is noteworthy as it used directly measured indicators of health facility resources—rather than government planning estimates which are significantly divorced from reality—and also controlled for the potential endogeneity of household income with respect to health by using education of household members as a proxy for long-run resource availability.

In a recent study from Indonesia, Deolalikar (1992) used a reduced form of the demand approach to estimate the distributional impact of public expenditures. In this study, government health expenditure was treated as a fixed factor which influenced household health behavior conditional on household income, education, and family size. The study provided fairly convincing evidence that government health expenditures are associated with greater use of preventative services (namely immunization) and with better child outcomes (namely shorter spells of illness and greater weight for age). Furthermore, Deolalikar's results show that the beneficial impact of government health spending on child health outcomes and the likelihood of use of services for children are significantly greater for the poor than for the nonpoor. As the author hypothesized, the greater benefit for the poor is most likely a result of two major factors: (i) the first being the greater marginal product enjoyed by the poor (due to their lower level of health) for an extra available unit of health services and health infrastructure; and (ii) the greater price elasticity of demand for health services for the poor relative to the nonpoor which leads to a more than proportionate increase in utilization of health services as prices of services decrease due to an improved supply of government subsidized services.

All the studies cited above (and in the notes at the end of this chapter) focused on child health outcomes rather than adult health outcomes. Thomas, Lavy and Strauss (1991) do report that in the Cote d'Ivoire data, in contrast to child health outcomes, they found no significant relationship between health infrastructure and adult body mass index, although this may be a function of the method used for measuring adult health which is subject to substantial reporting error. Recent data from Jamaica suggest that community characteristics (which can be used as a rough proxy for health/sanitation infrastructure) have a measurable impact on self-reported general adult health and limitations in activities of daily living (Strauss et al. 1992). This measure has proven to be substantially more reliable than morbidity measures. Indeed, a key problem in assessing the impact of health infrastructure on adult health is the lack of reliable, reproducible indices. Much more attention needs to be given to this area.

Another important methodological caveat to be considered in evaluating the true impact of public sector investments in health on individual health behavior and outcomes is the potential endogeneity of program placement. Governments may target programs to the locations that most need the services. If government programs and expenditures are specifically targeted to the poor and those in poor health, cross-sectional estimates of the effects of government health expenditure on individual health behavior and health outcomes will be biased. However, estimates of how changes in programs affect changes in health outcomes (fixed effects estimates) are free from such bias.

Pitt, Rosenzweig, and Gibbons (1992) examined the impact of government programs on child fertility and child mortality in Indonesia and found that the placement of health and family planning programs is not random, implying that cross-sectional analyses that ignore this endogeneity provide seriously biased estimates of the impact of public programs. In a fixed-effect analysis that controls for the endogeneity of program placement, they found significant impact of the availability of health programs on child mortality and the availability of family planning on fertility. In a more detailed fixed-effects analysis, also using Indonesian data, Gertler and Molyneaux (1994) found that family planning inputs such as the availability of clinics, village contraception distribution centers, targeted educational activities, and family planning personnel lead to significant increases in contraceptive use and reductions in fertility.

Demand for Education

Research has demonstrated a strong link between schooling (both quantity and quality) and economic productivity. Hence, the impact of public expenditures in terms of reducing access costs and improving school quality inputs on educational attainment and on cognitive development are examined here.

While there have been numerous studies of educational attainment, few have included indicators of school accessibility. Gertler and Glewwe (1990) found that school accessibility is especially important in the developing country setting because children both work and go to school. Further, a key determinant of a households' decision to

Table 4.18

**Distribution of Health and Family Welfare Expenditure
Between Urban and Rural Areas, India, 1983**

(per cent)

State	Urban	Rural	Common	Urban Bias
Andhra Pradesh	46.7	18.3	35.0	2.4
Assam	33.6	21.2	45.2	3.7
Bihar	23.5	28.4	48.1	2.4
Gujarat	43.0	13.2	43.8	1.8
Haryana	43.3	19.5	37.2	2.4
Himachal Pradesh	22.0	25.6	52.4	3.4
Jammu and Kashmir	52.5	18.1	29.4	2.8
Karnataka	44.1	17.5	38.4	1.9
Kerala	59.1	12.4	28.5	3.4
Madhya Pradesh	26.5	20.9	52.6	1.8
Maharashtra	47.7	7.8	44.5	1.8
Nagaland	39.0	17.1	43.9	3.0
Orissa	34.5	28.1	37.4	3.3
Rajasthan	44.6	17.4	38.0	2.5
Tamil Nadu	51.3	17.4	31.3	1.9
Tripura	43.4	18.3	38.3	4.3
Uttar Pradesh	36.1	18.4	45.5	2.5
West Bengal	48.1	16.0	35.9	2.2
States	41.1	18.6	40.3	2.6
Central Government	55.4	0.9	43.7	
All India	44.0	15.1	40.9	2.3

Note: The calculation of urban bias is explained in the text.
Source: Rao et al. 1987.

enroll children and hours of attendance in another year of school are based on the opportunity cost of foregone income to the household. Using Peruvian data, they found significant effects of distance on both secondary enrollment and time spent in school, and found that the greater the foregone income as a percentage of total family income, the less likely families are to enroll their children in school. This suggests that accessibility of schools may have a greater impact on poorer households. King (1993) found similar effects of distance on the probability of completing primary and secondary school in Indonesia, and also found that the negative distance effects are greater in lower-income households. Finally, Pitt, Rosenzwieg, and Gibbons (1992), using fixed effects analysis, found that the availability of primary and secondary schools in Indonesian villages greatly increased the probability of enrollment. They also demonstrated that the placement of schools is non-random in Indonesia and that cross-sectional estimates provide seriously biased estimates of the impact of school availability.

A number of authors have recently investigated the effects of school quality inputs (such as teachers' schooling and ability, books, and libraries) on enrollment and student achievement. In a recent study in Pakistan, Alderman et al. (1992) found that school quality measures such as student-teacher ratios, teacher quality (measured in terms of tests of reading and math ability), and teacher experience are highly significant predictors of student cognitive achievement, controlling for household economic and family background characteristics. Similar results have been found in Brazil (Hanushek 1986) and in Ghana. These latter studies found educational infrastructure to be important as well.

FERTILITY AND HUMAN CAPITAL ACCUMULATION[2]

Another social service that can be used to increase investments in human capital is the family planning program. Because of the increased competition for scarce resources, children from large families are disadvantaged in terms of schooling, nutrition, and health opportunities. Reducing the number of children in a household may cause families to invest in schooling and health (quality) of children. Indeed, reducing the number of children is equivalent to an income effect, increasing available resources to the household. If children are normal goods, then an increase in income will be partly spent on improving the quality of life for the children, i.e. better schooling and health.

There is a large literature documenting the inverse relationship between family size and the educational and health status of children (see the reviews by Wray 1971; King 1985; Birdsall 1988). Studies have found high parity and/or close birth-spacing to be associated with lower average levels of child nutrient intake, such as calorie, protein, and calcium (Behrman and Deolalikar 1991), lower nutritional quality of food intake (Mahmud and McIntosh 1980), poorer nutritional status for children (i.e., height and weight) (Wolfe and Behrman 1982; Scott and Matthew 1983), higher levels of infant and child mortality (Frenzen and Hogan 1982; Simmons et al. 1982; Wolfe and Behrman 1982), smaller per capita health and food expenditures (Wray 1971; Rodgers 1984), poorer access to preventive and curative medical care (Deolalikar 1992), lower schooling expenditures per child (Miyashita et al. 1982; Tan and Haines 1983), lower grades for children enrolled in school (Ernst and Angst 1983), and child intelligence (King 1985). In general, the negative relationship between family size and indicators of child health, education, and development is more pronounced in poor than in nonpoor families, indicating that poverty exacerbates the adverse effects of large family size (Birdsall 1980).

However, the above studies typically treat family size as an exogenous or predetermined variable. Since fertility is a decision variable at the household level, the above results cannot be interpreted as larger family size "causing" low accumulation of human capital per child. A few studies have attempted to separate the causality by examining how other exogenous factors jointly influence (in opposite directions) household decisions on fertility and child human capital accumulation. Rosenzweig and Evenson (1977) and Rosenzweig and Wolpin (1982) demonstrated this result with data from India; they found that a number of variables exogenous to household decision-making, such as technical changes in agriculture, presence of family planning programs and primary health centers in a community, agricultural wage rates for females, and female literacy, simultaneously reduced fertility and improved the average schooling of children. Foster and Roy (1993) found that the experimental family planning invention in Matlab, Bangladesh simultaneously reduced fertility and increased educational enrollment of children.

In countries where awareness of contraceptive methods is not widespread and access to family planning services is limited, the actual fertility of couples may differ significantly from desired fertility so that there are a large number of unwanted births. In developing countries, the incidence of unwanted births is concentrated among

Table 4.19

Indicators of Overall Educational Development, Selected Asian Countries, Mid-1980s

Country	Per Capita GNP 1985 (US$)	Literate Adults (per cent)	Public Spending on Education In Budget (per cent)	In GNP (per cent)	Gross Enrollment Ratio (per cent) Primary	Secondary	Higher[a]	Average Grade Attained[b]
Bangladesh	159	33	10.3	1.5	60	18	5.2	3.9
Bhutan	151	15	7.3	3.8	25	4	0.1	1.4
China, People's Rep. of	273	69	7.8	3.3	118	39	1.7	5.1
India	259	43	13.7	3.0	92	41	9.0	4.8
Indonesia	470	74	15.0	3.7	118	42	6.5	7.3
Korea, Rep. of	2,040	92	16.6	3.4	96	75	31.6	11.4
Lao PDR	332	44	...	...	94	19	1.5	4.8
Malaysia	1,860	74	16.0	6.0	99	53	6.0 (9.0)	9.2
Myanmar	184	...	10.9	1.8	107	23	5.4	7.0
Nepal	142	26	9.6	1.8	82	25	4.6	3.6
Papua New Guinea	621	45	17.9	6.9	70	13	2.0	4.3
Philippines	581	86	11.5	1.8	106	65	38.0	10.2
Singapore	7,093	86	...	...	115	71	11.8	9.9
Sri Lanka	374	87	8.1	2.8	103	63	4.6 (5.1)	9.5
Thailand	712	91	19.4	3.6	97	30	19.6	7.0
Regional Averages	1,017	65	12.6	3.3	92	39	9.8	6.6

... means data are not available.

a   Data in parentheses refer to the enrollment ratio if nationals studying abroad are included in the numerator.

b   Variable refers to the average educational status that the current school-age population is likely to attain given the current structure of the enrollment pyramid and the pattern of cohort survival in the system. The figure for Myanmar is not strictly comparable to those for other countries as it is based only on the enrollment structure. It is excluded from the regional average calculations.

low-income groups (Brackett 1978; Westoff 1978; Birdsall 1980), and unwanted children have significantly lower levels of schooling and are at higher risk of mortality than wanted children (Rosenzweig and Wolpin 1980; Rodgers 1984). Thus, to the extent that family planning programs reduce the incidence of unwanted births, especially among the poor, average levels of schooling and health as well as mortality risk among children are likely to improve.

USER FEE FINANCING

As noted above, governments can improve health and educational outcomes through expanding social infrastructure in terms of access and quality. However, such expansion requires additional resources, and while some of this may come from general government allocations, most must come from nongovernment sources (Jimenez 1987, 1989). There are two general complementary approaches to mobilizing more resources into the social sectors; the first is to charge user fees and the second is to better target existing subsidies to desired groups, especially the poor.

User Fees

Evaluation of the benefits and costs of potential fee increases depends on the revenue-equity trade-off. Over the last several years, a great deal of literature examining the pros and cons of user fee-financed social services has been produced (e.g., Jimenez 1986, 1989; Cornia et al. 1987; Gertler and van der Gaag 1990). Most focus on the trade-off between revenue generation and the effect of increased fees on utilization, especially by the poor. Proponents of user fees point to the revenue potential, arguing that revenues are critical to expanding accessibility and quality of health care.

Revenue potential depends on the price elasticity of demand. This can be seen from the following formula for predicting revenues:

Revenues = (# of people needing medical care
or wanting to enroll in school)
* (1 - per cent fee deters from seeking care or enrolling in school)
* Fee

When demand is inelastic, a 1 per cent rise in the fee will lead to a less than 1 per cent increase in the per cent the fee deters from seeking care. This implies that the effect of the increase in revenues generated

Table 4.20
Distribution of Public Spending on Education, Selected Asian Countries, Mid-1980s

Country	Gini Coefficient[a]	Cumulative Spending Received by 10 Per Cent Best-Educated (percentage of total cumulative spending)
Bangladesh	81.9	71.7
China, People's Rep. of	44.4	31.1
India	65.8	60.8
Indonesia	27.3	21.4
Korea, Rep. of	15.9	13.4
Malaysia	37.9	32.0
Nepal	57.9	53.5
Papua New Guinea	62.1	53.5
Philippines	18.6	14.1
Sri Lanka	32.6	28.1
Thailand	32.9	23.3
Regional Average	43.4	36.3

[a]   This statistic has a range of 0–100. The closer it is to 100, the more unequal the distribution of public spending on education in a generation of school-age population.
Source: Tan and Mingat 1992.

from the increase in revenue per patient is greater than the loss in revenue from the reduction in the number people seeking care. Therefore, as long as demand is price inelastic, increases in the fees will lead to increases in revenues.

The revenue potential from user fees in the social sector is likely to be very large in most countries. Most studies of the demand for medical care and education throughout the world indicate that demand is relatively insensitive to prices, i.e., price inelastic (Jimenez 1989). While the general belief is that demand is inelastic in most countries, there is little research on the price sensitivity of the demand for medical care and education in Asian countries. Such research is critical for countries to be able to better project potential revenues from user fees and consequently to be able to estimate the resources available to expand their social services.

A major concern about user fees are their impact on access to social services. If the poor are more price elastic than the nonpoor, then raising user fees will lower utilization by the poor more than by the wealthy. Gertler, Locay and Sanderson (1987) provide a theoretical argument that the price elasticity of demand should fall with income for discrete goods such as medical care and education. Recent empirical work on the demand for medical care in urban Pakistan (Alderman and Gertler 1989), in urban Peru (Gertler et al. 1987), in Cote d'Ivoire (Gertler and van der Gaag 1990), in Kenya (Ellis and Mwabu 1992), and in Ghana (Lavy and Quigley 1992) report that the poor are indeed substantially more price elastic. Similar empirical work on Peru and Ghana (Gertler and Glewwe 1992) and on Indonesia (King 1993) shows that the price elasticity of demand for education falls with income as well.

However, price elasticities do not provide a complete evaluation of the user fee proposal. Implicit in the arguments for user fee-financed improvements in social services is the assumption that the revenue generated from the user fees will be reinvested in the system to improve access and quality. User fees will be welfare improving only if people are willing to pay more than the assessed fee for improvements, i.e., that the increase in utilization derived from the improvements in the system are greater than the reductions in utilization resulting from the increased fee. This is clearly an empirical situation which is dependent on the relative sensitivity (elasticity) of the demand for medical care to prices, accessibility, and quality. If consumers are willing to pay the full cost of the improvement, the user fee expansion will increase utilization and access. If consumers are unwilling to pay for additional costs, then government subsidies will be required for the improvement to raise utilization.

Another consideration with the user fee proposal is that willingness to pay differs by socioeconomic status. Ignoring this fact in the implementation of user fee-financed expansion could lead to a redistribution of access to social services from the poor to the nonpoor. For example, if, on average, households are willing to pay for the full cost of better and wider availability of drugs and poor households are not willing, then increasing fees to pay for more drugs reduces the use of drugs by the poor and increases their use by the nonpoor. In this case mechanisms would be required to exempt the poor from having to pay the fee, while charging the fee to those willing to pay. Thus, implementation of fee discrimination based on willingness to pay requires information on who is willing to pay. This information can be obtained from demand studies.

Unfortunately, there are very few studies that have assessed the willingness to pay for social services. Gertler and van der Gaag (1990) examined the willingness to pay for improved access to public medical services in Cote d'Ivoire and Peru and found that households in middle-income villages are willing to pay 20–30 per cent of the cost of operating new clinics so as to reduce their travel time to a clinic by two hours. Poor villages, on the other hand, were only willing to pay less than 10 per cent of the cost. This suggests that governments would need to subsidize 70–90 per cent of the costs of new clinics to ensure that they improve the welfare of the people. Gertler and Glewwe (1990, 1992) investigated the willingness to pay for improved education and found that even poor households in Peru are willing to pay the cost of secondary schools to improve access and that even poor households in Ghana are willing to pay to improve teacher quality and school physical infrastructure.

The potential benefits of user fees as a financing mechanism will vary from location to location. The willingness to pay will depend on the returns to human capital in the market, the productivity of social infrastructure in producing human capital, and preferences. To determine the maximum fee that can be charged, information is needed on price, access and quality elasticities by income group, and the cost of producing the services. However, the expected increases in fees and possibly the expected improvements in quality are beyond the range of variation in the few cross-sectional data bases currently available, thus there is a need for a set of country pilot studies to evaluate the effect of price changes. Such evaluation requires longitudinal household and provider data collected before and after the price changes.[3]

Practical Options for Price Discrimination in the Public Sector

The success of increasing social sector user fees depends on the revenue-equity trade-off. Revenues depend on price elasticities, i.e., the proportion of patients exempted from fees and the administrative costs of identifying the poor. The goal of price discrimination is to identify a group of individuals who the government wants to exempt from paying the fee. The criteria for success are in minimizing type I and type II errors and administrative costs:

> A type I error is failing to exempt someone who should be exempted. The greater the type I error, the fewer is the number of poor protected by the price discrimination method. An extreme example of a type I error is when everyone is charged the full cost of delivering the service. In this case, the type I error is 100 per cent.

A type II error occurs when someone who should not be exempt from paying the fee is exempted. The greater the type II error, the greater the leakage of potential revenues. An extreme example of a type II error is when everyone is given free care. In this case, all potential revenues are lost and the type II error is 100 per cent.

Administrative costs of price discrimination methods can overwhelm all of the gains from price discrimination. There are clearly diminishing returns to making price discrimination methods more precise. Administrative methods vary from the inexpensive, such as geographic price discrimination and targeting by age and gender, to the costly, such as a sliding fee system with social worker verification. The additional benefits of better targeting need to be compared to the additional administrative costs of implementation.

Table 4.21

Average Public Subsidies Per Pupil, Selected Asian Countries, Mid-1980s

Country	Subsidies by Level of Education[a]			Cumulative Subsidies[b]		
	Primary	Secondary	Higher	Primary	Secondary	Higher
Bangladesh	5.3	28.0	250	27	223	1,223
China, People's Rep. of	6.3	21.9	199	38	169	964
India	5.2	15.0	180	26	116	836
Indonesia	10.8	16.3	30	65	163	283
Korea, Rep. of	16.6	8.3	12	100	149	197
Malaysia	13.6	20.5	170	82	225	905
Nepal	8.5	7.2	170	43	79	759
Papua New Guinea	26.4	39.0	978	158	392	4,304
Philippines	5.5	4.5	6	33	51	77
Sri Lanka	5.8	8.8	77	35	96	404
Thailand	11.6	13.3	30	70	149	269
Regional Average	10.5	16.6	191	61	165	929

Note: Spending per pupil is expressed as a percentage of per capita GNP.

[a]   The data refer to the average for the public and private sectors at each level. They reflect overall operating costs per pupil minus the amount financed through fees, and are adjusted for the share of private education and the extent of government subsidization of that sector.

[b]   The data reflect the annual recurrent subsidies multiplied by the number of years in the cycle; the figures for secondary and higher education include the subsidies received in the previous cycles of education.

Source: Tan and Mingat 1992.

Table 4.22
Projected Distribution of Educational Attainment and Cumulative Public Subsidies Among Members of Current School-Age Population, Selected Asian Countries, Mid-1980s
(per cent)

Country	Educational Attainment (percentage of school-age population)				Share of Cumulative Subsidies (per cent)			
	No Schooling[a]	Primary	Secondary	Higher	No Schooling[a]	Primary	Secondary	Higher
Bangladesh	40	42	13	5	0	11	28	61
China, People's Rep. of	0	61	37	2	0	22	60	18
India	8	51	32	9	0	11	30	60
Indonesia	0	58	36	7	0	33	50	12
Korea, Rep. of	4	21	43	32	0	14	43	43
Malaysia	1	46	47	6	0	19	54	27
Nepal	18	57	20	5	0	31	20	49
Papua New Guinea	30	57	11	2	0	41	20	39
Philippines	0	35	27	38	0	21	25	54
Sri Lanka	0	37	58	5	0	14	63	23
Thailand	3	67	10	20	0	40	13	47
Regional Average	9	48	30	12	0	23	37	40

[a] This population did not in fact enter the education system.
Source: Tan and Mingat 1992.

Practical options for price discrimination as a method of targeting subsidies to the poor are discussed below. Individual price discrimination is the ideal method for minimizing the revenue lost. However, practical administrative considerations and experience render it ineffective in many settings. Three additional types of price discrimination include geography, self-selection and indicator targeting.

Individual Price Discrimination. A common method of price discrimination is to provide exemption on an individual-by-individual basis. In some countries, this can be done in the community or at the point at which services are delivered. Facility-based mechanisms are used by India, Malaysia, Papua New Guinea, Philippines, and Singapore, whereas Indonesia, Republic of Korea, and Thailand have community-based systems.

Indonesia's current mechanism for ensuring the poor's access to care is through the affidavit of indigence, the *Surat Lurah*. Financially indigent persons can request that their village headman issue an affidavit which exempts them from paying fees for health services at all public health facilities and schools. Unfortunately, few people take advantage of the opportunity. Results from the 1990 SUSENAS and the 1994 Indonesian Resource Mobilization Study indicate that less than 1 per cent of the poor paid zero for their health care. Several site visits to public health centers and hospitals indicated that very few affidavits were presented. Although it is not clear why the system is failing, several possibilities exist: (i) people may not be aware of the benefits; (ii) prices are so low that the benefit is not worth the time cost of obtaining it; (iii) village headman may be charging a fee to issue the affidavit; and (iv) facilities may charge a fee to accept the affidavit.

However, even if individuals were taking advantage of the *Surat Lurah*, it is not clear that a reliance solely on individual exemptions is the best option for the country. It is difficult to measure economic well-being in an economy with no income tax and where a good portion of economic resources are home produced, and without accurate, fast, and administratively simple methods of identifying poor individuals, an individual exemption mechanism may exempt too many people and consequently sacrifice substantial revenues. Another consequence is that a large portion of the poor may not have access to the *Surat Lurah*. While the Government may not want to use the *Surat Lurah* universally, it may be useful in certain circumstances where other methods of protecting the poor are unavailable or in cases where the poor cannot be easily identified.

Geographic Price Discrimination. An alternative method of implementing a pricing policy which protects the poor is geographic price discrimination. The policy aims to tailor the fee structure to the socioeconomic makeup of the population served by each facility. Facilities that serve primarily poor households would charge zero or near zero fees, and facilities that serve primarily nonpoor households would charge larger fees. The fee charged by a facility would rise with the average economic status of the households in its service region. Indeed, facilities in wealthier areas could charge fees equal to or in excess of unit costs. A facility-level fee schedule increasing with the economic status of the households in the facility's service region would imply that government subsidies are pro-poor in that they are largest in the poorest areas.

While in principle the idea of geographic price discrimination is straightforward, its implementation is quite complex. Several steps are involved in the process. First, the geographic area served by the facility must be identified. Second, the economic status of the population living in those areas must be estimated. Third, the level of income below which the government does not want people to pay must be established.

Populations within a service region will not be homogeneous; every service region will have some households whose income is below the government's definition of ability to pay. In those regions where a large percentage of the population are unable to pay, the government could keep fees low enough so as to protect the poor without sacrificing substantial revenues. However, in regions with a small percentage of households being unable to pay, the government would forgo substantial revenues from those able to pay to protect a small number of poor. In this case, it would be cost-effective to screen the poor at the facilities themselves or employ an individual discrimination method. Based on service region and income distribution information, health planners can better implement fee and program characteristics based on economic status.

The implementation of a price discrimination policy requires identifying the population to be served and those that cannot afford the service at a proposed price level. The latter is the population that the government may want to exempt from paying the fees or at least for whom the fees may be reduced. This notion of affordability, of course, has no precise definition and is a policy decision, as is the assessment of the percentage of a household's budget which could be used to pay for services. More factors than just price elasticities of poor households must, therefore, be taken into account. Specifically, inelastic demand among the poor does not indicate an ability to pay. Poor households may borrow heavily or sell assets such as land to pay for medical care. In this case, households place themselves in financial ruin or may forgo food consumption to pay for medical care, and the long-term effects on health and welfare are likely to be very large.

Self-Selection for Medical Care. Using service region price discrimination in areas where the poor are concentrated is a promising method for protecting the poor, without a large sacrifice of revenues. Long travel times prevent people living in wealthier areas from switching to the lower fee facilities in poorer areas once fees in the area have been increased. However, the method has limited potential in urban areas where most facilities are easily accessed by both poor and nonpoor.

An alternative in urban areas is to protect the poor by self-selection. The goal is to keep fees low at health subcenters and much higher at health centers and hospital outpatient clinics. If an individual first goes to the health subcenter and requires a higher level of care at the health center or hospital, the registration fees are waived at the higher levels of care. In this pricing structure, fees are lower if the patient enters the system at the lowest level, and progressively higher the further up the system the patient enters. This pricing structure provides an affordable portal of entry into the health care system through the health subcenter and allows those willing to pay to bypass the health subcenter and to go directly to higher levels of care.

The self-selection method of protecting the poor depends on the poor entering the system at the lowest level of care, and the nonpoor choosing to enter the system at the higher levels. The government can maximize the number of poor protected and revenue generated by setting the price differential between the health subcenter and higher levels of care so that only the poor enter the health care system through the health subcenters. However, the identification of the appropriate price differential depends on cross-price elasticities of demand and how these elasticities vary by income level. Information on both price and cross-price elasticities are currently unavailable.

Self-selection may have its greatest potential in terms of generating additional revenues from wealthier populations. This population may be willing to pay for better services. For example, wealthier patients may be willing to pay out-of-pocket to have a class I bed instead of a class III bed. Setting fees below the willingness to pay will induce these patients to self-select the higher class of service. If the fee for the higher class of service is greater than the cost of providing those services, excess revenues generated can be used to subsidize the care of the poor. At a minimum, the fee should be set at the cost of delivering the higher class of service to ensure that the care of those willing to pay is not subsidized. In any event, effective price discrimination in urban areas can be achieved by self-selection through service-level fee differentials rather than through facility-wide (geographic) price differentials.

Indicator Targeting. Finally, a method of charging those most able to pay at least the full cost of care is to target identifiable groups. Insurance status is a good indicator of those most able to pay, because the insured are wealthier than the general population, pay less under the current system of charges, and use more services. Thus, a greater than proportional share of public subsidies accrue to this wealthier group.

For example, in Indonesia, civil servants who are covered by ASKES insurance are concentrated at the top end of the income distribution. Over 50 per cent of civil servants are in the top 20 per cent of the overall income distribution and about 80 per cent of civil servants are in the top 40 per cent of the income distribution. However, at current prices, which are less than costs, ASKES patients are heavily subsidized by the public sector. The level of reimbursement for hospital care is only about 65 per cent of actual costs. Moreover, ASKES members have about 45 per cent more outpatient visits to government facilities and 65 per cent more inpatient visits than non-ASKES members. The higher utilization rates and lower charges imply that this relatively well-off population receives a greater-than-equitable share of public health care subsidies.

Thus, one method of retargeting public subsidies to the poor in Indonesia is to reduce the ASKES subsidy by raising prices to this well-identified population. Similar to lowering prices to the poor, the Government may opt to charge higher prices to these higher-income groups. However, increasing prices to ASKES members will greatly increase the expected liabilities incurred by ASKES. Therefore, if prices to ASKES patients are raised, PHB must be allowed to increase its premiums to cover the expected increase in liabilities.

Analogous to reducing prices to the poor, implementing price discrimination by raising prices to the wealthier group is a nontrivial administrative problem. Operationally, facilities can charge insured patients the full cost of care when they bill the insurance company and give cash paying customers a discount. However, for insurance companies not to game the system, the co-payment and deductible for the insured patients must be substantially less than the user fee charged to uninsured patients. Otherwise there is no incentive for households to purchase insurance and less incentive to use it if they have it. Additionally, if fees are increased to the insured population, premiums will have to be commensurately increased to maintain the financial viability of the insurance companies.

PRIVATE SECTOR DELIVERY OF SOCIAL SERVICES

An alternative to large public systems with administratively complex price discrimination mechanisms is to focus the public system on serving the poor. This can be accomplished by the existence of a higher quality fully priced private sector. The availability of such a private sector attracts those who are willing to pay for the improved quality and accessibility and results in a separating equilibrium where the poor remain in the lower quality, heavily subsidized public system and the nonpoor move to the private system. As income rises, households move out of the public sector into the private sector (Hammer et al. 1992).

One of the most debated mechanisms of promoting the private sector health sector is through prepayment or insurance schemes. While most countries in Asia have always had full insurance in the form of a national health care system financed through general tax revenues, the new insurance proposals are attempts to mandate individuals to privately contribute to prepayment funds that can be used to pay user fees at times of need. The goal is to smooth health care payments across times of good and ill-health, thus insuring against financial ruin during times of ill-health. Individuals become less price sensitive (moral hazard). Also, if health insurance plans are formulated so as to allow subscribers to access the private market, subscribers will shift out of the public sector into the private sector. If a large enough proportion of households currently served by the public sector shift to the private sector and the current subsidies to the public sector are not reduced, it is possible that the expenditures per person in the public sector will rise.

While the development of health insurance represents a huge potential benefit, care must be taken in structuring the design of benefits so as not to further exacerbate the regressivity of public subsidies. Since the insured population is primarily from the wage sector and therefore in the higher-income group, the government could retarget public subsidies to the poor by charging the full cost of care in public facilities to insured patients. In this way, the expansion of insurance would not lead to greater subsidy of the nonpoor.

CONCLUSIONS

A major public policy concern in Asia is the growing poverty associated with the rapid urbanization of many Asian countries. Governments need to develop poverty reduction policies that are targeted towards the urban poor. Unlike rural poverty reduction programs, urban programs cannot be based on agricultural technical assistance, and because the urban poor are geographically mixed with the nonpoor, the feasibility of community-level interventions is limited. Increased investments in the human capital of the children of the urban poor will help to remove the next generation from poverty, and expanded and improved education, family planning and health care programs are important vehicles for reducing urban poverty.

However, Asian countries face two interconnected problems in terms of the delivery of social services: (i) more resources must be generated to expand and improve the quality of the education, family planning and health care programs; and (ii) public subsidies are typically regressive in that more subsidies accrue to the nonpoor than to the poor.

Governments can raise additional resources through increased user fees at public facilities and by promoting the private sector. Both methods have great potential for generating substantial revenues. However, unless careful safeguards protecting the poor's access to social services are established at the same time, both of these financing proposals could dramatically increase the inequities between poor and nonpoor already in place.

The major obstacle to large increases in user fees is that a vast segment of the poor population may be priced out of the market. This chapter analyzed four methods of price discrimination that would allow governments to raise prices to the nonpoor and lower them to the poor: individual, geographic, self-selection, and wealth indicators. Further investigation of the feasibility of individual price discrimination is warranted because individual price discrimination, if administratively inexpensive, is the optimal level at which to implement a system of differential fees. Indeed, it is worth pilot testing several different alternatives to gain information about its potential.

The second method investigated was geographic price discrimination, i.e., charging lower prices at facilities that service poorer populations and higher prices in facilities that serve wealthier populations. Feasibility studies in two Indonesian provinces, Kalimantan-Timur (KALTIM) and Nusa Tengara Barat (NTB) indicated that this method is likely to be highly successful in areas where the poor are heavily concentrated (see Boxes 4.1, 4.2, and 4.3). However, information on price elasticity of demand and how the price elasticity differs by income is needed for full-scale implementation. Clearly, a pilot test of geographic price discrimination would be a major step toward geographic price discrimination.

While geographic price discrimination is feasible in some areas where public facilities are located at some distance from one another,

---

Box 4.1
Affordability of Medical Care in Indonesia

An upper bound on the notion of the price consumers are unable to pay is the price beyond which demand becomes elastic. Increasing prices beyond that point leads to large enough reductions in utilization so that revenues actually fall. Establishing such a point requires estimating price elasticities of demand by income level. Estimates of such price elasticities do not yet exist for most Asian countries. However, an idea of the price levels beyond which demand becomes elastic can be derived from demand functions estimated for other countries, such as estimates of price elasticities of the demand for medical care by income class obtained for Cote d'Ivoire, Pakistan, and Peru. A robust result across all three countries is that when outpatient prices rise above 5 per cent of nonfood household expenditures per capita, demand becomes elastic. Therefore, a general rule for setting the upper bound of ability to pay is that prices should be below 5 per cent of nonfood household expenditures.

While the definition of poverty is a policy decision, for the purpose of this analysis, those unable to pay for medical care were defined as households for whom the fee was greater than 5 per cent of nonfood expenditures per capita. This was based on the rule of thumb that demand becomes elastic when fees are above this level. Beyond this level, increases in fees lead to reductions in revenues. Using this affordability criterion, the percentage of households unable to pay various fee levels is graphed for two provinces in Indonesia (KALTIM and NTB) in Figure 3.8. The NTB curve is above that of KALTIM because NTB is substantially poorer. While only 10 per cent of households in KALTIM appear unable to pay the present outpatient fee of Rp300, nearly half of households in NTB (about 40 per cent) appear unable to pay the same fee. The percentage of households that are unable to pay rises very quickly in NTB, whereas in KALTIM it rises linearly.

other methods must be attempted in urban settings. Because public facilities are located accessibly close to one another, it is all but impossible to identify facilities that serve only the poor. An alternative

---

Box 4.2
Affordability of Education in Indonesia

The ratio of monthly schooling costs per enrolled child to the household's monthly income per capita suggests that the burden of education is on the family. This price/income ratio measures the affordability of education. The costs per student were computed using the 1989 SUSENAS, a nationally representative survey of over 60,000 households. Two caveats are valid: First, prices are observed mostly for those who have decided to enroll; hence, the price measures tend to be biased downward. Prices for those not in school are imputed based on the average prices paid for by those in school. One exception is the distance between the home and the nearest primary or secondary school which the SUSENAS asked of all households. Second, data limitations do not make it possible to control for quality of schooling; the price-income ratio, thus, implicitly assumes that one rupiah buys one unit of education of the same quality. One way to control for quality is by choosing, among the many components of price (e.g., tuition fees and extracurricular activity fees), those more exogenous to choices made regarding school quality. Though fees are likely to be used to ration seats in the better quality schools, they presumably reflect less variation due to quality than if price also included spending for learning materials.

On average, the price/income ratio for enrollees is 5 per cent for primary education, 24 per cent for lower secondary education, and 29 per cent for upper secondary education. However, at all levels the price/income ratio is higher for the poor, ranging from over 5 per cent for the lowest decile at primary, to 42 per cent at lower secondary and an enormous 82 per cent of income at senior secondary level. This ratio is highest for the poorest decile and lowest for the wealthiest at both of the secondary levels; at the primary level, it is lowest for the middle deciles. Private education incurs a larger share of family income than public education across all education levels. For each education level, the relative cost burden becomes much lighter for wealthier students. The price/income ratio then shows that, despite the widespread and increasing provision of public education, the burden of education expenditures is still most severely felt by low-income households.

By computing a price/income ratio, including those who had dropped out of school during the survey, this point becomes even clearer. Using the average price in the community as a proportion of the average income of those with school-age children, whether enrolled or not enrolled in school, the affordability of education for those whose children had dropped out of school can be compared with those whose children were enrolled. This ratio indicates that schooling indeed presented a greater burden for those whose children had left school than for those whose children were enrolled at all levels of education. Moreover, this difference was largest at the lowest decile.

to geographic price discrimination is self-selection. In health care, the government would maintain a set of facilities (health subcenters) with low prices that triage patients. Those requiring more sophisticated care would be referred at a reduced charge to health centers and hospitals. Those not willing to spend the time at the health subcenters could bypass them by paying a larger fee, thus the nonpoor would self-select out of the health subcenters. Another form of self-selection is through differential pricing of frills. The success of self-selection, however, requires getting the price differentials between the levels of care right, which requires knowledge of the price and time elasticities of demand for the various levels of care, the cross-price elasticities and how these vary by income.

The final method of protecting the poor is to use indicators of wealth to charge higher prices. For health care, one such indicator is insurance status, such as the Indonesian ASKES, which could be used to charge the wealthier customer the full cost of care. In this way public subsidies could be retargeted to the poor.

While the development of health insurance represents a huge potential for generating the resources necessary to expand the health care sector, care must be taken in structuring the design so as not to further exacerbate the regressivity of public subsides. Indeed, as insurance coverage grows and prices rise, governments need to guarantee the poor population access to insurance or provide low-cost alternative care. Moreover, as increased insurance coverage raises the flow of nongovernmental resources into the health care sector, mechanisms must still be identified which better target these resources to the poor. While insurance may generate additional resources, there is no guarantee that these will reduce the regressivity of public subsidies. Indeed, if the new resources are added to the current system, benefits will accrue in substantially greater proportion to the nonpoor. Methods must be found to retarget public subsidies towards the poor, possibly by increasing the public subsidy to the rural health care system and to the low-end public urban facilities. Most importantly, the position of the poor would be further eroded if government subsidies were reduced as nongovernmental resources increased.

The expansion of health insurance does improve the government's ability to price discriminate via target indicators. Since the insured population is primarily from the wage sector and, therefore, in higher income groups, the government could retarget public subsidies to the poor by charging the full cost of care in public facilities to insured patients. In this way, the expansion of insurance would not lead to greater subsidy of the nonpoor and avoid the current practice of large public subsidies accruing to insured patients.

Box 4.3
Geographic Price Discrimination in Indonesia

The possibility of employing geographic price discrimination for medical care has been investigated in two Indonesian provinces: KALTIM and NTB. Under consideration was an increase in health center fees from about Rp300 to between Rp600 and Rp900. Prior to implementation, there was substantial concern about the effect of these expected price increases on the poor's access to medical care and the ability of the Government to protect those unable to pay.

Service regions were constructed using village-level patient origin information. Rural service regions typically contain a single health provider serving a defined set of villages, while suburban service regions have populations in some villages that have access to more than one health facility and, therefore, may contain more than one facility. Finally, urban populations often have access to a large number of health providers and contain multiple facilities.

Information on village-level nonfood expenditures per capita was obtained from the 1987 SUSENAS. However, while the SUSENAS data are representative at the province level, they are not reliable for lower levels. Moreover, data were only collected for a sample of villages within each province. Hence, SUSENAS can only provide a province-level picture and not a service region-level picture. However, by merging the 1987 SUSENAS with the 1986 *Potensi Desa* (PODES) (a village level assets and infrastructure file), multivariate regression analysis was used to estimate average household level incomes (expenditures) at the village level based on community characteristics. All households in a village were defined as unable to pay a certain fee if the fee was greater than the village's average nonfood per capita expenditures. This information was then aggregated to the service level region to obtain the percentage of the population in the service region unable to pay the fee. These estimates were made for fees of Rp600 and Rp900.

Since service regions comprise households who are both able to pay and unable to pay, it is not clear which service regions should have low fees. Indeed, whether or not the facilities in a service region should raise their prices to a certain level depends on the percentage of the population who is unable to pay relative to the opportunity cost in terms of foregone revenues. The benefit to keeping fees low in the service region is measured as the number of persons unable to pay who are protected. The cost is measured in terms of the number of people exempted who are able to pay. By exempting people who are able to pay, the Government forgoes revenues.

In summary, geographic price discrimination has great potential in both KALTIM and NTB. However, the potential in KALTIM is much larger than in NTB. This is because the poor tend to be more concentrated in KALTIM than in NTB and the better transportation in NTB makes their service regions larger so that they encompass more heterogeneous populations.

A promising method of better targeting public subsidies to the poor is through the promotion of the private sector. Promotion of the private sector (by, for example, insurance in the health care sector) will expand the private market and improve the private market's accessibility to a wider class of individuals. If a large enough proportion of households currently served by the public sector shifts to the private sector and the current subsidies to the public sector are not reduced, it is possible that the expenditures per person in the public sector will rise.

Protection of the poor must be understood in the context of a broader philosophical discussion regarding the responsibilities and proper role of government in assuring public welfare. While some argue for national delivery of social services and its variants, others favor a private sector approach. The structuring mechanisms to ensure the poor's access to social services depends on the resolution of these two views. The approach that expands the public sector by installing user fee payments at government facilities requires the government to find methods of identifying the poor and price discriminating in favor of the poor at their facilities. There are three possible methods at hand. The first two, geographic price discrimination and self-selection, have been discussed in detail above. The third involves charging anyone with access to a prepayment fund a higher price, possibly full cost. The approach that emphasizes the development of the private sector depends on the nonpoor leaving the public sector. If existing subsidies to the public sector are not reduced, then this amounts to an increase in subsidies per poor person. In this case, the users of the public system would be the poor and there would not be a great need for incorporating price discrimination mechanisms in publicly provided health services.

Notes

1. Distance to medical care facilities has been found to be a key determinant of health care utilization by the following: Akin et al. (1986) for the Philippines; Dor et al. (1987) for Cote d'Ivoire; Gertler et al. (1987) for urban Peru; Alderman and Gertler (1989) for Pakistan; Gertler and van der Gaag (1990) for Cote d'Ivoire and Peru; Akin et al. (1993) for Nigeria; Ellis and Mwabu (1992) for Kenya; Lavy and Quigley (1992) for Ghana.
2. The discussion on fertility and human capital accumulation is based entirely on Deolalikar and Pernia (1993).

3. Such pilot studies are occurring as part of the Indonesian Resource Mobilization Study being conducted in two provinces and as part of the Chinese Health Insurance Project being conducted in four townships.

References

Akin, J.S., C. Griffin, D. Guilkey, and B. Popkin. 1986. "The Demand for Adult Outpatient Services in the Bicol Region of the Philippines." *Social Science and Medicine.* 22(3): 321–328.

Akin, J.S., D. K. Guilkey, and E. H. Denton. 1993. "Multinomial Probit Estimation of Health Care Demand: Ogun State Nigeria." Working Draft, University of North Carolina.

Alderman, H., and P. Gertler. 1989. "The Substitutability of Public and Private Medical Care for the Treatment of Childrens Illnesses in Pakistan." Living Standards Measurement Survey (LSMS) Working Paper 56. Washington, DC: The World Bank.

Alderman, H., J. Behrman, S. Kahn, D. Ross, and R. Sabot. 1992. "Public Schooling Expenditures in Rural Pakistan: Efficiently Targeting Girls and a Lagging Region." In *Public Spending and the Poor: Theory and Evidence,* edited by Dominique van de Walle and Kimberley Nead. Baltimore: Johns Hopkins University Press. Forthcoming.

Banerjee, Nirmala. 1983. "Women and Poverty: Report on a Workshop." *Economic and Political Weekly* 18(40)(October).

Barrera, A. 1990. "The Role of Maternal Schooling and Its Interaction with Public Health Programs in Child Health Production." *Journal of Development Economics.* 32:69–91.

Behrman, Jere R. 1990. "The Action of Human Resources and Poverty on One Another. What We Have Yet to Learn?" LSMS Working Paper, Number 74. Washington, DC: The World Bank.

Behrman, Jere R., and Nancy Birdsall. 1983. "The Quality of Schooling: Quantity Alone is Misleading." American Economic Review. 73:928–946.

Behrman, Jere R., and Anil B. Deolalikar. 1988a. "Unobserved House-hold and Community Heterogeneity and the Labor Market Impact of Schooling: A Case Study for Indonesia." Philadelphia: University of Pennsylvania. Mimeo.

_____ . 1988b. "Seasonal Demands for Nutrient Intakes and Health Status in Rural South India." In *Causes and Implications of Seasonal Variability in Household Food Security*, edited by David E. Sahn. Baltimore: The Johns Hopkins University Press. pp. 66–78.

_____ . 1989. "Seasonal Demands for Nutrient Intakes and Health Status in Rural South India." In *Seasonal Variability in Third World Agriculture*, edited by D. Sahn. Baltimore: Johns Hopkins Press.

_____ . 1991. "The Intrahousehold Demand for Nutrients: Individual Estimates, Fixed Effects and Permanent Income." *The Journal of Human Resources*. Winter.

Behrman, Jere R., and Chalongphob Sussangkarn. 1989. "Parental Schooling and Child Outcomes: Mother Versus Father, Schooling Quality, and Interactions." Philadelphia: University of Pennsylvania. Mimeo.

Besley, T., and S. Coate. September 1991. "Public Provision of Private Goods and the Redistribution of Income." *The American Economic Review*. 81(4):979–984.

Birdsall, Nancy. 1980. "The Cost of Siblings: Child Schooling in Urban Colombia." *Research in Population Economics*. 2:115–150.

_____ . 1988. "Economic Approaches to Population Growth." In *Handbook of Development Economics*, edited by Hollis Chenery and T.N. Srinivasan. Vol. 1, North Holland: Elsevier Science Publishers B.V.

_____ . 1992. "Another Look at Population and Global Warming." Policy Research Working Paper. WPS 1020, Washington, DC: The World Bank. November.

Birdsall, Nancy, and Jere R. Behrman. 1984. "Does Geographical Aggregation Cause Overestimates of the Returns to Schooling?" *Oxford Bulletin of Economics and Statistics*. 46, 55–72.

Boissiere, M., J. B. Knight, and R. H. Sabot. 1985. "Earnings, Schooling, Ability and Cognitive Skills." *American Economic Review.* 75:1016–1030.

Brackett, J. W. 1978. "Family Planning in Four Latin American Countries-Knowledge, Use and Unmet Needs: Some Findings from the World Fertility Survey." *International Family Planning Perspectives.* 4(4):116–123.

Chayovan, Napaporn, Peerasit Kamnuansilpa, and John Knodel. 1988. *Thailand Demographic and Health Survey 1987.* Bangkok: Institute of Population Studies, Chulalongkorn University, and Columbia, MD: Institute for Resource Development, Westinghouse.

China (Peoples Education Press). 1984 and 1986. *Achievement of Education in China.* Beijing.

Cornia, G.A., R. Jolly, and F. Stewart. 1987. *Adjustment with a Human Face.* Oxford: Clarendon Press.

Das Gupta, Monica. 1987. "Selective Discrimination Against Female Children in Rural Punjab, India." *Population and Development Review.* 13(1):77–100.

_____ . 1990. "Gender Discrimination in the Intrahousehold Allocation of Health Inputs and Distribution of Health Outcomes among Children under 5: Results from Indonesia." The Robert S. McNamara Fellowship Report. The World Bank. October.

Deolalikar, Anil B. 1988. "Nutrition and Labor Productivity in Agriculture: Estimates for Rural South India." *Review of Economics and Statistics.* 70:3(August), 406–413.

_____ . 1992. "Does the Impact of Government Health Expenditures on the Utilization of Health Services and Health Outcomes of Individuals Differ Across Expenditure Classes?" World Bank Conference on Public Expenditures and the Poor: Incidence and Targeting. Washington, DC: The World Bank.

Deolalikar, Anil, and Ernesto Pernia. 1993. "Population Growth in Asia: Trends and Implications for Economic Growth, Ecology and Poverty." Paper presented at the Regional Symposium on Population Policy and Economic Development: Lessons of Experience. Manila: Asian Development Bank, 19–21 July. Mimeo.

Dor, A., P. Gertler, and J. Van der Gaag. 1987. "Non-Price Rationing and Medical Care Provider Choice in Rural Cote d'Ivoire." *Journal of Health Economics.* 6:291–304.

Ellis, R. P., and G. M. Mwabu. 1992. "The Demand for Health Care in Kenya." Processed. Boston University.

Ernst, C., and J. Angst. 1983. *Birth Order: Its Influence on Personality.* New York: Springer-Verglag.

Feachem, R., T. Kjellstrom, C. Murray, and M. Over. 1992. *The Health of Adults in the Developing World.* Oxford University Press.

Foster, A., and N. Roy. 1993. "The Dynamics of Education and Fertility: Evidence from a Family Planning Experiment." Paper presented at the Annual Meeting of the Population Association of America.

Frankenberg, E. 1992. "Infant and Early Childhood Mortality in Indonesia: The Impact of Access to Health Facilities and Other Community Characteristics on Mortality Risks." Dissertation in Demography. University of Pennsylvania.

Frenzen, Paul D., and Dennis P. Hogan. 1982. "The Impact of Class, Education and Health Care on Infant Mortality in a Developing Society: The Case of Rural Thailand." *Demography.* 19(3).

Gertler, P., and P. Glewwe. 1990. "The Willingness to Pay for Education in Developing Countries: Evidence from Rural Peru." *Journal of Public Economics.* 42:251–275.

_____ . 1992. "The Willingness to Pay for Education for Daughters in Contrast to Sons: Evidence from Rural Peru." *The World Bank Economic Review.* 6(1):171–188.

Gertler, P., and J. van der Gaag. 1990. *The Willingness to Pay for Medical Care in Developing Countries: Evidence from Two Developing Countries.* Baltimore: Johns Hopkins Press.

Gertler, P., and J. W. Molyneaux. 1994. "How Economic Development and Family Planning Programs Combined to Reduce Indonesian Fertility." *Demography.* 31(1):33–63.

Gertler, P., L. Locay, and W. Sanderson. 1987. "Are User Fees Regressive? The Welfare Implications of Health Care Financing Proposals in Peru." *Journal of Econometrics.* 36:67–88.

Griffin, Charles C. 1992. *Health Care in Asia: A Comparative Study of Cost and Financing.* Washington, DC: The World Bank.

Hammer, J. S., I. Nabi, and J. A. Cercone. 1992. "Distributional Impact of Social Sector Expenditures in Malaysia." Paper presented at the World Bank Conference on Public Expenditures and the Poor: Incidence and Targeting. Washington, DC, The World Bank, 17–19 June.

Hanushek, Eric. 1986. "The Economics of Schooling: Production and Efficiency in Public Schools." *Journal of Economic Literature.* 24(3):1141–77.

Hobcraft, J. 1985. "The Interplay of Health and Society: Towards New Surveys of Mortality Determinants." In *The Collection and Analysis of Community Data,* edited by J. Casterline. Voorburg, Netherlands: International Statistical Institute. 144–155.

Horn, Robin, and Anna-Maria Arriagada. 1986. "The Educational Attainment of the World's Population: Three Decades of Progress." World Bank, Education and Training Department Discussion Paper EDT 37, Washington, DC.

Indonesian Resource Mobilization Study. 1994. "Financing Health Care: Lessons from the Indonesian Resource Mobilization Study." Santa Monica, CA: RAND.

Institute for Resource Development, Westinghouse, and Sri Lanka, Janalekhanaha Sankhyalekhana Departamentuva. 1988. *Sri Lanka 1987: Demographic Health Survey: Summary Report.* Colombo: Department of Census and Statistics, Ministry of Plan Implementation.

International Centre for Diarrheal Disease Research, Bangladesh, 1991. "Project Proposal: Urban Health Extension Project (UHEP)."

Jimenez, Emmanuel. 1986. "The Structure of Educational Costs: Multiproduct Cost Functions for Primary and Secondary Schools in Latin America." *Economics of Education Review.* 5(1):25–29.

_____ . 1987. *Pricing Policy in the Social Sectors: Cost Recovery for Education and Health in Developing Countries.* Baltimore: Johns Hopkins University Press.

_____ . 1989. "Social Sector Pricing Policy Revisited: A Survey of Some Recent Controversies." Proceedings of the World Bank Annual Conference on Development Economics. 109–138.

King, E.M. 1985. "Consequences of Population Pressure in the Family's Welfare." Background paper prepared for the Working Group on Population Growth and Economic Development, Committee on Population, National Research Council, Washington, DC.

King, E. 1993. "Changing Pricing Policy in Education." In *Indonesia Public Expenditures, Prices and the Poor*, Report No. 11293-IND, chapter 5, edited by Nicholas Prescott. Washington, DC: The World Bank.

King, E. M., and R. Bellew. 1988. "Education Policy and Schooling Levels in Peru." Washington, DC: The World Bank. Mimeo.

Kinsella, K. 1988. "Aging in the Third World." US Bureau of the Census. International Population Reports Series P-95, no. 79. Washington, DC.

Lavy, V., and J. Quigley. 1992. "Quality and the Willingness to Pay for Medical Care in Ghana." Processed. Washington, DC: The World Bank.

Mahmud, S., and J.P. McIntosh. 1980. "Returns to Scale to Family Size–Who Gains from High Fertility?" *Population Studies*. 34(3).

Meerman, J. 1979. *Public Expenditure in Malaysia: Who Benefits and Why*. New York: Oxford University Press.

Miyashita, H., et al. 1982. "The Effect of Population Growth on the Quantity of Education Children Receive: A Reply." *Review of Economics and Statistics*. 64.

Over, M., R. Ellis, J. Huber, and O. Solon. 1992. "The Consequences of Adult Ill-health." In *The Health of Adults in the Developing World*, edited by R. Feachem, T. Kjellstrom, C. Murray, M. Over, and M. Phillips. Oxford University Press.

Pitt, Mark, M. Rosenzweig, R. Mark, and Donna M. Gibbons. 1992. "The Determinants and Consequences of the Placement of Government Programs in Indonesia." World Bank Conference on Public Expenditures and the Poor: Incidence and Targeting. Washington, DC: The World Bank.

Prescott, N. 1993. *Indonesia Public Expenditures, Prices and the Poor*. Report No. 11293-IND. Washington, DC: The World Bank.

Psacharopoulos, G. 1985. "Returns to Education: A Further International Update and Implications." *Journal of Human Resources*. 20, 583–597.

Rahman, M.O., A. Foster, and J. Menken. 1992a. "Gender Differences in Marriage and Mortality For Older Adults in Rural Bangladesh: Is Widowhood More Dangerous For Women Than Men?" Paper presented at the annual meeting of the Population Association of America, Denver, Colorado, May 1992.

Rahman, M.O., J. Strauss, P. Gertler, and K. Fox. 1992b. "Gender Differences in Adult Health, An International Comparison." Forthcoming in *The Gerontologist*, 1994.

Rao, N. Bhaskara, M.E. Kahn, and C.V.S. Prasad. 1987. *Health Sector Expenditure Differentials in India*. Baroda, India: Operations Research Group for the Ministry of Health and Family Welfare.

Rodgers, Gerry. 1984. *Poverty and Population: Approaches and Evidence.* Geneva: International Labour Organisation.

Rosenzweig, M.R., and R.E. Evenson. 1977. "Fertility, Schooling and the Economic Contribution of Children in Rural India." *Econometrica.* 45(5)(July):1065–1080.

Rosenzweig, M.R., and K.J. Wolpin. 1980. "Testing the Quantity-Quality Fertility Model: The Use of Twins as a Natural Experiment." *Econometrica.* 48(1):227–240.

_____ . 1982. "Governmental Interventions and Household Behavior in a Developing Country: Anticipating the Unanticipated Consequences of Social Programs." *Journal of Development Economics.* 10(2)(April):209–225.

Ross, John A., Marjorie Rich, Janet P. Molzan, and Michael Pensak. 1988. *Family Planning and Child Survival: 100 Developing Countries.* New York: Columbia University Center for Population and Family Health.

Sahn, David E., and Harold Alderman. 1988. "The Effect of Human Capital on Wages, and the Determinants of Labor Supply in a Developing Country." *Journal of Development Economics.* 29:2-(September):157–184.

Schultz, T.P. 1985. "School Expenditures and Enrollment, 1960-80: The Effects of Incomes, Prices and Population Growth." Background paper prepared for the Working Group on Population Growth and Economic Development. Committee on Population, National Research Council, Washington, DC.

Scott, Wolf, and N.T. Mathew. 1983. *Levels of Living and Poverty in Kerala.* Geneva: United Nations Research Institute for Social Development.

Selowsky, M. 1979. "Who Benefits from Government Expenditures? A Case Study of Colombia." New York: Oxford University Press.

Sen, A. 1992. *Inequality Reexamined.* Oxford: Clarendon Press, and Cambridge, MA: Harvard University Press.

Simmons, George B., C. Smucker, S. Bernstein, and E. Jensen. 1982. "Post-Neonatal Mortality in Rural India: Implications of an Economic Model." *Demography*. 19(3):371–389.

Smith, W.J. 1988. "Chapter III: Education and Training." Contribution to 1988 Country Economic Report for Sri Lanka. World Bank, Asia Country Department 1, Washington, DC.

Statistical Pocketbook of Bangladesh. 1987. Bangladesh Bureau of Statistics, Statistics Division, Ministry of Planning. Government of the Peoples Republic of Bangladesh, Dhaka, Bangladesh.

Strauss, John. 1986. "Does Better Nutrition Raise Farm Productivity?" *Journal of Political Economy*. 94(April):297–320.

Strauss, John, Paul Gertler, Omar Rahman, and Kristin Fox. 1994. "Gender and Life-Cycle Differentials in the Patterns and Determinants of Adult Health." *Journal of Human Resources*. Forthcoming.

Strong, Michael. 1992. "The Impact of Adult Health on Child Health." Paper presented at the annual meeting of the Population Association of America, Denver, Colorado, May, 1992.

Tan, J.P., and M. Haines. 1983. "Schooling and the Demand for Children: Historical Perspectives." Background paper prepared for the *World Development Report 1984*. Washington, DC: The World Bank.

Tan, Jee-Peng, and Alan Mingat. 1992. *Education in Asia: A Comparative Study of Cost and Financing*. Washington, DC: The World Bank.

Thomas, Duncan, John Strauss, and Maria Helena Henriques. 1990. "Child Survival, Height for Age and Household Characteristics in Brazil." *Journal of Development Economics*. Vol. 33:197–234.

Thomas, Duncan, Victor Lavy, and John Strauss. 1991. "Public Policy and Anthropometric Outcomes in the Cote d'Ivoire." Processed, RAND, Santa Monica, CA.

Thomas, D., and J. Strauss. 1992. Prices, Infrastructure, Household Characteristics and Child Height. *Journal of Development Economics*. 32(2):301–322.

Trussell, J., and A.R. Pebley. 1984. "The Potential Impact of Changes in Fertility on Infant, Child, and Maternal Mortality." Unpublished manuscript, Princeton University.

UNESCO. 1987a. *Statistical Digest 1987*. Paris..

UNESCO. 1987b. *Statistical Yearbook 1987*. Paris.

UNICEF. 1987. *An Analysis of the Situation of Children and Women in the Lao People's Democratic Republic*. Vientianne.

van de Walle, Dominique. 1992. "The Distribution of Benefits from Social Services in Indonesia, 1978–87." World Bank Conference on Public Expenditures and the Poor: Incidence and Targeting. Washington, DC: The World Bank.

Westoff, C.F. 1978. "The Unmet Need for Birth Control in Five Asian Countries." *International Family Planning Perspectives*. 4(1):9–17.

Wolfe, Barbara L., and Jere R. Behrman. 1982. "Determinants of Child Mortality, Health, and Nutrition in a Developing Country." *Journal of Development Economics*. 11:163–193.

_____ . 1987. "Women's Schooling and Children's Health: Are the Effects Robust with Adult Sibling Control for the Women's Childhood Background?" *Journal of Health Economics*. 6:3(239–254).

World Bank. 1980. *World Development Report, 1980*. Washington, DC: The World Bank.

_____ . 1988. "Indonesia: Poverty Assessment and Strategy Report." Report No. 8034-IND, Country Department V, Asia Region. Washington, DC: The World Bank. Mimeo.

_____ . 1989. "Indonesia Basic Education Study." Asia Country Department V, Report 7841-IND, Washington, DC.

_____ . 1991. "Indonesia: Issues in Health Planning and Budgeting." A World Bank Country Study, Department V, Asia Region. Washington, DC: The World Bank.

Wray, J.D. 1971. "Population Pressure on Families: Family Size and Child Spacing." National Academy of Sciences, ed. *Rapid Population Growth, Consequences and Policy Implications*. Baltimore: The Johns Hopkins University Press.

Chapter Five

Urban Shelter, Municipal Services, and the Poor

Emiel A. Wegelin

With urbanization, the poor are increasingly found in urban areas. This reflects, in large measure, the attraction of the city as an economic entity. The high productivity of its industry generates the wealth which "trickles down" to reduce some poverty. In general, the rural poor have less money income than their city counterparts, but do not necessarily show worse levels of nutrition or life expectancy. Higher urban incomes are often offset by a worse physical situation, especially with respect to crowding, pollution and access to shelter.[1]

The poor are employed, often from early childhood and for long hours, mostly in physical labor. Women often have dual child care and income earner roles. Single parents (usually women) are particularly disadvantaged. They do not own, or have the capacity to purchase, assets such as land, housing or simple capital equipment (e.g., tools). They have few skills. Informal sector jobs are the main source of livelihood for the urban poor. They are lowly paid and insecure and sometimes income is intermittent. In some countries, transfers from friends or relatives constitute a substantial proportion of the income of the poor, most particularly for the unemployed poor.[2] Because of the characteristics of their livelihood, the poor are risk averse in their spending. They spend for consumption (at least half on food) or for directly profitable investments (e.g., boys' schooling) which have the shortest term returns. Men tend to spend less of their earnings on the family than do women.

The poor have little or no access to publicly provided goods and infrastructure, i.e., land serviced with public infrastructure, education, and health care. They are denied access through their inability to pay for these services and through their inability to negotiate the institutional impediments to access.[3] Cultural, educational, racial, and ethnic backgrounds often set poor communities apart. Overt or unthinking prejudice on the part of the dominant class in a community often hinders access to goods and services to which the poor are entitled.

In sum, the urban poor are placed in a position where they lack: (i) access to income-earning possibilities and to urban amenities including shelter and related infrastructure such as water supply and sanitation; and (ii) the capacity to respond to these possibilities if they arise.

SHELTER

Demand and Supply

The backdrop of urbanization and urban poverty presented in earlier chapters of this volume clearly implies enormous requirements for urban shelter. In the absence of significant subsidized housing schemes, this amounts to an effective demand in the various legal and illegal housing submarkets that can be identified, ranging from squatter housing through to legal and illegal low-income housing subdivisions to "regular" developer-provided middle-class housing and higher-income housing. Typologies vary from city to city[4] but typically about one third of the urban population in major Asian cities live in slums and squatter settlements, and about 60–80 per cent of housing supply is provided and financed through informal sector mechanisms (ADB 1983; Wegelin 1989).

In Dhaka, housing is supplied overwhelmingly by the informal sector. The informal private sector has two major subsystems: (i) the private household sector in which a middle-class household operates either as a builder occupier, or as a small entrepreneur of 2–10 units of apartments which serve the middle-class tenants; and (ii) the slum entrepreneur who builds very low-cost units and rents these to low-income people. Most of the shelters are built by individual efforts and on a per household basis. *Pucca* housing, which comprises 28 per cent of the housing stock, and semi-*pucca* housing, which comprises 13 per cent, are generally legal, including land title and approval of the planning authority. Financing is largely from personal savings and informal credit. Semi-legal shelters, including both semi-*pucca* and *kutcha* housing (*kutcha* housing comprises 59 per cent of the stock), have a legal title to land but do not have approval for construction. Financing is almost wholly from own savings and informal credit. Slums as a subsystem come under this category and are one of the largest suppliers of housing, particularly to lower-income groups. Squatters build mostly on government land and have neither a legal title nor the approval of planning agencies. Shelters are mostly rudimentary shacks, and services are procured illegally or are absent (UNDP and USAID 1992, 18–19; Islam 1990). Public sector involvement is limited to allotting plots to middle-income and lower-income groups. The number of land developers and apartment builders (nearly 50 in Dhaka) is growing, with increasing activities in the production of residential plots and housing units. Most of the commercial companies are catering to the needs of the upper-middle and higher-income groups. The number of houses built is small, and mostly consists of multi-storey apartments (10,000 units constructed and 5,000 planned), fitted with all standard utility services. Buyers have to make advance payments. Cooperative societies assemble land for housing and services, generally at the fringes of Dhaka. Additionally, some cooperative societies also build houses besides providing land development and services, generally within the city limits. Both types of development cater to middle-income and higher-income groups (UNDP and USAID 1992, 16–18, 36; Khundker et al. 1994).

In Ahmadabad, five major groups can be identified who are involved in different activities in the housing supply process: public sector, private developers, petty landlords, community groups, and individual households (Mehta and Mehta 1989, 67–68), with the most dominant system being the formal private sector and the informal sector. The share of the public sector in terms of provision is only 10 per cent of total supply, while the formal private developers contribute almost 60 per cent, even outpacing the informal sector. This is reflected in the fact that the rate of ownership more than doubled in Ahmadabad during two decades, from 17.6 per cent in 1961 to 36 per cent in 1981. This average of 36 per cent includes 58 per cent of the elite areas and 28 per cent of the slum settlements. Another significant trend in Ahmadabad is that of unauthorized construction. Almost 50 per cent of the net additions to the housing supply were made without the requisite permission and, of that 50 per cent, the informal sector supplies about 89 per cent and the private formal sector supplies the remainder (Mehta and Mehta 1989, 70, 77–78). Formal housing efforts have catered only to the middle classes and above; the only recourse for the lower-income groups has been to live in "hutments" (slum housing). In the informal sector, slum landlordism and quasi-legal developments are becoming increasingly commonplace. This not only applies to new housing but affects existing stock as well, especially in areas which lack effective and representative community control (Mehta and Mehta 1989, 80, 96).

A study of housing in Bangkok identified the following five major housing submarkets catering to the needs of low-income groups (Angel 1987):

(i)   National Housing Authority (NHA) land-and-house projects which take the form of subsidized walk-up apartments, the construction of houses on serviced plots and core houses in sites-and-services projects;

(ii) low-cost houses produced by the private sector, which has recently moved into mass production of housing, selling three times as fast as other land and house packages on the market;

(iii) informal land subdivisions, which play an important role in low-income housing in Bangkok. These are effectively a form of sites-and-services projects provided by the private sector which include plots, unpaved roads, water, and electricity. For many, such subdivisions are the first step on the housing ladder;

(iv) slums and squatter settlements: Over 80 per cent of all slum dwellers rent land legally and live in houses which they have owned for long periods; and

(v)   low-cost rental housing provided by the informal as well as the formal private sector.

In Karachi, the individual owner has been the main producer of housing (83.7 per cent). As developers produce relatively small numbers of expensive units, low-income and medium-income groups have to opt for shelter in the informal sector, which provides about 60 per cent of the total housing production (Kinhill/NESPAK 1990, 13). The poor are also effectively excluded from access to government plot development schemes, "firstly by standards and prices which cannot be afforded by 40–50 per cent of the population; secondly by the long waiting period before a plot can be occupied; thirdly by the allocation procedure" (van der Linden 1990, 7). Consequently, the poor are forced to rely on illegal subdivisions (van der Linden 1990, 7). Among the sources of financing, own savings are prominent (74 per cent of the households). Such savings are often mobilized through informal rotating saving and credit associations (Sultan and van der Linden 1991, 20).

A survey of urban households in the following sample cities—Jakarta, Bandung, and Medan (large cities), Yogyakarta, Bandar Lampung, and Balikpapan (medium cities), and Serang, Jambi, and Pukang (small cities)—showed that urban Indonesia has two systems for the delivery of housing, i.e., the popular or household-based system and the formal system. The popular system provides houses through incremental construction (80 per cent of all housing) and is highly responsive to consumer demand. The formal system provides moderate-income to high-income housing, is often heavily subsidized, and is constrained in its ability to provide both housing and housing finance (Struyk et al. 1990, 9). The formal sector comprises housing directly developed by Perumnas, a state agency, and housing supplied by private professional real estate developers—combined providing about 20 per cent of annual production. The housing career path of the majority or 46 per cent of the people begins with the purchase of a vacant lot, or for 37 per cent, a lot with a semi-permanent unit to which they make major improvements, and for 16 per cent, a lot to which they make minor or no improvements. Only a few are able to purchase a formally financed unit. The purchase of property is made through savings from wages (cash or gold), sale of personal property, or funds obtained from family (Struyk et al. 1990, 74, 102). Land which can be developed may be purchased either directly or by an investor or agent. Informal subdivision of land is a major way in which land enters the residential housing market (Struyk et al. 1990, 80). Lower-income rental units are developed by individual property owners. The main groups who provide these units are family entrepreneurs, commercial entrepreneurs, or employers (Struyk et al. 1990, 108).

The above cases illustrate that in most countries formal sector response, and particularly direct housing or land provision by government, has been woefully inadequate to meet the demand for shelter.[5] This has led to sharp increases in housing costs, and, as this is virtually risk-free in the above circumstances, to substantial speculation in undeveloped urban and peri-urban land. This, of course, has further fueled the vicious spiral of demand-supply imbalance, explaining the often noted phenomenon of very substantial housing and land shortages alongside significant undeveloped tracks of lands in the same city.[6] Some spectacular crashes in speculative property prices can be observed when alternative investment opportunities present themselves, as happened in Karachi and Lahore in Pakistan in 1992 when the Government liberalized foreign exchange transactions, allowed the holding of foreign currency accounts in the country, and revitalized the Karachi stock market, *inter alia*, by increasing access for intending local equity investors. Admittedly, the property market downturn was also stimulated by declining remittances from overseas Pakistanis.

A large and increasing proportion of housing demand is exercised in the informal land market by the poor, and increasingly by middle-class urban dwellers, to whom housing options provided through the formal sector (government and private developer/contractor supplied) are no longer affordable. It appears that in the informal sector itself, as a result of this demand pressure, there is an increasing trend of commercialization: in the 1970s and 1980s, there were comparatively fewer "spontaneous" squatter settlement patterns which were a predominant pattern in the 1950s and 1960s. Instead, semi-legal or illegal commercial land subdivisions became the dominant provision mode in many developing countries (Baross and van der Linden 1990).

This is not surprising considering the enormous demand-supply imbalance implied in the above demographic dynamics. By their very nature, commercialized informal housing opportunities are more expensive than squatter arrangements, hence this transformation has increased shelter costs to the urban poor, and in the absence of cheap new settlement opportunities, has contributed to increased housing densities in existing developed areas. This is noticeable not only in already established informal settlements, but also in areas which had been established through a formal sector development process, such as government or developer-built housing estates, and in the older central city areas.

Obviously, these patterns are not identical from country to country. They are influenced by substantial differentials in demand resulting from differences in demographic pressures and housing affordability ratios, by differences in existing rules and regulations and in land ownership patterns, and by differences in the effectiveness of government and private formal sector interventions. The latter are not only in the area of housing, but also in the provision of neighborhood infrastructure and services and in the supply of housing-related credit.

In the Philippines, for example, government assistance for housing construction and development has increased considerably since the 1970s. Government-supported supply, however, still only meets about 16 per cent of demand (Balisacan 1994). Apart from its limited contribution, over half of the government-supported investment in housing units has gone to middle-income and upper-middle-income groups, mostly using provident funds collected from low-income groups (Balisacan 1994). In Bangladesh, the high price of buildable urban land and the deliberate policy of the Government favoring the higher-income groups have left the urban poor in a vulnerable position, virtually without legal access to housing of reasonable quality (Khundker et al. 1994).

Demand factors appear to vary along relatively stable and predictable lines: as GNP per capita increases, the average fraction of household income spent on housing increases, from 5 per cent in countries with very low GNP per capita to about 35 per cent, before beginning to decrease again at yet higher levels of prosperity (IBRD 1992a, 10). Across income levels within any country, the typical pattern is for the proportion of household income spent on housing to decline with rising incomes.

However, aggregate housing price/income ratios in developing countries vary widely from country to country, from a low of 2.5 for Thailand to a high of 7.8 for Tunisia, largely resulting from wide variations in the extent to which distortions in housing supply are operative and the extent to which such distortions result in price increases (IBRD 1992a, Table A.1.1, 60).

Although the extent of supply constraints varies widely, the following broad policy issue generalizations may be inferred:

(i)   Direct government provision of low-cost housing and/or sites-and-services arrangements to meet the needs of the urban poor has generally not been successful: not enough units have been provided; they were generally too expensive and in the wrong places, often provided to the allottees below cost and, hence, often preempted by groups for which they were not intended.

(ii) Virtually nowhere has the government been able to remedy this lack of sufficient public supply by ensuring adequate private supply of serviced, buildable land accessible both physically and administratively to the urban poor. More often than not, government interventions in the land market have been counterproductive and have actually made the situation worse for the urban poor.[7]

(iii) Speculative forces have tended to widen this gap even more, particularly in situations where there were few profitable investment options other than investment in urban land.

Functions of Housing

The provision of shelter is an important element of the living conditions of the urban poor, affecting material and psychological well-being, health, school performance of children and, through the health impact, productivity at work (Burns et al. 1970; Wegelin 1978). Hence, its improvement directly and indirectly increases the welfare of the urban poor.

Apart from the above, the auxiliary functions that housing fulfill in the survival strategies of the poor, its potential for employment creation and its relation to the quality of the urban environment are important additional considerations.

Housing and the Survival Strategy of the Poor. A first important function of housing is that it provides some socioeconomic stability to the urban poor, who are, relative to the rural poor, much less protected by an emergency network of relatives/kinsmen. In the absence of a formal social security safety net, ownership of a house has an important insurance value in that it is an asset that can be sold or let, if necessary.[8] Additionally, an investment in housing is an important means of channeling savings: in many countries the poor have limited alternatives for savings and for maintaining the value of these savings in real terms, i.e., protected from erosion by inflation (Lall 1989). Home ownership is also often a major condition to obtaining credit in the informal market (van der Linden 1986).

Second, a house provides the basis for economic activities, both at the nonmonetary subsistence level (vegetable gardening, animal husbandry, self-help home maintenance and/or improvement)[9] and in the monetized informal sector. This latter element is probably most significant: part of the home may be let for residential and/or other activities, or used as a base for home industry activities, such as for food vending, dressmaking, barber shops, and recycling of used materials/garbage scavenging.[10] In fact, more often than not, there is no other location for such work that can be procured at low cost.[11] Additionally, in some societies the home is the only place where women can work and hence contribute to the household income—and occasionally to neighborhood education, as demonstrated by the slum home school system in various areas in Karachi (Bakhtiari and Wegelin-Schuringa 1992). On the above grounds, it may be argued that housing provides access to the urban economy for the urban poor (Peattie 1979).

Finally, secure land tenure/home ownership reduces the dependency of the urban poor on middlemen, neighborhood leaders, and local politicians, thus reducing or eliminating transaction costs associated therewith, and increasing access to bargaining power for the delivery of urban services (Mitra and Nientied 1989).

Housing, on these three counts, therefore, is clearly an important element in the survival strategy of the urban poor.

Housing Investment, Services, and Employment. Investment in housing or housing improvements, which generally accounts for 2–8 per cent of GNP and 10–30 per cent of gross domestic capital formation in developing countries (IBRD 1992a, 2), itself forms an important source of employment, both in the construction industry and, through backward linkages, in construction materials and other auxiliary industries. International studies suggest consistently high employment multipliers for the construction industry as compared to other industries and aggregate production (Burns and Grebler 1977; Wegelin 1978), irrespective of levels of GDP. This is due to the labor-intensive nature of the construction industry and the building materials industry in combination with the low import contents of housing.

These findings are even more persuasive when related to informal sector housing, where labor intensity is higher than in the formal sector and where the "import leak" is smaller, as such housing will normally contain fewer (luxury) elements requiring imports. The employment generated in informal sector housing investment is largely unskilled, semi-skilled, and/or requiring skills accessible to the urban poor such as block making, carpentry, masonry, bar bending, and cement-mixing.[12]

Apart from the income and employment generated through housing investment, housing services (comprising operation and maintenance services as well as pure rent) additionally account for a varying proportion of 5–10 per cent of GNP (IBRD 1992a, 2). As the magnitude of the rental element in the housing services sector is generally imputed in national accounts data, irrespective of actual rent levels paid, such data must be treated with caution, but it is clear that the combined investment and services share in GNP has a very significant expenditure and employment impact.

Housing and the Urban Environment. A final function of improved housing which deserves reference is its potential impact in ameliorating urban environmental degradation. As neighborhoods are upgraded and provided with municipal infrastructure, environmental problems associated with uncollected garbage, clogged drainage channels and unhealthy sanitary conditions will be addressed, and garbage scavenging and recycling activities can be organized more effectively.

This presumes that, in one way or the other, improvements in housing are associated with improvements in municipal services. While this is intuitively clear for neighborhood infrastructure associated with the provision of formal housing, the experience with more organic, gradual housing environment improvement suggests the same, whether as part of a concerted effort at neighborhood upgrading such as the Kampung Improvement Program in Indonesia, or through the more common "muddling through" process.

SHELTER-RELATED MUNICIPAL SERVICES AND THE POOR

Municipal services, *inter alia*, comprise water supply, sewerage, drainage, flood protection, solid waste collection and disposal, local roads, public transport, street lighting, and traffic management. All, in greater or lesser degree, can be considered to be shelter-related, even though, as noted above, such service systems should be planned and programmed on an integrated citywide basis, and as such extend beyond the neighborhood level.

Lack of Access to Services

For all such municipal services, the poor essentially face the problem of limited access: poor neighborhoods are not usually the first target for road upgrading, water supply, sewerage, drainage, or municipal solid waste collection.

For example, the results of a recent survey in India showed a disparity in the access to water and sanitation/sewerage facilities of people in different levels of consumption expenditure in urban areas. Among the bottom 40 per cent households, 66 per cent of the population have average access to tap water whereas the corresponding figure for the total urban population is as high as 72.4 per cent. For sources of water other than through taps, 18.7 per cent and 13 per cent of households in the bottom 40 per cent of the population obtain water from handpumps and *pucca* wells respectively, whereas the average for all fractiles is 15.4 per cent and 10.3 per cent only for these two sources. About 34 per cent of the poor are not covered by formal piped water supply subsidized and provided largely (85 per cent) by the government. These people are obliged to draw water from sources that are mostly private, at prices higher than in the formal system. Water from these sources generally is less hygienic and less reliable (Kundu 1991).

In many Indian cities, per capita water supply to the poorer sections of the population is much below the recommended minimum. For example, in Ahmadabad, the wealthier 25 per cent of the population consume 90 per cent of the water supplied, while the remaining 75 per cent of the population have to make do with only 10 per cent of the water. In Calcutta and Bombay also, the supply of water to slum areas through public standposts is much less than in other areas. In Calcutta, water supply in slums is about 75 liters per capita per day (lcd) whereas in non-slum areas it is about 220 lcd. The corresponding figures in Bombay are 90 lcd and 130 lcd, respectively. These figures substantiate the conclusion that the distribution of water in urban areas is extremely inequitable and biased against the poor.

The disparity and the gap between the lower and upper fractiles in terms of sanitation facilities is significantly higher than in the case of water. In the bottom fractile, only about 30 per cent of the population have latrine facilities as compared to 80 per cent in the top fractiles. About 50 per cent of the people in the higher expenditure categories have flush latrines connected to the sewerage system. The sewerage system is often managed and maintained by the local authorities with a nominal user charge levied on the households; hence, subsidized sanitation facilities are available to the relatively well-off sections of the population. While people with higher consumption not only have the privilege of latrine facilities but also their exclusive use, the pattern for the poor households is just the opposite. "For households with monthly per capita expenditure of less than Rs85, less than 40 per cent have a toilet facility and about 70 per cent of these share it with others. Only the top three fractiles have a percentage of households dependent on shared latrines, less than the national average of 58 per cent" (Kundu 1991). An average of 51.8 per cent of the bottom 40 per cent households (per capita expenditure up to Rs125) do not have any latrine facility. The corresponding figure for all expenditure groups is substantially lower, namely 36.8 per cent. A field survey in Delhi noted that of 44 resettlement colonies in the city, only nine are connected to the sewerage system. In others, the sewerage lines are partly laid or have not been laid at all. The conditions in *jhuggi jhompri* clusters in Delhi are much worse. Nearly 37 per cent of the households do not have access to any type of latrine or sanitation facility, while another 26 per cent use community toilets, and only 2.4 per cent have individual toilet facilities.

According to Mathur, a similar situation applies nationally with regard to access to latrines and sanitation. Twelve per cent of the urban population do not have access to water supply, and 57 per cent do not have access to sanitation. In states where the poverty incidence is high, the percentage of population without access to water supply and sanitation is extremely high (Mathur 1994, 49).

The Republic of Korea's urban population is not yet adequately covered by the water supply system. Supply is intermittent, unstable and inadequate in the hilly areas because of low water pressure, and water supply systems have not been extended into the slum areas. In conjunction with dilapidated pipeline systems, low water pressure also causes water pollution through infiltration of polluted subsoil water, a problem which is exacerbated by the inadequacy of the sewerage system in most cities. The average sewerage treatment coverage ratio for all ordinary cities in 1991 was only 6.6 per cent (Kim 1994).

In Sri Lanka, centralized water supply systems designed to serve urban areas do not meet the continuing and increasing demand (Gunatilleke and Perera 1994). At least two thirds of the urban population use water that cannot be classified as safe. Despite the supply of safe water that is available for the urban population, 1.1 million people, mostly from among the urban poor, do not have access to safe water.

According to the National Housing Authority of Thailand, lack of infrastructure and public services is a severe and major condition of slums which results in a poor environment such as polluted water and narrow and unplanned catwalks (Ratanakomut et al. 1994). While the situation elsewhere in Thailand is improved (Thailand Development Research Institute Foundation 1991, 43), in the southern region of Thailand, 34 per cent of those living in slums have no access to electricity and 92 per cent have no access to piped water.

Findings from Indonesia also indicate that improvements in the provision of housing services, electricity, and water supply in urban areas mostly benefit the nonpoor (Firdausy 1994).

For sewerage and solid waste collection and disposal, public provision coverage levels usually are substantially lower than those for water supply. For instance, in 1992, about 85 per cent of the urban population in Pakistan had access to safe drinkable water, while on average only about 30 per cent of solid waste generated per day is properly collected and less still is treated (ADB 1993a, 25, 27). In another example, it was estimated in 1989 that 550 cities in Indonesia were provided with water supply systems while only 10 cities were provided with a solid waste management system (ADB 1989, 17). Dhaka is the only city in Bangladesh where there is a waterborne sewerage system covering parts of the city, but only 35 per cent of the city's households have access to the sewerage lines. Further, the garbage collection and disposal system in Bangladesh is very poor; only an estimated 20 per cent of the urban households have access to municipal garbage dustbins (Khundker et al. 1994).

On the other hand, it is often somewhat easier for the urban poor to develop their own neighborhood solutions to such deficiencies, both through individual household arrangements (such as the conventional hiring of sweepers for both solid and human waste disposal, as is common throughout the South Asian continent, and through the implementation of on-plot, low-cost sanitation solutions such as soak-pits) or on a neighborhood/community basis. Examples of the latter are communal toilets, shallow lane sewers as developed in Karachi, Pakistan with NGO assistance, and collective community solid waste collection arrangements, often on a lane basis, as are common in low-income areas in Indonesian and Thai cities (see Hasan 1988; SELAVIP 1992; McManus 1991; Savasdisara et al. 1987).

The Poor Pay More for Inferior Services

For those services which can be individualized and for which a price can be charged, such as water supply, solid waste collection, and public transport, inadequate municipal/public supply to poor neighborhoods is usually substituted for by informal sector supply. Informal supply of such services is usually provided at prices which the low-income market can bear, whereas public provision more often than not is subsidized directly or indirectly. In consequence, the poor usually pay more for comparable services, or sometimes for services of lower quality, as noted in the following examples.

In *jhuggi jhompri* clusters and unauthorized colonies in Dehli, Ghaziabad, and Hyderabad in India, the levels of payment people are willing to make for an improved water delivery system are higher than what they are presently paying to either a public or private agency for meeting their water needs. As supply of a community tap is insufficient for 40 households, some households jointly contribute an amount of about Rs3,000 to Rs4,000 to install a handpump which meets the water needs of 10–15 households. However, operational costs of the handpump become a real financial burden for these households. Moreover, handpumped water is not always of good quality. The households would prefer to pay the same monthly amount or even more for the piped water supply provided by the local authorities as they would then be assured of a sufficient supply of safe water (Lall 1991, 78, 80).

The price of water from a government-assisted public hydrant or water terminal charged by caretakers in North Jakarta was lower than before the provision of these services. The price, however, is still much higher than the formal water enterprise tariff for clean water (National Development Planning Board [BAPPENAS] et al. 1990, Ex-9). Additional factors affecting the quality of water directly or indirectly provided by the caretakers are (i) floods in the *kampungs* during high tide and during the rainy seasons which cause contamination; and (ii) additional concrete reservoirs built by the caretakers which are located near public bathrooms and toilets. Moreover, people store water in drums near their garbage sites and the pit latrine. According to a BAPPENAS report, a water container appeared to be too expensive for the poorer households (BAPPENAS et al. 1990, 4–18, 19).

A survey in various low-income areas across developing countries confirms the above-mentioned problems of quality and high price of water from vendors. Households frequently pay 30 per cent of their monthly income for water from vendors, whereas they pay 1–5 per cent for water from piped water systems. Containers are frequently filled with water from local polluted rivers and open wells. Even where the initial quality of the water is acceptable, containers are often dirty, and the water is contaminated in its handling. Further, delivery is often unreliable (Zaroff and Okun 1984, 290, 292).

Supply through the publicly provided piped water supply network often does not extend, or only partially extends into the urban slum areas, which forces the residents to rely on other sources. Unless they can rely on private wells, they are dependent on water vendors, who often pirate their supply from the official network. Vendors' supplies take various shapes—bottles, donkey cart loads or tankers, depending on the storage capacity at the neighborhood or household level. Typically, consumption levels are lower, but unit prices higher than for consumption of water taken from public supply sources. A review of vending in sixteen cities showed that the unit cost of vended water is always much higher than that of water from a piped city supply—from 4 to 100 times higher, with a median of about 12 (IBRD 1992b, 100).

In Bangkok, the poor often buy water from nearby households at prices approaching six times the formal supply price (Ratanakomut et al. 1994). As a consequence, they can only afford to buy water for drinking and sometimes for cooking, and obtain cheaper water of lower quality for other uses (Ratanakomut et al. 1994).

Finally, in the Republic of Korea, the benefits of subsidizing water production and distribution by the Central Government mostly accrue to the rich. As a consequence, their consumption is virtually unrestrained and the poor end up paying more for less (Kim 1994).

Inappropriate Pricing Policies and Delivery Standards

Well-intended subsidies on supply often do not reach the lower-income groups for which they are intended. As a result, the main impact of these subsidies is to undermine the financial sustainability of the municipal water supply operations, leading to inadequacies in the operation and maintenance of existing systems as well as limiting their ability to extend those systems into areas presently unserved (see Raj 1991; Lovei and Whittington 1991).

These problems are aggravated by the issue of standards: frequently systems are designed to deliver unduly high levels of water per capita in areas served, thus further reducing the possibility of extending service to areas as yet unserved. In many Asian cities, therefore, subsidized water is supplied in relatively large quantities to those who do not really need such subsidized provision. Obviously there are fewer checks on such situations if water is not priced per unit actually consumed (e.g., because of the practical difficulties associated with installing and operating a metering system), but rather on the basis of house floor space or rental value, which provides no incentive to economize on water use.

For example, in India, the state-sponsored water supply and sewerage boards or municipal authorities are providing water free or at highly subsidized rates to domestic consumers. Wherever water is priced, its price level varies from city to city (Raj 1991, 10). In some states of India, the price of water is linked to a home's rental value, which makes project cost recovery difficult and also provides little incentive for rationalization in water rates. Further, it creates operational problems. In Uttar Pradesh, it is proposed to undertake water supply projects in over a dozen towns. The per capita cost of water supply varies from Rs455 to Rs885, but the tariff proposed is at the rate of 10 per cent of the annual rental value of the houses. Operational problems arise if rental values are only infrequently updated, as is common. In consequence, it is difficult to adopt a flexible price structure to recover capital and operation and maintenance costs (Raj 1991, 11). A recent survey of slums in Hyderabad shows another effect of access to water supply on the quantity consumed. Remarkably, consumption patterns in the slums of the city indicated a sharp decrease in consumption with increase in supply periods (Bijlani and Rao 1990, 29). People tend to use more water when the supply is intermittent.

Water meters, along with appropriate rates and efficient billing and collection systems, are essential if consumers are to economize on water use. Arlosoroff (1989) argues that either the government or water companies should finance installation costs and deduct the amount from the monthly water bill, which would allow low-income households to be provided with a meter (Urban Edge 1991). However, even if a metering system has been installed, it does not always promote water conservation or benefit low-income households because the water bill is often calculated on an increasing block tariff (IBT). Low-income households tend to use less water than high-income households. The price of water in the initial block, therefore, may be set very low, usually at a subsidized rate to ensure the poor are not discouraged from using the amount of water essential for human needs. Low-income households sometimes share a water meter if they live in apartment buildings or shared compounds. Households without connections often obtain their water from public systems indirectly, purchasing it either from neighbors who do have connections or from water vendors. Hence, to the extent that people are more apt to live in high-density housing and share a common metered water connection or buy water from vendors or their neighbors, they will pay higher average prices (Whittington 1992, 75–77).

The constraints operating on the public provision of sanitation services are, as they are for water, largely a combination of financial and institutional inability to adequately operate and maintain existing systems and to extend such systems into low-income areas, in combination with unrealistically high design standards of provision. Unlike for water, however, once the system is designed and in operation, individual "consumption" levels can only vary between being served or not being served by the system. Where sewerage and/or solid waste charges are incorporated in water charges (often for collection convenience, as the supply agencies often have responsibility both for water and sanitation services), financial sustainability of sanitation operations becomes dependent on the effectiveness of the water charges collection system.

For other municipal services and infrastructure, such as roads, drainage, and flood protection, similar provision/coverage deficiencies and problems of standards apply. These are often more serious than for water and sanitation because the absence of the direct cost-recovery option in principle precludes the possibility that such services can be provided in a free-standing, financially sustainable way.

Instead, provision levels depend on the limited financial and institutional capability of municipal governments or specialized delivery agencies, such as development authorities, public works departments of higher levels of government, and on the priority such provision enjoys among other development spending priorities of such agencies.

Need for Citywide Integrated Municipal Service Delivery

The poor, like other urban dwellers, need access to municipal services, as access to such services directly influences their living conditions, and particularly impacts on their health status. Also, if, as was argued above, housing has a vital role to play in the survival strategy of the poor, it is evident that well-serviced housing fulfills that role much more effectively than inaccessible housing devoid of water supply and reasonable sanitary conditions.

As the above examples illustrate, the environmental impact of isolated neighborhood upgrading alone will be limited in the absence of an effective hook-up to citywide infrastructure/services systems. Problems are often encountered at the trunk end of the municipal infrastructure provision, for instance in organizing safe final garbage disposal sites, and in developing effective citywide drainage and sewerage systems, including adequate treatment facilities.

Additionally, there is the issue of service interrelationships: the cost-effectiveness of municipal service delivery is obviously enhanced if the above services are delivered in an integrated way, both in a physical sense (e.g., the effectiveness of a drainage system is obviously enhanced if solid waste management deficiencies are addressed simultaneously, so that new drains will not become clogged as a result of indiscriminately dumped garbage; likewise, a sewerage system will not function without levels of water consumption/supply adequate for self-flushing of the sewers by the wastewater generated from the households) as well as in a financial sense to ensure the adequacy of intersectoral priority setting.

Nonmunicipal Services

The poor also need access to public services such as transport, telephone, electricity, and gas, which are not normally the responsibility of the local government. As the examples below demonstrate, levels of access to electricity supply vary substantially. For this service, for which individualized provision is possible, the poor in some cases have demonstrated a willingness and ability to pay market prices, but, as is the case for water supply, often at reduced levels of consumption.

People living (illegally) in squatter settlement areas in Thailand have to buy electricity by the bulb at 70–80 baht each per month which is seven times higher than the price charged by the Metropolitan Electricity Authority (Ratanakomut et al. 1994). A number of dwellers, however, are not eligible to subscribe to the public supply, and must instead sublease electricity from nearby households at a price 3–5 baht higher for each unit consumed (Ratanakomut et al. 1994). In this case, the poor are willing and able to pay market prices but are forced to pay higher prices than public supply prices because their houses are not registered. In Bangladesh, electricity is also widely distributed in many low-income areas. However, many households cannot afford the connections and resort to illegal connections to gain access to this service. Approximately 25 per cent of supply in Dhaka is consumed in this way. Electricity is well supplied in the slum areas in the Republic of Korea and most poor families in the city areas use basic electric appliances (Kim 1994). In all major cities in Indonesia (except Dili), the percentage of households with access to electricity is greater than 70 per cent, whereas the percentage of urban households with access to piped water and pumps varies widely from 23.9 per cent in Mataram to 98.1 per cent in Surabaya (Firdausy 1994).

LESSONS, ISSUES, AND POLICY CONCERNS

Having established that on several counts housing improvements and the associated delivery of municipal services should be seen as instruments to strengthen the position of the urban poor, the next issue to be considered is ways in which shelter and municipal services development can contribute most effectively to urban poverty reduction; i.e., what pattern of shelter and associated services delivery is most effective?

Lessons from Public Housing

A lesson that has clearly emerged from past practices is that the provision of direct, government low-cost housing is rarely appropriate. The units are generally provided at an arbitrarily set level of minimum planning and building standards, normally substantially higher than that of informal housing. Hence, the units are too expensive for the poor, unless at substantial subsidies. Further, such subsidies in combination with the generally attractive minimum standards have often led to "downward raiding" of public housing, either at the stage of initial unit allocation, or in subsequent resale or subletting, by those who do not need the lower-cost housing.[13] Problems of limited financial resources and limited available land have resulted in too few units being built, often at unattractive locations. To some extent this has also resulted from administrative constraints imposed on land acquisition by the agencies concerned. In the case of public rental housing, adequate operation and maintenance (estate management) has often not been possible, leading to dilapidation, vandalism, and environmental degradation (as, for example, has been witnessed in public housing schemes in Bangkok, Jakarta, and Kuala Lumpur).

There are exceptions to this general litany of problems, such as the well-run public housing program in Singapore. Moreover, Singapore, being an island state with moderate natural population growth at relatively high levels of prosperity, has been able to provide political continuity and stability, social control, sophisticated operational arrangements, relatively well-paid staff, and corruption-free management for its public housing stock. This situation is unique in many ways, and is not a model that can be easily emulated elsewhere.

Another form of housing provision is (public or private) employer-provided housing, which in the public sector still has a quantitatively important role, housing civil servants across the former British colonies, particularly employees of public works and communication departments. Some of the above ailments associated with public housing also apply to this type of housing, particularly the managerial and financial problems, which raises the question of the cost-effectiveness of public expenditure on such housing. More directly to the point, access to such housing is constrained by its very nature to the departments' staff, most of whom cannot be considered particularly poor. On the other hand, their being housed by their employer reduces pressure elsewhere in the housing market, including the downward-raiding prospect of public housing.

Enabling Approach

From the mid-1960s onwards, increasing disenchantment with the lack of effectiveness of public housing led to the rediscovery of the vitality of incremental housing by the poor. While scholars on all continents conducted research on this theme, public recognition came largely through the seminal work of John F.C. Turner, who, based on initial research work in squatter areas in Lima, Peru, presented the most cogent and forceful case for housing by the people instead of for the people (Turner 1976).

From the realization that the creative building energies of dwellers in slums and squatter settlements themselves needed to be recognized as the most cost-effective ingredient in housing the poor, the focus of attention shifted to defining the prerequisites for effectively harnessing this creative energy. This led to the identification of the following three major clusters of prerequisites to be arranged by (local) governments to galvanize the housing action of low-income slum dwellers: (i) land tenure security; (ii) availability of adequate shelter-related infrastructure and municipal services; and (iii) adequate access to housing finance.

The strategy required to bring these about, now generally known as the enabling strategy, has been adopted and promoted by international agencies such as the World Bank, United Nations Centre for Human Settlements/United Nations Development Programme (UNCHS/UNDP), regional development banks, including ADB, and bilateral donor agencies from the early 1970s onwards (ADB 1987; IBRD 1975, 1980, 1983, 1991, 1992; UNCHS 1987; UNDP 1991). The strategy has also been adopted by many governments in the region, some of whom had themselves already adjusted their housing policies in the same direction (note, for example, the origins of Indonesia's Kampung Improvement Program). Generally this strategy has been given expression in the form of slum improvement and sites-and-services programs. These programs, in principle, provide more room for harnessing the housing efforts of the urban poor themselves, but program evaluations to date suggest the outcomes have been a mixture of successes and failures.[14]

Slum Improvement. Slum improvement programs have generally comprised neighborhood infrastructure upgrading, often complemented by legalization of land tenure, and sometimes dovetailed with a home improvement loan and/or small business development loan scheme. Some of the major implementation difficulties of slum improvement programs are discussed below.

A major problem has been the apparent incongruence between the need for cost recovery and the need to keep solutions affordable for the urban poor. Programs which did not have a land tenure regularization component have generally relied on indirect cost recovery through local (mainly land/property) taxation, or have accepted that neighborhood infrastructure is a part of the wider urban infrastructure network and its associated financing problems. Cost recovery in the narrow context of slum upgrading is, therefore, not appropriate in such cases. The broader issue of equitable yet viable financing of urban infrastructure has virtually nowhere been resolved satisfactorily (Skinner et al. 1987).

Where programs have included explicit measures to legalize land tenure (generally through the provision of stay permits or long-term leases; occasionally through conferring freehold ownership), additional complications have arisen, particularly where such land titling was also intended to contribute directly to cost recovery of infrastructure investments. More often than not, land title charges did not adequately reflect the cost of developed urban land (i.e., the cost of land plus infrastructure/services). As noted in the earlier discussion, tariffs for billable services provided, such as water supply, sewerage, and solid waste removal, are often equally insufficient to cover costs of provision. This obviously adversely affects the sustainability of serviced urban land supply and the supply of the above public services.

Simultaneously, as noted above, the poor often pay substantially higher prices in the informal market for urban land and services (particularly water supply) as evidenced by program evaluations in many countries (see IBRD 1992a, 49; DGIS 1990). This indicates an ability and willingness to pay market prices for such services, although admittedly at lower consumption levels than would be the case for subsidized public provision.

When services are provided at a price below cost in obvious scarcity, this "administrative pricing" practice is open to abuse and corruption, and leads to the emergence of middlemen, brokers, and vendors. This tends to achieve the opposite of the intended result, reducing the likelihood that the urban poor will gain adequate access to land and services. Mitra and Nientied (1989) suggest, moreover, that large-scale, transparent legal provision at cost-plus prices is ultimately likely to be a cheaper solution for slum dwellers than illegal subdivision followed by the gradual provision of services, which is the more dominant delivery pattern.

In some cities, where public land ownership is predominant (e.g., in Karachi where about 94 per cent of urban land is in public ownership), implementation of the slum improvement strategy is further hampered by the fact that the occupants who often acquired their land through the illegal land subdivision process, correctly perceive that their leaders and/or middlemen would successfully be able to use their influence to protect them from eviction, perhaps out of enlightened self-interest. Hence the occupants' perceived security of land tenure is high, even without a formal land lease title. Furthermore, land titling procedures are usually cumbersome, requiring a substantial number of administrative steps and the collection and preparation of various, sometimes numerous, documents in support of the title application. These factors combined remove much of the incentive on the part of the occupants to be quick in applying for a land title. This further weakens the cost recovery, and hence replicability potential of the approach.

Where slum dwellers live on private land, land titling problems are compounded by delays resulting from land acquisition procedures. This is one reason why in several countries, for example, in Thailand and in Indonesia, land tenure issues were not addressed in the context of slum improvement, and reliance was placed on the *de facto* recognition implicit in the provision of neighborhood services and infrastructure.

Where home improvement and/or small enterprise development loans have been included in the delivery package, it has generally been found that such "packaging" has not been very successful. This is largely because the sponsoring agencies were usually housing agencies with little experience and ability to run credit programs (IBRD 1983).

Nevertheless, despite these problems, evaluation studies suggest substantial positive features (Skinner et al. 1987):[15]

   (i)   In most settlements, the provision of infrastructure improved dramatically over time, leading to improved sanitary conditions, improved health conditions, and reduced infant mortality.

   (ii) Individual households have made substantial complementary investments in improving and extending their houses; partly as a result, property values in the settlements have increased substantially, sometimes at more than double the rate of inflation, providing a significant social safety net for the owner-occupants.

   (iii) Rental values have also increased significantly, but this has not led to an (expected) exodus of renters, who generally have a weaker socioeconomic profile than owner-occupants. More generally, the turnover of population was low and not significantly different from that in other areas.

   (iv) Ultimately, residents will take land titles despite the above-cited difficulties. Given existing levels of *de facto* security of tenure and supply barriers this may not have the same priority as home improvements, but a steady gradual increase in the percentage of households with titles has been the dominant pattern.

The overall picture that emerges is that of a moderate acceleration of the normal, organic process of settlement formation and consolidation. This gradual development, while it misses some of the cost-recovery and efficiency opportunities a more rapid and concerted approach would have offered, at least has avoided some of the undesirable by-products, such as displacement of poorer residents.

However, upgrading is not always possible or desirable because of physical reasons—for example, if slums are located in river beds or on steep hills, or administrative reasons—for example, settlements established after a certain date are often not eligible. Additionally, in the upgrading process there is often a need to relocate some households who are affected by road realignments or to make way for other infrastructural facilities in the area. While first priority would obviously be to relocate such households within the settlement itself, this is not always feasible.

Sites-and-Services Approach

Because of the physical and administrative reasons mentioned above, there is a need for a complementary strategy of development of new serviced sites for shelter. The sites-and-services approach has been tried in most of Asia's developing countries, although its implementation has often failed for the following reasons, mostly similar to the problems encountered in public housing provision discussed earlier (van der Linden 1986, 1992; Swan et al. 1983):

(i)   lack of coordination of trunk infrastructure design with planning of individual schemes, as a result of which schemes could not be provided with water and access; the resulting delays in allocation and occupation adversely affected the cash flow of the implementing agencies, which often theoretically work on a "no profit–no loss" basis;

(ii) unduly high planning and infrastructure standards, leading to high cost levels per unit;

(iii) administrative plot allocation policies, which result in (subsidized) plots ending up in the hands of land speculators rather than the target groups, including displaced slum area occupants; and

(iv)   administrative/organizational inability to recover costs through hire-purchase or mortgage financing arrangements; credit schemes for home upgrading/extension or small business development often met the same fate.

The result has generally been that not enough plots have been developed or those developed have been in the wrong places, were developed at high costs (often only partially passed on to the plot holders), or were partly occupied or preempted by groups for which the implicit subsidies were not intended. Cost recovery has only partially succeeded, and in the process, the development agencies which relied on land development for their financial sustainability were confronted with adverse financial consequences.[16]

There are exceptions to this pattern, however, such as the early sites-and-services schemes in Madras, India and the more recent attempt in Hyderabad, Pakistan to pattern the approach more closely to illegal land subdivision (Siddiqui and Khan 1990). These exceptions suggest that the sites-and-services approach is valid. However, to avoid the management problems discussed above, the rules governing its implementation should be as simple and transparent as possible, perhaps comparable to what occurs in informal land subdivision.

Housing Finance

Adequate access for the poor to housing finance at reasonable terms has not generally been achieved. Although housing finance institutions were ostensibly established to provide cheap housing credit to deserving (i.e., poor) groups, they have generally failed to realize their objectives: typically only a limited number of loans could be provided, and procedural obstacles and terms and conditions were such that, at best, middle-income groups captured the benefits of subsidized credit. Well-known examples are the performance of Bank Tabungan Negara (BTN) in Indonesia and the mortgage program in the Philippines. Often the cause of failure has been a combination of factors, including the inability of the poor to provide adequate collateral for mortgage lending and restrictive financial sector regulations. Also, formal housing finance systems are often underdeveloped in the sense that only a limited range of financial instruments, if any, exists. Further, these are usually not well integrated in the savings and loan industry and the capital market at large. Whatever instruments exist are usually not well-tailored to the requirements of the urban poor.

Hence, for lack of alternatives, the urban poor must rely to a large extent on informal sector finance, which often is provided at relatively unattractive terms and conditions.[17]

Moreover, there are also some interesting successes, such as the experience of the Government Housing Bank in Thailand and the largely rural housing loan program of the Grameen Bank in Bangladesh.[18] These two very different operations suggest that:

(i) the chances of success are greater if an institution is well-embedded in the financial sector: a prerequisite for both was being allowed to take deposits from their clients and therefore act as a savings-and-loan bank; and

(ii) individual loans may need to be quite small, not necessarily requiring a property title as collateral, but may be backed by prior savings or by a form of community collateral; this effectively amounts to a marriage between the formal and informal housing finance sector (see also Wegelin 1989).

Providing Municipal Infrastructure and Services

The above strategic changes in approaches to shelter, *inter alia*, placed increased emphasis on shelter-related municipal infrastructure and services. On-site provision of such services forms only part of the solution; the effective connections to citywide networks is a major concern, raising entirely different sets of issues, all related to the technical, financial, and institutional viability of such networks.

The link with shelter programs increased the need for sectoral infrastructure programs such as water supply, sanitation, urban drainage, and solid waste disposal to be increasingly based on sectoral master plans for the entire city. As implementation of such master plans cannot be carried out for all sectors simultaneously, due to financial and administrative constraints, the issue of intersectoral investment priority-setting assumes increasing importance.

Thus, the 1980s witnessed a movement to internalize these strands in a framework of increasingly integrated urban infrastructure programs.[19]

Ingredients for Success

The slum upgrading and sites-and-services approaches discussed above are perhaps best characterized as a half-way house in shaping the enabling approach: they are still conceived as "projects" (or marginally better, as "programs") to be delivered by government executing agencies. Hence, the same type of supply constraints which have frustrated public housing delivery, have, to a large extent, also impinged on the effectiveness of slum upgrading and the sites-and-services approach. This has been reinforced by the tendency to further burden agencies that are already suffering limited delivery capabilities with additional tasks, such as the administration of credit schemes for a variety of purposes.

The most successful schemes are those where government initiatives and interventions have been limited to those that, by their very nature, the community or the private sector are unable to perform, such as freeing land and providing major municipal infrastructure, and where all other developmental roles have been carried out either by the community itself and/or by qualified private sector entities, be they private enterprise or NGOs. In view of the nature of these schemes, it is perhaps not surprising that implementation has generally been somewhat easier in the slum improvement area than for sites-and-services programs. The more successful slum improvement programs have been the less complicated ones which could be implemented on a relatively large scale, such as the Bustee Improvement Program in Calcutta, India and the Kampung Improvement Program in Indonesia.[20]

The link between major municipal infrastructure and the reinforcement of integrative trends in municipal infrastructure and services delivery is of relative recent origin, and has not yet taken firm roots. This is partly because it is inextricably connected to the decentralization of responsibilities for such delivery to local and sometimes sub-local government levels that, of course, have much wider sociopolitical and administrative ramifications. While the general trend is clear, with major benefits being more cost-effective investment programs and easier assumption of operation and maintenance responsibilities by local governments, the initial experience with these programs suggests that the transition from sectoral, technically oriented, and centralized decision-making and implementation to doing this in a more decentralized and integrated way is difficult and time-consuming. The process also predictably tends to raise new issues, such as overall responsibilities for services provision between the various levels of governments and municipal financing patterns (see Morfit 1986; Utoro 1990; van der Hoff and Steinberg 1992; de Guzman 1988; Bastin and Hidayat 1992; Devas 1989).

Issues and Policy Concerns

Clearly the project/program-oriented strategy has not been able to deal with many important shelter issues outside the framework of the specific projects/programs, but which form the main impediments to adequate shelter supply, and in the process have hampered the implementation of the schemes themselves. In this regard, the following main issues stand out:

(i) Adequate land supply for shelter in the right location, particularly for housing the poor (i.e., close to employment opportunities), has been identified as a problem virtually everywhere. As noted above, this is not normally a problem of physical shortage of buildable land. However, virtually everywhere the existing regulatory framework (i.e., planning and building control regulations, land expropriation and land transfer regulations, land/property tax regulations, public land disposal policies and procedures, and land titling procedures) have tended to stifle land supply. Clearly, this has affected land supply for housing the urban poor most of all.

(ii) Formal housing finance systems are usually underdeveloped in the sense that only a limited range of financial instruments, if any, exists. Further, these are usually not well integrated in the savings and loan industry and the capital market at large. Whatever instruments exist are usually not tailored to the requirements of the urban poor. Hence, for lack of alternatives, the urban poor must rely to a large extent on informal sector finance, which often is provided at relatively unattractive terms and conditions.[21]

(iii) Neighborhood infrastructure and services such as local roads, electricity and water supply, drainage, sewerage/sanitation, garbage collection and disposal, and public transport are not only essential in housing development, but their provision/denial is an important potential instrument (often the only one realistically at the local government's disposal) to guide the direction and pattern of urban growth. While generally there has been gradual progress in the supply of infrastructure and services to already settled low-income areas as these are legalized, coordination between supply of services and urban land development needs to be strengthened for this to work. The modalities of providing such services in an integrated, coordinated way, taking cognisance of financial and administrative constraints at the local government level in infrastructure planning, programming, budgeting, and implementation need to be explored further, building on the emerging experience with such approaches in an increasing number of South Asian and Southeast Asian countries.

(iv) It has become increasingly clear that renting a house or a room is often the only housing option open to sizeable segments of the urban poor. However, government intervention has not generally been directed at stimulating private sector supply of rental housing. In some countries, a concern with rental housing supply has led to public housing projects for rent, but as noted earlier, these have suffered from a number of unintended by-products, and in any event the limited magnitude of such projects have prevented them from making any serious impact. Relevant rules and regulations such as rent control regulations and regulations on subletting in public housing schemes and sites-and-services projects have tended to discourage investment in rental housing rather than stimulate it (see for example, Kalim 1988).

(v)   Virtually nowhere have governments dealt effectively with the complexities of inner city redevelopment, although it is clear that large sections of the urban poor are vitally dependent for their livelihood on locations in or close to the city center. Planning and building control regulations, which could be used to guide such processes appropriately, have at best had a neutral impact, or have actually accelerated the process of decay. The impact of rent control in inner city areas has been to reinforce this process (Kalim 1983, 1988).

(vi) To seriously embark on an enabling approach in shelter delivery, to develop housing finance adequately as part of financial sector development, to provide municipal services in an integrated and decentralized approach, and to modify the regulatory environment to ensure that it encourages the enabling approach rather than stifles it, all require substantial institutional reorientation and capacity building, particularly but not exclusively at the local government level. It is clear that this is a long-term concern, for which there are no easy shortcuts. In conjunction, part of the institutional reorientation must be towards recognition of the importance of community participation in urban shelter, services delivery, and resource mobilization and towards an understanding of the imperative of close cooperation between local governments, NGOs and community-based organizations (CBOs) in achieving this.

POLICY OPTIONS AND APPROACHES TO FINANCING

From the above it may be clear that all realistic options in housing and urban services for the urban poor will be variations on the theme of the enabling approach. Generally this will require that the informal sector shelter delivery be made to function more effectively, by improving access and lowering costs. The overriding role for government is to ease market supply constraints and exercise strategic interventions to strengthen the position of the urban poor. The precise combination of policy elements will necessarily vary from country to country, but the following major aspects will require consideration:

(i) *Housing policy program*: Approaches to assist the urban poor in obtaining appropriate shelter, which will allow the best possible use of that shelter considering all aspects discussed above, are best formulated as part of an overall medium-term housing policy program, in which the housing sector is considered as part of the national economy, and in which low-income housing demand and supply are seen as part of aggregate housing demand and supply. Housing actions by other groups impact directly on housing opportunities for the poor. Further, many of the enabling actions required of government are not necessarily in the housing area per se, and must be considered in a broader perspective. These are notably land issues, housing finance and subsidies, and regulatory frameworks.

(ii) *Review of and modifications in the regulatory framework impinging on urban land supply*: The above housing policy program should contain a review of the regulatory framework, including planning and building control regulations, land expropriation and land transfer regulations, land/property tax regulations, public land disposal policies and procedures, and land titling procedures with the objective of removing barriers to an effective and affordable land supply.

(iii) *Enhancing the quality of the housing finance system*: Housing finance institutions must be authorized and strengthened to compete for savings with other financing institutions at market rates of interest. Access of the poor to housing finance must be enhanced by ensuring that the relevant institutions are physically accessible, and offer housing loan "products" and, where appropriate, savings "products" which meet the demand of the lower-income groups. In many cases this will require a link with informal housing finance systems, effectively capitalizing such systems and making use of their network and organization. The range of financial instruments should be broadened to also include small loans for upgrading or extending homes. However, this may only be possible through the establishment/provision of incentives for savings and loans associations/credit unions, with appropriate provisions for systems of uncollateralized loans through group and/or mutual guarantees. Secondary mortgage markets may need to be established. Further, the government may be required to stimulate the development of the housing finance system through the institution of a guarantee system or through fiscal facilities.

(iv) *Neighborhood infrastructure and services*: Municipal infrastructure and services such as local roads, electricity and water supply, drainage, sewerage/sanitation, garbage collection and disposal, and public transport need be provided in conjunction with and in support of new residential land development. Further, these services should be provided in an integrated fashion to maximize the benefits of infrastructure and services supply and to facilitate efficient land use (see ADB 1991). Through the provision/denial of infrastructure and services, the local government will be able to guide the direction and pattern of urban growth away from areas where settlement is dangerous (e.g., hillsites where there are substantial risks of landslides) or where the provision of services is prohibitively expensive. This provision policy needs to be clear and consistent, and needs to be supported by the regulatory framework concerned with land titling/subdivision and planning and building control. A similar policy is required for already settled low-income areas: legalization of land tenure needs to be in close association with the coordinated supply of municipal infrastructure and services.

(v) **Rental housing and inner cities' rehabilitation**: In many cases the (local) government may not have the institutional strength to undertake positive action to stimulate supply of rental housing and to ensure sensitive redevelopment of inner city areas to protect the interest of the urban poor. In those cases, the government should at least desist from regulations and actions which run counter to the development of rental housing supply (e.g., rent control regulations) and which may adversely affect the position of the urban poor.

(vi) **Minimizing relocation**: As noted earlier, the poor use their shelter for more purposes than to simply have a roof over their head. The location of their shelter vis-a-vis employment opportunities, infrastructure, and services is of paramount importance. Forced relocation must, therefore, be avoided as much as possible. Where this cannot be avoided, simple, transparent and enforceable rules dealing with forced relocation will be required, based on the principle that those persons relocated will be at least as well off after relocation as before.

(vii) **Targeted subsidies**: Housing and municipal services delivery systems in almost any country contain explicit or implicit subsidies. More often than not these subsidies would be unaffordable to the government if the housing and municipal services programs actually met demand—in which case there is a case for abandoning such subsidies altogether. Where there is financial room for subsidies, they should be as directed to the specific target (low-income) groups as possible. Generalizations are difficult in this area, except that there is a prima facie case against price subsidies (e.g., interest subsidies, below market land prices, rent control, below market service charges for such services as water or solid waste) on two counts: first, they distort the pricing system, often achieving the opposite from what was intended; and second, they tend to be preempted by non-deserving groups.

Direct income supplements to deserving households do not distort the pricing system and may be easier to target—depending on the degree of sophistication of the administrative system—but have the drawback that they are open-ended from a budgeting point of view. In the services area, specific subsidized provision may be considered for common facilities well-targeted to poor neighborhoods, such as providing water standpipes, but such subsidy provision needs to be explicit, transparent and provided by the government, and not at the expense of the financial sustainabilty of water supply operations generally.

(viii) *Incentives for the commercial and noncommercial private sector*: Experience has shown that both the private commercial sector (formal and informal) and the NGO sector have important roles to play in the development of shelter and associated infrastructure. The role of the private commercial sector is constrained to profitable activities, which obviously may include design, building activities, building materials production, and housing finance. The government's role is to promote transparent competition in all these areas, to ensure functional building standards (with realistic minimum standards relating to the prevention of fire and other natural hazards), and to ensure and promote the commercial attractiveness of environmentally and technologically appropriate building materials.

The role of the NGO/CBO may be manifold, ranging from building cooperatives (such as the Building Together Company in Thailand), savings and loan associations and financial intermediation (such as the Community Mortgage Program in the Philippines) and intermediating organizations in infrastructure delivery (such as the Orangi Pilot Project in Karachi) to advocacy groups (e.g., those supported in various Asian countries by the Asian Coalition on Housing Rights) (see Murphy et al. 1990). In relation to such groups, the first maxim to governments and their agencies should be to regard NGOs and CBOs not as adversaries but as productive, legitimate participants in the housing process, whose programs are often more effective in reaching the poor than are government programs. Such cooperation could lead to a more active, stimulating role, *inter alia*, to develop rules and regulations to make legitimate working agreements possible and to facilitate coordination. Such cooperation is not easily achieved, given the small-scale and often project-specific, non-replicable nature of many NGO/CBO activities, and the mutual suspicions between NGOs/CBOs and (local) governments. Care must be taken to stimulate and facilitate the sustainability of NGO/CBO activities, yet to avoid the impression that NGOs have been simply co-opted in government programs.

STRATEGIES AND OPERATIONAL MEASURES FOR DONOR ASSISTANCE

International development institutions, including ADB and World Bank, have, in the past, provided substantial support to the shelter and urban services sector in a number of Asian developing countries (ADCs). The nature of this support has developed over time in keeping with the development of sector policy thinking. Much of what is suggested below, therefore, is not new to ADB, but rather reinforces the direction in which it and donor assistance in the sector has developed during the past few years.

It is important, however, that all international development institutions, including ADB, become more selective in providing support for the sector only in those cases where the government has committed itself to an enabling approach. In this regard, an ADB sector review, including a regulatory audit to identify those regulations causing the most serious distortions in sector performance, and an urban land market assessment (as land supply has been demonstrated to be a major constraint) should be able to:

(i)   determine the actual *modus operandi* of the government sector agencies; and,

(ii) establish if there is enough basis/common ground to enter into sector policy dialogue to identify and agree to required regulatory and operational changes, thus ensuring an effective enabling role of the government, as well as defining and agreeing on ways and means to ensure that possible ADB shelter and urban services sector support adequately benefits the urban poor.

Such sectoral policy dialogue may often require substantial consultation/review among the government agencies involved and, hence, may require substantial time and effort. It should preferably be carried out in conjunction with other institutions and donors, particularly the World Bank. Sectoral policy dialogues should be supported with technical assistance to facilitate the process which should preferably lead to the formulation of a sector policy program (where necessary, again, supported by technical assistance), which should form the framework for further support. As noted above, the most effective support to housing efforts of the poor is through removing constraints on the housing market as a whole. Therefore, it is necessary to consider the sector comprehensively in view of the interdependency of the various housing submarkets and the "envelope" nature of many of the enabling measures required to be implemented by governments.

It follows that funding institutions should generally avoid financing isolated individual (housing) projects, unless these mark the first entry into the sector in a country. Rather, assistance should preferably be directed to support the government in implementing its enabling role in the sector in a programmatic way through:

(i)   wholesale DFI-type loans to housing finance institutions (with conditionalities related to such institutions' lending policies and criteria—both in terms of effectiveness and of accessibility for the poor—as well as to their management capabilities for dealing with a sizeable loan portfolio). A good example of this type of support is provided by the Low-income Housing Development Project in Sri Lanka, approved by ADB in 1991;

(ii) urban land management/land development sector loans to well-established land development agencies which amounts to supporting an appropriate mix of slum improvement/sites-and-services/guided land development schemes. This was intended in the Shelter Sector Project in Thailand, approved by ADB in 1985. During project implementation it became clear that regulatory and procedural land acquisition constraints on the National Housing Authority formed a much more serious obstacle to effective sites-and-services development than anticipated. This, in combination with the remarkable growth of the Government Housing Bank's housing finance activities (particularly through linking the mobilization of domestic savings through attractive deposit terms and outreach policy with flexible financing for housing development) during the same period, suggests that, in retrospect, shelter finance was not a bottleneck requiring external support, but that sector problems were more institutional in nature;

(iii)   broader support for the urban sector, where the focus could be the integrated, decentralized delivery of municipal infrastructure and/or urban land management/development. This support could be direct, through support to the implementation of an infrastructure program, or indirect through a DFI-type credit line to a municipal development bank or fund. Most of the loans provided by ADB to date for urban infrastructure in Indonesia are in the former category, as are the Second Urban Development Project in Pakistan (approved in 1989) and the recently (1992) approved Urban Development Sector Project in Sri Lanka; and

(iv)   sectoral technical assistance grants and loans to assist governments to formulate, develop, and implement the regulatory and operational measures required for the government to shape its enabling role. Though ADB has not yet provided technical assistance loans exclusively for the urban sector, several advisory technical assistance grants have been provided for such purposes to a number of developing countries, including Bangladesh, Bhutan, Fiji, Pakistan, Sri Lanka, and Western Samoa.

In all types of assistance, a strong emphasis should continue to be given to institutional strengthening of sector agencies to ensure adequate sector coordination and sustainability of urban development. This element is likely to assume increasing importance in the context of implementing the enabling strategy, particularly as responsibilities shift between different levels of government with the evolution of decentralized and integrated municipal services delivery, and with increasing formal-informal sector interaction in the area of housing finance.

In summary, the new element proposed in the above discussion is not a radical departure from past practices. Rather, it builds on and extends what is currently being done, emphasizing more comprehensiveness. An increased emphasis on sector reviews, including regulatory audits and urban land market assessments, policy dialogue, and institutional capacity building is required by the international development and donor agencies. Patience in determining project processing schedules is needed, as is an effort to devote more staff resources to front-end activities than presently occurs.

Operational guidelines should reflect the above, reiterating the development agency's support of the enabling approach as well as its emphasis on sector study work—specifying regulatory audits and urban land assessments as essential ingredients—and policy dialogue on its impact on the poor and on the need to avoid forced relocation—including clear guidance on conditionalities, if this appears unavoidable.

Notes

1. See also the Asian Development Bank's *Annual Report 1992* theme paper on urbanization (1993b).
2. See Mazumdar (Chapter Three of this volume) for a detailed study of urban poverty and urban labor markets.
3. See Gertler (Chapter Five of this volume) for a detailed study of the urban poor, education, and health.
4. See, for example, Payne (1989) for a review on informal housing and land subdivisions.
5. The inadequate response of the formal sector in meeting the demand for shelter was confirmed by the country contributions at ADB's 1993 Workshop on the Critical Issues and Policy Measures to Address Urban Poverty: see Mathur (1994), Kim (1994), Balisacan (1994), Perera (1994), Khundker and Mahmud (1994) and Firdausy (1994).
6. See UNCHS (1987, 131–145) for an overview description of this phenomena; van der Linden (1990), Kinhill/NESPAK (1990), and Lindfield and Barker (1991) describe some specific instances in Pakistan and Fiji.
7. Well-known examples are the impact of the Urban Land Ceiling and Regulation Act in India (IBRD 1992a, 17) and the Ceiling on Housing Property Law in Sri Lanka (Selvarajah 1983).
8. Some examples of this for Karachi, Pakistan are provided by van der Linden (1981).
9. See Evers (1980) for an estimate of housings' basis for economic activities at the nonmonetary subsistence level in *kampungs* in Jakarta.
10. See also Balisacan (1994); and Thailand Development Research Institute Foundation (1991, 41) for examples from the Philippines and Thailand.

11. See Jellinek (1991) for a description of a food vendor's life in Jakarta and the role that the house plays as production location and security.
12. An instructive example of how this may also generate substantial employment and income for women is provided by the Save the Children US-supported Kirillapone Project in Colombo (see Fernando 1985).
13. While downward-raiding is a common experience of public housing schemes throughout the region, such problems have been particularly pronounced in the *Bagong Lipunan* Sites and Services (BLISS) housing schemes developed in the early 1980s in Manila, in the low-cost housing flats developed by the National Housing Authority in Bangkok, and in some of the PERUMNAS housing schemes in Indonesia in the 1970s and 1980s.
14. See, for example, Swan et al. (1983) for a review of the sites-and-services strategy in Asia, and Skinner et al. (1987) for an evaluation of the slum improvement experience.
15. See also Sultan and van der Linden (1991) for some evidence resulting from unusually long-term longitudinal studies in two settlements in Karachi.
16. The most notable case is that of the Karachi Development Authority, which as a result of this—largely political—mismanagement was barely able to pay its staff salaries by 1991.
17. See ADB (1990a, 187–215) for a comprehensive, wide-ranging discussion of informal sector finance issues.
18. Another success is the Community Mortgage Program in the Philippines. This Program, as a provision of the new Urban Development law, seems to have successfully acquired land for housing the poor (Murphy 1992).
19. These programs, as they have emerged in several of the countries in the present study—the IUIDP in Indonesia; RCDP/PREMIUMED in the Philippines; RCDP in Thailand; and IDSMT in India are good examples (see Wegelin 1990 for an overview)—are all bound by financial and administrative program implementation constraints at the local government level, have intersectoral priority setting procedures and, by virtue of these features, have gravitated towards decentralization of decision-making on program priorities (see e.g., Indian Human Settlements Program 1989; ADB vols. I and II 1991; Sidabutar 1992; Philippines Regional Municipal Development Project 1992).

20. An early example of a successful sites-and-services area is the IBRD-supported sites-and services program in El Salvador, implemented by FUNDASAL (an NGO) with government concurrence. A more recent example is the Khuda-ki-basti in Hyderabad (Siddiqui and Khan 1990; van der Linden 1992).
21. See ADB (1990a, 187–215) for a comprehensive, wide-ranging discussion of informal sector finance issues.

References

Angel, Shlomo. 1987. "The Land and Housing Markets of Bangkok: Strategies for Public Sector Participation." *The Bangkok Land Management Study*, Volume I: Final Report. Manila: Asian Development Bank. pp. v–vi.

Angel, Shlomo and Sopon Pornchokchai. 1990. "The Informal Land Subdivision Market in Bangkok." In *The Transformation of Land Supply Systems in Third World Cities*, by Paul Baróss and Jan van der Linden. Avebury: Alderschot.

Arlosoroff, Saul. 1989. *Issues in Water Management for Urban Centers in the Developing World*. Washington DC: The World Bank, Water and Sanitation, Infrastructure and Urban Development Department.

Asian Development Bank (ADB). 1983. *Regional Seminar on Financing of Low-income Housing, A Summary Report*. Manila: Asian Development Bank.

_____ . 1987. "Urban Development and Housing Sector Operations Paper." Doc.In. 290–87. Manila: Asian Development Bank. p. 17.

_____ . 1989. *Appraisal of the Secondary Cities Urban Development (Sector) Project in Indonesia*. Manila: Asian Development Bank. p. 17.

_____ . 1990a. *Asian Development Outlook 1990*. Manila: Asian Development Bank. pp. 187–215.

_____ . 1990b. *Water Supply and Sanitation Sector Study of Indonesia*. Manila: Asian Development Bank.

_____ . 1991. *The Urban Poor and Basic Infrastructure Services in Asia and the Pacific*. Manila: Asian Development Bank.

_____ . 1993a. "Pakistan Urban Sector Profile Study." Discussion draft. Manila: Asian Development Bank. pp. 15, 25, 27.

_____ . 1993b. *Annual Report 1992*. Theme Paper on Urbanization. Manila: Asian Development Bank.

Bakhtiari, Qurat-ul-Ein, and M. Wegelin-Schuringa. 1992. *From Sanitation to Development—The Case of Baldia Soakpit Pilot Project*. The Haque: IRC.

Balisacan, Arsenio M. 1994. "Urban Poverty in the Philippines: Nature, Causes, and Policy Measures." *Asian Development Review*. vol. 12, no. 1.

Baross Paul, and Jan van der Linden, eds. 1990. *The Transformation of Land Supply Systems in Third World Cities*. Avebury: Aldershot.

Bastin, Johan, and Wahju Hidayat. 1992. "Financing the Integrated Urban Infrastructure Development Program." In *Innovative Approaches to Urban Management, Institute for Housing and Urban Development Studies*, edited by Robert van der Hoff and Florian Steinberg. Avebury: Aldershot.

Bhattacharya, Swades Kumar. 1985. "Pricing Urban Domestic Water Supply in Developing Countries." *Journal of the Institution of Public Health Engineers*. India. no. 2, April–June.

Bijlani, H.U., and P.S.N. Rao. 1990. *Water Supply and Sanitation in India*. New Delhi: Oxford and IBH Publishing Co. p. 29.

Burns, L.S., R.G. Healy, D.M. McAllister, and B. Khing Tjioe. 1970. *Housing, Symbol and Shelter*. Los Angeles: University of California at Los Angeles (UCLA).

Burns, L.S., and L. Grebler. 1977. *The Housing of Nations: Advice and Policy in a Comparative Framework*. London: Macmillan.

Cairncross, Sandy, Jorge E. Hardoy, and David Satterthwaite. 1990. *The Poor Die Young, Housing and Health in Third World Cities*. London: Earthscan Publications Ltd.

de Guzman, R.P. 1988. "Decentralization as a Strategy for Redemocratization in the Philippine Political System." In *Philippine Journal of Public Administration.* vol. XXXII, nos. 3, 4.

Devas, Nick. 1989. "Issues in the Financing of Local Government in Indonesia." In *Planning and Administration.* no. 2.

Directorate General of International Development Cooperation (DGIS). 1990. *Evaluation of IKK Water Supply Program Batch 3, West Java, Indonesia.* The Hague: DGIS.

Evers, H.D. 1980. "Subsistence Economy and the Jakarta Floating Mass." In *Prisma.* Jakarta: M. Dawam Rahardjo and Harselan Haralap. pp. 27–35.

Fernando, Marina. 1985. "Women's Participation in the Housing Process: the Case of Kirillapone, Sri Lanka." Gender and Planning Working Paper no. 3. London: Development Planning Unit, University College.

Firdausy, Carunia Mulya. 1994. "Urban Poverty in Indonesia: Trends, Issues, and Policies." *Asian Development Review.* vol. 12. no. 1.

Gertler, Paul. J., and Omar Rahman. 1994. "Social Infrastructure and Urban Poverty in Asia." Chapter Four in this Volume.

Gunatilleke, Godfrey, and Perera, Myrtle. 1994. "Urban Poverty in Sri Lanka: Critical Issues and Policy Measures." *Asian Development Review.* vol. 12. no. 1.

Hasan, Arif. 1988. "Low-cost Sanitation for a Squatter Community." In *Health Forum. An International Journal of Health Development.* vol. 9.

Indian Human Settlements Program, Phase II. 1989. Extension Proposal 1991–1994, Annex 6.10, Documentary Material.

International Bank for Reconstruction and Development (IBRD). 1975. *Housing Sector Policy Paper.* Washington DC: The World Bank.

_____ . 1980. *Shelter, Poverty and Basic Needs Series.* Washington DC: The World Bank.

_____ . 1983. *Learning by Doing: Retrospective Review of Urban Operations.* Washington DC: The World Bank.

_____ . 1990. *World Development Report 1990: World Development Indicators.* New York: Oxford University Press.

_____ . 1991. *Urban Policy and Economic Development: An Agenda for the 1990s.* Washington DC: The World Bank.

_____ . 1992a. "Housing: Enabling Markets to Work." A World Bank Policy Paper, draft. Washington DC: The World Bank. pp. 2, 10, 17, 49, 60.

_____ . 1992b. *World Development Report 1992: Development and the Environment.* New York: Oxford University Press. p. 100.

Islam, Nazrul. 1990. *Dhaka Metropolitan Fringe Land and Housing Development.* Dhaka Study Series no. 10. Dhaka: Dhaka City Museum.

Jellinek, Lea. 1991. *The Wheel of Fortune—The History of a Poor Community in Jakarta.* Asian Studies Association of Australia, Southeast Asian publication series no. 18. Sydney: Allen and Unwin.

Kalim, S. Iqbal. 1983. "Incorporating Slumdwellers into Redevelopment Schemes." In *Land for Housing the Poor,* edited by S. Angel, R.W. Archer, S. Tanpiphat, and E.A. Wegelin. Singapore: Select Books.

_____ . 1988. "The Inner City Tenant: The Missing Category in Housing Policy." Working Paper no. 19. Alumni Paper Series. East-West Center Association.

Khundker, Nasreen, Wahiduddin Mahmud, Binayak Sen, and Monawar Uddin Ahmed. 1994. "Urban Poverty in Bangladesh: Trends, Determinants and Policy Issues." *Asian Development Review.* vol. 12. no. 1.

Kim, Jong-Gie. 1994. "Urban Poverty in Korea: Critical Issues and Policy Measures." *Asian Development Review.* vol. 12. no. 1.

Kinhill Engineers/NESPAK. 1990. *Karachi Urban Land Management Study, Final Report.* Karachi: Kinhill Engineers/Nespak. p. 13.

Kundu, Amitabh. 1991. "Micro-Environment in Urban Planning. Access of Poor to Water Supply and Sanitation." *Economic and Political Weekly*. vol. 26, no. 37. pp. 2168–70.

Lall, Vinay D. ed. 1989. *Resource Mobilization, International Experiences of the Informal Sector*. New Delhi: Society for Development Studies.

_____ . 1991. *Drinking Water Delivery System in Urban Settlements: Status, Development Strategy and Action Plan*. New Delhi: Society for Development Studies. pp. 78, 80.

Lindfield, M.L., and T.B. Barker. 1991. *Fiji Housing Sector Resource Mobilization Study*. Fiji: Asian Development Bank and Government of Fiji.

Lovei, Laszlo, and Dale Whittington. 1991. "Rent Seeking in Water Supply." Discussion Paper, Report INU 85. Washington DC: The World Bank, Sector Policy and Research, Infrastructure and Urban Development Department.

Mathur, Om Prakash. 1994. "The State of India's Urban Poverty." *Asian Development Review*. vol. 12. no. 1.

Mazumdar, Dipak. 1994. "Urban Poverty and Urban Labor Markets." Chapter Three in this Volume.

McManus, Gerald M. 1991. *Consulting Assignment 1989–91, Solid Waste Management Adviser, Second Bandung Urban Development Project*. Final Report. Australia: Kinhill Engineers Pty. Ltd.

Mehta, Meera, and Dinesh Mehta. 1989. *Metropolitan Housing Market—A Study of Ahmedabad*. London: Sage Publications. pp. 67–68, 70, 77–78, 80, 96.

Mitra, B.C., and Peter Nientied. 1989. *Land Supply and Housing Expenses for Low-income Families: A Rationale for Government Intervention*. Urban Research Working Paper no. 19. Amsterdam: Amsterdam Free University.

Morfit, M. 1986. "Strengthening the Capacities of Local Government: Policies and Constraints." In *Central Government and Local Development in Indonesia*, edited by C. MacAndrews. Singapore: Oxford University Press.

Murphy, Dennis. et al. 1990. *A Decent Place to Live: Urban Poor in Asia.* Manila: Asian Coalition for Housing Rights.

_____ . 1992. *Initial Information 1992 Region Action Project.* Philippines, Draft Interim Report. Manila: Asian Coalition for Housing Rights.

National Development Planning Board (BAPPENAS), United Nations Children's Fund (UNICEF), and Yayasan Dian Desa. 1990. *Monitoring and Evaluation of Public Hydrants and Water Terminals in North Jakarta, Final Report.* Yogyakarta: Yayasan Dian Desa. pp. Ex–9, 4–18, 19.

Nientied, Peter, and Jan van der Linden. 1990. "The Role of the Government in the Supply of Legal and Illegal Land in Karachi." In *The Transformation of Land Supply Systems in Third World Cities,* by Paul Baróss and Jan van der Linden. Avebury: Aldershot.

Payne, Geoffrey. 1989. *Informal Housing and Land Subdivisions in Third World Cities: A Review of the Literature.* Prepared for the Oversees Development Administration (ODA) by the Center for Development and Environmental Planning (CENDEP). Oxford: Oxford Polytechnic.

Peattie, L. 1979. "Housing Policy in Developing Countries: Two Puzzles." *World Development.* vol. 7. pp. 1017–22.

Philippines. 1992. *Regional Municipal Development Project.* Project Brief. Manila: Asian Development Bank.

Raj, Mulkh. 1991. *Financing of Urban Infrastructure in India.* New Delhi: Housing and Urban Development Corporation (HUDCO). pp. 10, 11.

Ratanakomut, Somchai, Charuma Ashakul, and Thienchay Kirananda. 1994. "Urban Poverty in Thailand: Critical Issues and Policy Measures." *Asian Development Review.* vol. 12. no. 1.

Savasdisara, Tongchai, Walter E.J. Tips, and Sunata Suwamodom. 1987. *Final Report on the Belgian Low-Cost Housing Project.* Residential Satisfaction, Mobility and Estate Management in Private Lower Cost Housing Estates in Thailand, Research Monograph No.13. Bangkok: Division of Human Settlements.

SELAVIP. 1992. *Latin America and Asian Low-Income Housing Service.* Santiago.

Selvarajah, Eswaran. 1983. "The Impact of the Ceiling on Housing Property Law on the Slum and Shanty Improvement Program in Sri Lanka." In *Land for Housing the Poor,* edited by S. Angel, R.W. Archer, S. Tanpiphat, and E.A. Wegelin. Singapore: Select Books.

Sidabutar, Parulian. 1992. "The Origin and Concept of the Integrated Urban Infrastructure Development Program." In *Innovative Approaches to Urban Management,* edited by Robert van der Hoff and Florian Steinberg. Institute for Housing and Urban Development Studies. Avebury: Aldershot.

Siddiqui, T.A., and M.A. Khan. 1990. "Land Supply to the Urban Poor: Hyderabad's Incremental Development Scheme." In *The Transformation of Land Supply Systems in Third World Cities,* edited by P. Baross, and J. van der Linden. Avebury: Aldershot.

Skinner, Reinhard J., John L. Taylor, and Emiel A. Wegelin, eds. 1987. *Shelter Upgrading for the Urban Poor—Evaluation of Third World Experience.* Manila: Island Publishing House.

Struyk, Raymond J., Michael L. Hoffman, and Harold M. Katsura. 1990. *The Market for Shelter in Indonesian Cities.* Washington: The Urban Institute. pp. 9, 74, 80, 102, 108.

Sultan, Jawaid, and Jan van der Linden. 1991. *Squatment Upgrading in Karachi – A Review of Longitudinal Research on Policy, Implementation and Impacts.* Urban Research Working Paper No. 27. Amsterdam: Amsterdam Free University. 20.

Sutmuller, Paul. 1992. "Multi-Year Investment Planning for the IUIDP." In *Innovative Approaches to Urban Management.* Institute for Housing and Urban Development Studies, edited by Robert van der Hoff and Florian Steinberg. Avebury: Aldershot.

Swan, Peter, Emiel A. Wegelin, and Komol Panchee. 1983. *Management of Sites and Services Housing Schemes: The Asian Experience.* Chichester: John Wiley and Sons.

Thailand Development Research Institute Foundation, NESDB. 1991. *National Urban Development Policy Framework, Draft Final Report Area 6: Urban Poor Upgrading.* Bangkok: NESDB. pp. 41, 43.

Turner, John F.C. 1976. *Housing by People.* London: Marion Boyars.

United Nations Centre for Human Settlements (UNCHS). 1987. *Global Report on Human Settlements 1986.* New York: Oxford University Press. pp. 131–145.

United Nations Development Programme (UNDP). 1990. *Human Development Report 1990.* New York: Oxford University Press. p. 174.

_____. 1991. *Cities, People and Poverty—Urban Development Cooperation for the 1990s.* A UNDP Strategy Paper. New York: UNDP.

_____. 1992. *Human Development Report 1992.* New York: Oxford University Press.

UNDP and United States Agency for International Development (USAID). 1992. *Bangladesh Country Paper.* Regional Seminar on Private Sector Initiatives in Urban Housing and Services in Asia and the Pacific. Bali. pp. 2, 16–19, 36.

Urban Edge. 1991. *Water: Save Now or Pay Later, The Urban Edge Issues and Innovations.* vol. 15, no. 3. Washington DC: The World Bank. pp. 2, 3.

Utoro, Sutikni. 1990. "Implementation Problems of Local Level." Workshop on Integrated Spatial and Infrastructure Development. Bandung.

van der Hoff, Robert, and Florian Steinberg. 1992. "The Integrated Urban Infrastructure Development Program: Innovative Approaches to Urban Management in Indonesia." In *Innovative Approaches to Urban Management, Institute for Housing and Urban Development Studies,* edited by Robert van der Hoff and Florian Steinberg. Avebury: Aldershot.

van der Linden, Jan. 1986. *The Sites and Services Approach Reviewed.* Hants: Gower.

_____ . 1988. "The Squatter's House as a Source of Security in Pakistan." *Ekistics*. no. 48. Athens: Athens Center of Ekistics of the Athens Technological Organization. pp. 44–48.

_____ . 1990. "The Limited Impact of Some 'Major Determinants' of the Land Market; Supply of Land for Housing in Lahore and Karachi, Pakistan." Paper presented at the European Conference of Asian Studies. Amsterdam. p. 7.

_____ . 1992. "Back to the Roots: Successful Implementation of Sites-and-Services." In *Beyond Self-help Housing*, edited by Kosta Mathey. London: Mansell.

Wegelin, Emiel A. 1978. *Urban Low-income Housing and Development – A Case Study in Peninsular Malaysia*. Leiden/Boston: Martinus Nijhoff.

_____ . 1989. "Housing Finance: Bridge-building Between the Formal and Informal Sectors." In *Resource Mobilization, International Experiences of the Informal Sector*, edited by Vinay D. Lall. New Delhi: Society for Development Studies.

_____ . 1990. "New Approaches in Urban Services Delivery: A Comparison of Emerging Experience in Selected Asian Countries." In *Cities*. vol. 7, no. 3.

Wegelin, Emiel A., Michael R. Lindfield, and Ferry van Wilgenburg. 1991. *Urban Poverty Indicators – A Review of Urban Poverty Indicators, and a Practical Application for Pakistan and Indonesia*. Rotterdam: Netherlands Economic Institute.

Whittington, Dale. 1992. "Possible Adverse Effects of Increasing Block Water Tariffs in Developing Countries." In *Economic Development and Cultural Change*. vol. 41, no. 1. pp. 75–77.

Zaroff, Barbara, and Daniel A. Okun. 1984. "Water Vending in Developing Countries." In *Aqua*. no. 5. pp. 290, 292.

Chapter Six

Improving Urban Environmental Quality: Socioeconomic Possibilities and Limits

Peter Nijkamp

This chapter focuses on the increasing gap between economic progress and urban quality of life in many Asian cities. Its aim is to identify critical success factors for urban sustainable development, based on empirical illustrations from Asian countries.

After a background sketch of growth and environmental issues in these cities, the chapter introduces the concept of local sustainable development (LSD) as a strategy. It is argued that urban sustainability indicators ought to be developed as guidelines for effective policy-making. Experiences from both the developed and developing world are reported, with particular attention to the triangular relationship among efficiency, equity, and sustainability.

A major portion of the chapter is devoted to the assessment of urban sustainability in Asia. The analysis uses a pentagon prism of critical success factors, comprised of hardware, socioware, orgware, ecoware, and finware, to illustrate urban sustainability issues.

The feasibility of various sustainability policies is judged by investigating four important fields: (i) urban resources and waste management; (ii) urban quality of life; (iii) urban transport; and (iv) urban sustainability finance policy. Each of these fields is analyzed and illustrated from the perspective of the pentagon prism.

The chapter concludes by discussing the need for effective private and public sustainability strategies. Decentralized policy initiatives are advocated as the most plausible.

CONCEPT OF SUSTAINABILITY

An Urban World and a Threatened Environment

Despite wars and natural disasters, the planet's population is steadily increasing. In the past 200 years, an average fivefold increase has occurred and there is no clear end to this trend expected. Some regions show even higher growth rates. For example, on the island of Java in Indonesia the population size has risen in the past century from five million to nearly 95 million people, causing unprecedented stress on land use, resources, and amenities.

The world's population growth rates place a severe stress on the environment and on the earth's natural resources. In addition, besides the sheer quantitative trends regarding population and environmental decay, two qualitative trends reflecting structural or systematic changes on environmental quality are also of concern here.

First, the gradually rising living standards in many developing countries will cause environmental decay or threat which far exceeds the linear growth of environmental stress as a fixed proportion of population members. Since industrial products in a modern society are far more environmentally harmful than commodities in a rural society, a nonlinear exponentially growing environmental stress curve is plausible. The resulting environmental threat is, without doubt, at odds with the notion of sustainable development in both the developing and the developed world.

Second, the spatial dispersion of population and economic activities will have an impact on the environment. Apart from some local and temporary exceptions, there is a continuing urbanization trend in almost all countries, often quickening in many developing countries (shown in Chapter Two). In fact, developing countries are following the pace set by the industrial countries, so that by the turn of the century, more than one half of world's population will be living in cities. There is a threat that, without effective environmental policies, the urban lifestyle of the world will cause even more environmental disturbance in terms of noise, congestion, pollution, and waste, mainly as a result of density and poverty (Lea and Courtney 1985).

Many developing countries will likely even become the forerunners in this global megatrend towards massive urbanization. Some numerical information on this trend towards "third world megalopolization" can be found, inter alia, in Fuchs et al. (1987), Linn (1983), and Lo (1992). Figure 6.1 illustrates this also.

A few numbers also illustrate the above point. Nearly 1.5 billion people in the world's developing countries are living in urban areas. Further, at the beginning of this century, there were only 11 cities with over one million inhabitants; at the turn of the century there will be approximately 400 such cities and in approximately 30 years, there will be nearly 500 such cities in the developing countries.

Figure 6.1
Ranking of Megacities According to Population Size

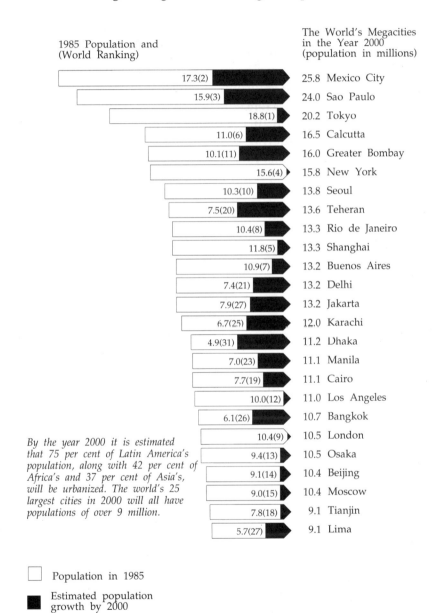

1985 Population and
(World Ranking)

The World's Megacities
in the Year 2000
(population in millions)

17.3(2)	25.8 Mexico City
15.9(3)	24.0 Sao Paulo
18.8(1)	20.2 Tokyo
11.0(6)	16.5 Calcutta
10.1(11)	16.0 Greater Bombay
15.6(4)	15.8 New York
10.3(10)	13.8 Seoul
7.5(20)	13.6 Teheran
10.4(8)	13.3 Rio de Janeiro
11.8(5)	13.3 Shanghai
10.9(7)	13.2 Buenos Aires
7.4(21)	13.2 Delhi
7.9(27)	13.2 Jakarta
6.7(25)	12.0 Karachi
4.9(31)	11.2 Dhaka
7.0(23)	11.1 Manila
7.7(19)	11.1 Cairo
10.0(12)	11.0 Los Angeles
6.1(26)	10.7 Bangkok
10.4(9)	10.5 London
9.4(13)	10.5 Osaka
9.1(14)	10.4 Beijing
9.0(15)	10.4 Moscow
7.8(18)	9.1 Tianjin
5.7(27)	9.1 Lima

*By the year 2000 it is estimated
that 75 per cent of Latin America's
population, along with 42 per cent of
Africa's and 37 per cent of Asia's,
will be urbanized. The world's 25
largest cities in 2000 will all have
populations of over 9 million.*

☐   Population in 1985

■   Estimated population
growth by 2000

Source: Lo 1992.

Welfare increases, in terms of gross national product (GNP) per capita, play a major role in the ongoing urbanization trend. Clearly, rising GNP levels per capita induce a trend toward an urban way of living which often leads to a conflict with conditions for sustainable environmental quality, as is witnessed in cities such as Bangkok, Bombay, Jakarta, and other metropolises.

The size, density, complexity, and poverty levels in many cities appear to cause massive environmental decay, especially in the developing countries of Asia. Hence, megacity or metropolis management will be a necessary but difficult planning mission for many governments, especially considering the volumes of material resources consumed and of waste generated in densely populated urban areas.

However, megacity development is certainly not the only important pattern of structural change. Especially in developing countries there is an extremely rapid growth in the number of medium-size cities (Figure 6.2). The quality conditions in such cities are by no means significantly better than those in megacities. The conditions which impact on megacities, i.e., lack of resources, urban poverty, insufficient public interest, and failure of environmental management, apparently impact on these medium-size cities as well, leading to worsening urban environmental quality.

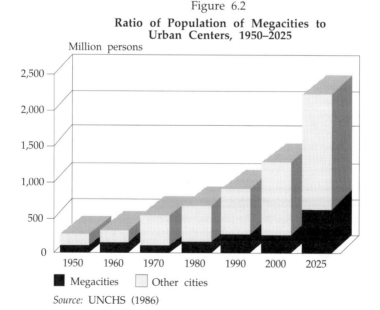

Figure 6.2
Ratio of Population of Megacities to Urban Centers, 1950–2025

Million persons

Source: UNCHS (1986)

Consequently, in many countries, it is not absolute population figures which are the sole contributor to environmental degradation; further industrialization also leads to more environmental pollution. Bangkok, Jakarta, and Seoul are glaring examples of the above phenomenon, with high congestion causing industry and the population to move to the fringe of the city ("urban sprawl") thus leading to a spillover of the social costs of massive urbanization. The lack of effective abatement measures, such as sewage treatment plants, prohibition of toxic materials, filters in chimneys, and catalytic converters in cars, reinforces the above problem. Lo (1992, 193) recently concluded that: "... megacities in developing countries are aggravated by the pressures of mounting population and cumulative economic activities. The need for service and infrastructure to accommodate these growing megacities far exceeds the financial means and capabilities of their urban administrations, often resulting in chaotic situations. The lack of basic urban services has contributed to inadequate housing for low-income residents, unemployment among the urban poor, traffic congestion, irregular land use patterns, and environmental deterioration." It is certainly not an overstatement to claim that sustainable development is one of the most difficult challenges for urban policies in developing countries.

Nevertheless, a massive concentration of people in a large agglomeration does not necessarily create an environmental problem, as is witnessed by Singapore. Even a high population density is not by definition disastrous to the urban environment. There is often not an overall shortage of space; the main problem is that a large share of the population is living in an extremely small part of the urban territory. For example, in Manila the poorest 45 per cent of the population live in settlements which occupy less than 6 per cent of the land area (Hardoy et al. 1992). Thus, the problem of sustainability in urban areas is a complex one, and some general reflections on the issue of urban sustainability are warranted.

The Spatial Dimension of Sustainable Development

The modern city is embedded in a complex force field of economic survival, "creative destruction" (à la Schumpeter) and the "home of man" (Ward 1976). Expansion, restructuring, and maintenance of quality often form competing forces that place the city at a dynamic and vulnerable edge.

The world's cities are becoming increasingly centrifugal and centripetal nodes in a national and more and more international society. In connection with the urgent need to solve problems of poverty, housing, and unemployment, cities are also facing the need to generate competitive advantages to be sustainable and to survive in fierce national/international competition (Nijkamp 1990; Porter 1990). Against the background of international competition and gains/losses of trade, the idea of sustainable development is increasingly coming to the fore.

The notion of sustainable development (SD) has been discussed extensively at numerous fora in recent years (see Archibugi and Nijkamp 1989; Carley and Cristie 1992; International Institute for Applied Systems Analysis 1992; WCED 1987). However, these discussions were often globally and conceptually focused. Consequently, there is a noticeable lack of empirical applicability, a major source of criticism of these fora. A more operational treatment of this appealing but still abstract concept of SD is the only way for it to survive in the current debate. The practical applicability of this concept must be emphasized, a need which was strongly advocated at the United Nations Conference on Environment and Development held in Rio de Janeiro (June 1992).

The World Commission on Environment and Development defines sustainable development as "a pattern of development that meets the needs of present generations without jeopardizing the ability of future generations to meet their own needs" (WCED 1987). However, SD has not only an intergenerational dimension, but also contains other aspects, notably spatial, allocative, and quality of life aspects. Such spatial dimensions range from the global to the local. Global examples are the rise in the level of oceans caused mainly by global warming or climatic changes, depletion of the ozone layer, deforestation, desertification, and extinction of species. Local examples are pollution in areas that face strong urban expansion, local hazards from chemical, nuclear, and radioactive toxic industries, extinction of specific species through uncontrolled hunting, road construction, and local catastrophes.

A common attribute of the global and local examples is that they threaten human and environmental survival and hence are "negative" changes in social welfare that should be avoided. "Positive" changes—such as regeneration of natural environmental stocks, and advances in environmental technology regarding optimal resource allocation and exploitation—are by definition welcome changes. Clearly, intensified scientific action is needed to support and enhance the latter.

The previous discussion can also be illustrated by referring to current attempts at correcting GDP for various material and environmental depreciations. Such depreciations may relate to manmade capital (MC_d) and natural resources (NR_d). Such an ecological domestic product (EDP) is thus equal to:

$$EDP = GDP - MC_d - NR_d$$

This equation is valid for national accounts and for regional and local accounts as well. The previous definition also has relevance for sustainability analysis at a local or regional level, but has as yet not found many applications because the openness of a spatial system often precludes an operational application of this otherwise sound economic framework. This means that environmental policies in cities are more often based on systems of standards, prohibitions, or quotas than on market-oriented instruments such as charges, although a combined use of such instruments does also occur. An example is Singapore's traffic policy.

In general, an SD analysis should offer operational guidelines for the contents and the steps to be taken to meet the objective of sustainable development. These range from the adoption of market principles to technology design/implementation or prohibitions/regulations (Young 1992). Such strategies would not only have global significance, but would offer many possibilities for effective local or regional sustainability strategies. The inherent logic of an LSD analysis stems from the belief that this analysis may make functional interdependencies at the local level more manageable in view of a given desired development of cities and regions. From a management and policy point of view, a local scale is more suitable for policy control and transformation than is a global scale.[1] Hence, it is evident that the objective of SD may be achieved more easily if the processes of socioeconomic development and environmental change at the local level are clearly understood and properly managed (Kairiukstis 1989). Local development planning may vary from analytical-theoretical to descriptive-empirical or to prescriptive guidelines. A unidimensional SD objective may be operationalized by means of conventional optimization strategies, whereas with a multidimensional policy analysis, a "satisficing" strategy may be more appropriate (Simon 1967).

In the framework of LSD, an integrated economic and environmental approach to policy-making is needed to minimize conflicts between resource-using activities to enhance socioeconomic opportunities (such as optimizing employment opportunities), and to bequeath an environmental estate for the benefit of future generations (Cloke and Park 1985). Quite often an LSD-oriented strategy is carried out by evaluating the implications of environmental standards or by putting constraints on industrial land use, housing, or transport development. A particular project should aim to increase welfare levels of society at different points in time and space, recognizing that there are distributive implications for income, employment, and environmental amenities over space and time.

In light of these observations, it is meaningful from a welfare viewpoint to redefine LSD as development which ensures that the local population can attain an acceptable level of welfare, both now and in the future, and that this local development is compatible with ecological circumstances in the long run, while at the same time it tries to accomplish supralocal and preferably global sustainable development (Bergh 1991; Nijkamp et al. 1992). Consequently, LSD has to fulfill two goals: (i) it should ensure for the local population an acceptable level of welfare, which can be sustained in the future; and (ii) it should not be in conflict with SD at a supralocal level.

Of course, LSD does not mean to transfer the "global rhetoric" (Pezzy 1989) of sustainability as an abstract concept towards a micro-level (individual) or meso-level (regional, local, or sectoral) of application. Clearly, local treatment of sustainable development falls between a macro-systems or global level and a micro-level or project-level approach, and in this respect LSD focuses on a concrete policy analysis where practical, efficiency, or analytical reasons may necessitate a flexible use of different spatial scales. Also, management reasons may lead to a differentiated level of treatment of LSD, both for legislative tasks and for executive policy control tasks. Thus, LSD presupposes a meso-level analysis, mainly based on a flexible spatial scale of a region of city.

Consequently, LSD differs from SD on three essential aspects: (i) the openness or interrelatedness of a city or region; (ii) socioeconomic imbalances which are, in contrast to global treatment, not aligned on a local or regional scale; and (iii) the local or regional authority of common goods. These aspects should be considered explicitly to make SD operational on the basis of supralocal, regional, or supraregional but locally or regionally differentiated policies. These three dimensions justify separate attention for LSD.

If sustainability analysis is restricted to economic and ecological coevolutionary development on a local scale (Nijkamp 1990), LSD may form a formal economic viewpoint to be conceived of as non-negative changes of local social welfare over time, with social welfare being made up of two correlated components (see also Nijkamp and Soeteman 1990; Van Pelt et al. 1991a; 1991b; Van Pelt 1993), namely the consumption of manmade products and services (the socioeconomic system) and the consumption of environmental amenities (the ecological system). In Figure 6.3, a schematic simplified representation is given of the above interpretation of social welfare. Both systems (the socioeconomic and the environmental system) produce important functions that include quantitative and qualitative components which influence human welfare.

It is evident, using Figure 6.3 as a general reference, that the condition that social welfare function changes should be positive ($dW/dt \geq 0$) may hold in two different ways: either the change in one welfare constituent is positive and in the other negative (provided the net overall change in W is still positive) or all changes in both welfare constituents are positive. In the first case, "weak sustainability" exists, whereas in the second case there is a condition of "strong sustainability" (Daly 1991; Opschoor and Reijnders 1991). Although these distinctions are conceptually sound, the absence of a "numéraire" makes an actual

Figure 6.3

An Economic-Ecological Interaction Systems Model

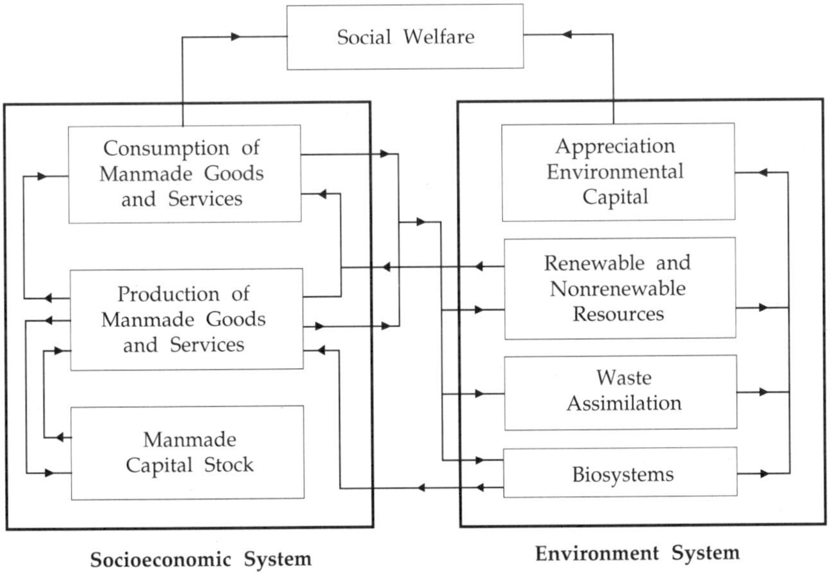

Socioeconomic System   Environment System

numerical illustration or application difficult. It is clear that spatial substitution within one of the two subsystems and substitution between welfare components are closely related phenomena. The nature of such substitution phenomena may be brought to light more adequately and in a visually appealing way by using geographic information systems (GIS).[2]

Based on this broad exposition of sustainability issues, the question arises whether such issues have the same relevance for the developing countries as for the industrial ones. In this regard, developing countries have a socioeconomic structure which differs in many significant ways from that in developed countries:

(i) In general, the market system in the developing countries is characterized by serious price distortions.

(ii) There is a substantially unequal distribution of income and access to basic infrastructure services (such as water supply, solid waste collection, public lighting, and public transport).

(iii) In general, the informal sector is well developed.

(iv) Most developing countries have pronounced characteristics of a dual economy.

(v) Urban housing for the poor (slums and squatter settlements) is usually of very low quality.

(vi) Given the low levels of human welfare, the perception of environmental quality is often of less concern among the people of the developing countries than those in developed countries.

The Concept of Sustainable Cities

The need to favor and support LSD has provoked the awareness of the idea of sustainable cities as a strategic guideline for urban environmental policy.

In recent years the interest in the urban environment has risen to an unprecedented degree. The Commission of the European Communities launched its *Greenbook on the Urban Environment in 1990;* OECD published its report on Environmental Policies for Cities in the

1990s; and many other international, national, regional, and local institutions followed this new wave of interest in urban quality of life by organizing meetings of experts, undertaking urban environmental research projects, and, among other activities, preparing programs on urban quality of life. Various new concepts were advocated, such as the "green city," the "eco-city," and the "environmental city." All of these activities reflect a broad concern about the future of the world's cities.

Sustainable development of cities refers to continuity in a changing situation. In the history of most cities in the past century, it is possible to identify shifts in the role that the city plays within the (changing) national system of cities and within the changing national (and international) economy (Nijkamp 1991).

In some cases—such as war, catastrophes, a decline of a dominant employer, or a major new policy initiative—external developments may induce a very clear role change of a city leading, for instance, to a decline of its economic base, as reflected, *inter alia*, in population decline, environmental degradation, inefficient energy systems, loss of employment, ex-migration of industries and services, and unbalanced socio-demographic composition. In general, if the self-organization of an urban system fails, for example, because of a lack of consensus among different individual institutions, a phase of non-sustainability is likely to begin. Environmental decay is one of the first signs of non-sustainability.

Policies addressing sustainable development of cities should thus cover multiple fields, such as urban pollution, rehabilitation, land use, transport, energy management, sanitation, health care, water supply, architecture and conservation policy, and even cultural heritage. Of course, a major task is to specify operational criteria for evaluating LSD. Measurable indicators, including minimum performance and critical threshold levels, will have to be defined, estimated, and used in forecasting so as to improve awareness of sustainable development issues of modern cities. Local authorities will have to share their tasks with all other actors in the urban space, including the private sector. Unfortunately, urban sustainable development is a process rife with conflicts and incompatibilities. Commitment to a strict environmentally sustainable urban development program by key actors in a city is critical. Within this context, strict market-based economic incentives may be desirable to cope with the negative externalities of modern city life. Failure to develop an effective and balanced urban development policy will reinforce urban sprawl and will externalize inner city problems to a much larger area.

A necessary condition for implementing an effective planning system for urban environmental management is the development of a system of suitable urban environmental quality indicators (OECD 1978). Such indicators, which should represent a balance between the necessary quality of information and the costs involved, would have to be related to economic, ecological, social, spatial, and cultural dimensions of the city. The OECD has drawn up a long list of elements for urban environmental quality which would have to be included in such an indicator system. These elements include housing, services and employment, ambient environment and nuisances, and social and cultural concerns. It is extremely difficult to operationalize such an indicator system, however, especially while at the same time guaranteeing cross-comparative urban analysis. This means that precise empirical evidence on long-run urban environmental quality and on the implications for both the household sector and the business sector is not always available.

Therefore, in the context of a balanced urban development policy, it is necessary that systematic attempts be made to assess, monitor, and evaluate the various elements of urban development. Within this framework, environment and community impact analysis (ECIA) might be developed (Lichfield 1990), which, analogous to environmental impact analysis (EIA) in many countries, would provide policymakers with all relevant information for sustainable city planning.

To explain urban dynamics from the viewpoint of spatial externalities, it is necessary to recognize that cities throughout the world have played a critical role as nodal points in the spatial-economic network of a country. In this role, the city—in both the developed and the developing world—has always attracted urban in-migrants. At the same time, the movement toward the urban territory has caused high density, resulting in urban sprawl, leading to city regions or functional urban regions. Both land prices and environmental externalities in central areas of the cities were often impediments to new household and firm locations, so that an outward shift took place. Industries moved to the urban fringe or to special industrial parks in the neighborhood of cities. People moved to suburban and even more distant locations. This massive movement was essentially only an expansion of the functional urban territory. Hence, despite a broadening of the spatial range, the urban system has kept its original function and has even reinforced its position. Urban environmental damage thus tends to show a wider spatial coverage (see also Orishimo 1982).

Urban sprawl rests on a trade-off of agglomeration economies, notably economies of scale and scope, including higher wages, versus diseconomies (e.g., population density and environmental decay). In most cases, the external costs of diseconomies are not fully internalized in the price system, so that a distorted urban locational pattern will likely emerge. In addition, government policies aimed at restoring the balance are often hampered by severe failures so that the ultimate situation may become worse. Thus, centripetal and centrifugal spatial processes are interchangeably determining the spatial layout of an urban system (city, fringe, rural areas).

Although it is likely that problems of environmental quality may become more severe with urban size, there is no clear evidence that size as such causes environmental decay. According to Orishimo (1982), it is not the sheer city size, but rather the land use, the transport system, and the spatial layout of a city which are critical factors for urban environmental quality.

Cities throughout the world are experiencing a process of economic restructuring, accompanied by technological, environmental, cultural, transport, and socio-demographic changes. Further, in many countries, public policies, within the framework of an overall national policy or of regional policies, have shown in the recent past a market shift from direct interference to indirect (or conditional) policies (e.g., incubation policies and innovation policies). Altogether, modern cities tend to show drastic evolutionary changes.

In a recent article, Nijkamp (1993) showed the dichotomy of successful and failing cities using the notion of a 3C-city introduced by Andersson and Strömqvist (1989). Successful cities are characterized as 3C+ (plus) areas exhibiting the following three positive features: creativity, competence, and communication. Unsuccessful cities, denoted as 3C- (minus) areas suffer from congestion, criminality, and closure (or isolation). In this framework, technological innovation and new infrastructure and communication policies are increasingly advocated as effective tools in successful urban and regional development strategies.

As a result of a complex myriad of spatial-economic forces, modern urban systems, with their high density of population and economic activities, their nodal position in interwoven geographical and functional-economic (inter)national networks and their ambition to act as engines in the competitive process of open regions, are faced with increasingly severe environmental problems ranging from air, soil, and water pollution to intangible externalities such as noise annoyance, lack of safety, and visual pollution. Clearly, a wide variety of sources act to generate these urban environmental problems, such as demographic factors, socioeconomic development, inefficient energy consumption, inappropriate technologies, spatial behavioral patterns and, most important of all, inappropriate and/or badly enforced urban environmental policy measures. Thus, improvement of the current unfavorable situation requires a mobilization of all forces.

In the meantime, a new discipline—urban ecology—aims to design and implement principles for sound urban environmental policy (see also Marahrens et al. 1991). Concrete examples of such principles include:

(i)   minimizing space consumption in urban areas;

(ii) minimizing spatial mobility in the urban space by reducing the geographical separation between working, living, and facility spaces;

(iii) minimizing urban private transport (e.g., by creating pedestrian zones);

(iv) favoring the use of new information technology and telecommunication technology to minimize physical movements;

(v)   minimizing urban waste, favor recycling, and install proper sewage systems; and

(vi) minimizing urban energy waste (e.g., via combined heat and power systems and district heating).

The fulfillment of such principles will, of course, require an effective urban policy which is multifaceted in nature and which covers a great many aspects of current city life. Once implemented, the principles might turn cities into "islands of renewal in seas of decay" (Berry 1985). These cities and regions would then have to play a much more active role in mobilizing all actors in the urban territory to convince them that a sustainable city means a sustainable economy and society.

Further, as cities are the nodal points of people and their activities, and as they also face the most severe environmental problems, they should be the focal point for sustainability research and planning. Urban policies aiming to achieve sustainable development should be more strategic in nature, more integrative, more visionary regarding the role of the private sector, more focused on the provision of market incentives, and more oriented towards the needs of citizens. Finally, in view of their central role, the development of sustainable cities deserves absolute priority.

Unfortunately, despite the current popularity of the notion of sustainable cities, empirical practice is disappointing in that convincing examples of successful urban sustainability policies are still rare (for various European illustrations, see Nijkamp and Perrels 1993). The aims are noble though. Sustainable cities aim at achieving balanced (coevolutionary) development in which economic forces (e.g., efficiency), social considerations (e.g., equity and access to facilities) and environmental concerns (e.g., quality of life) are brought together from the viewpoint of a "green society" (see also Pearce et al. 1989). In many cities, improved local energy efficiency is likely to be one of the critical success factors for sustainable cities, as energy management and use provide substantial support to an improvement of the local economy (i.e., higher degree of competitiveness), to a more affordable and, hence, equitable distribution of scarce resources (i.e., better access to public services) and to a reduction in the environmental burden (e.g., reduction in emissions of CO_2). Thus, a more sustainable form of urban development requires an increase in pressure to reduce the consumption of fossil fuels, for instance, through the introduction of district heating, industrial cogeneration, combined heat and power technologies, biogas technology, or more efficient transport systems (see for details Nijkamp and Volwahsen 1990).

The main problem in building sustainable cities is not the lack of arguments supporting the need for "green-based" cities, but the question of designing proper concrete coevolutionary urban development strategies that can boast sufficient public support. As societies and cities move toward the end of the twentieth century, the case for improving drastically their energy and environmental base takes on steadily growing importance and urgency. If modern cities want to maintain and improve their role as the "home of man," intensified efforts are needed to safeguard both the historical-cultural heritage left to the present generation by our predecessors and the socioeconomic and environmental potential of modern cities needed to host the future generation. In this framework, it should be stressed that there are close mutual connections between urban economic policy objectives and environmental policy objectives:

(i) Urban development requires good environmental quality, as the latter dictates to a large extent the economic attractiveness profile of an area.

(ii) The achievement of a favorable level of quality of life needs a large amount of financial resources which often has to be generated at the local level.

(iii) Neglect of environmental quality conditions may have serious implications for human health at the local level, so much so that these externalities threaten urban growth objectives.

The question whether such issues have the same relevance for cities in the world's developing countries as in the developed was addressed by Hardoy et al. (1992, 21–22):

> The growing interest in urban environmental problems is based too much on Northern perceptions and precedents. It appears biased towards addressing the environmental problems which Third World cities have in common with cities in Europe and North America. This often means a greater attention to chemical agents in the air, rather than biological agents in water, food, air and soil—including those responsible for diarrhoeal diseases, dysentery and intestinal parasites. This bias often means that critical environmental problems such as the control of disease vectors which spread malaria, dengue fever, filariasis and yellow fever are forgotten. It can mean more attention to the loss of agricultural land due to urban spread than to the fact that half, or more, of the urban population lack access to safe and sufficient water supplies.

In light of the specific nature of socioeconomic conditions and environmental sustainability problems in cities in the developing world, more explicit attention to the issue of sustainable cities is warranted.

ACHIEVING SUSTAINABILITY

Sustainability Issues in Developing Countries

Cities and regions are important key actors for sustainable development. Urban and regional environmental and energy planning is gaining increasing importance as an effective strategy for implementing ecologically sustainable economic development, as advocated in the Brundtland report. Does this also apply to urban policies in developing countries? Are there specific elements which make the notion of urban sustainability more problematic in developing countries? Is there sufficient evidence to warrant urban sustainability policies in developing countries? These questions are addressed below.

First, the massive density of people in the cities of many developing counties and the unequal access to resources, land, and housing aggravates environmental problems. Density and poverty lead to diseconomies of scale which interface exponentially with negative environmental externalities caused by polluting activities.

Second, environmental interests are usually not incorporated in regional and urban development planning in the developing countries, and normative guidelines—based, for example, on carrying capacity and regenerative capacity—are often absent from the planning process. Economic progress is often more focused on quantity than on quality.

Third, urban poverty itself complicates the problem of achieving sustainable development. According to the South Commission (1990), poverty causes environmental decay. Agarwal (1992) added to this conclusion by noting that, at international fora the main focus is on biodiversity and not on poverty abatement. The "fight for daily bread" leads to short-term decisions which shift environmental and multigenerational interests beyond the horizon. Some interesting figures on urban poverty in developing countries can be found in Table 6.1.

Fourth, there is a relatively unequal distribution of income and productive assets in the developing countries and cities, which is to the detriment of a rigorous and effective abatement policy for environmental decay.

Finally, the administrative ability to strictly enforce environmental measures and regulations is often lacking, thereby weakening the effectiveness of environmental policies. According to Hardoy et al. (1992):

> The scale and severity of environmental problems in Third World cities reflect the failure of governments. In most Third World nations, both national and urban governments have failed in three essential environmental actions: to enforce appropriate legislation (including that related to environmental health, occupational health and pollution control); to ensure adequate provision for water supply and solid and liquid waste collection and treatment systems; and to ensure adequate health care provision to treat not only environment-related illnesses but

also to implement preventive measures to limit their incidence and severity. The policies and actions that governments take in regard to the urban environment have profound implications for the health and well-being of urban citizens and, in the longer term, for the ecological sustainability of cities and the urban and regional systems of which they are part. The extent to which good environmental quality is achieved in cities may be one of the most revealing indicators of the competence and capacity of city and municipal government, and of the extent to which their policies respond to their populations' needs and priorities (pp. 20–21).

As noted earlier, urban environmental policy can be positioned at the crossroads of economic growth (the efficiency motive), distributional equity, and environmental concern seen from the viewpoint of urban land use and physical resources. The relationship among efficiency, equity, and sustainability as main appraisal criteria can be illustrated by the Dutch policy for development cooperation. Since the early 1980s, the overall objective of this policy has been the "structural combat of poverty" by combining the objectives of increasing production and income (efficiency) and fair distribution (intra-temporal equity). In 1990, without altering the overall objective, ecological sustainability was added as a third attribute.

Table 6.1
Incidence of Urban Poverty in Developing Countries, 1988

Region	Urban Population (million)	Share of Each Region (per cent)	Urban Population Below Poverty Line (million)	Share of Each Region (per cent)	Urban Population Below Poverty Line (million)
Africa	133.24	11.2	55.46	17.0	41.6
Asia	591.91	49.7	136.53	42.0	23.0
EMENA[a]	174.14	4.7	59.53	18.0	34.2
Latin America	291.66	24.5	77.27	24.0	26.5

[a] Europe, Middle East, and North Africa.
Source: World Bank 1989, as cited in Asian Development Bank 1991.

Efficiency. Cities tend to act as magnets for people. The efficiency motive related to urban economies of scale is dominant, causing an unprecedented urbanization process to occur. Even though negative externalities do exist (e.g., poor health conditions and congestion), many cities still exert a powerful gravity force based on efficiency grounds for socioeconomic activities. In conventional economic planning and program evaluation, the attributes of aggregate welfare have tended to be directly connected with the efficiency criterion, and efficiency has been a key criterion in policy frameworks in conventional (economic) project appraisal for developing countries (Little and Mirrlees 1974; UNIDO 1972; Squire and van der Tak 1975; Squire 1989).

Efficiency constitutes the difference between changes in gross aggregate welfare (benefits) and all uses of scarce resources (costs). In the past, welfare benefits tended to be equated with availability of material goods and services produced in the socioeconomic system (maximization of material consumption or income). Such goods are, in part, traded in markets, while others, such as social overhead and public goods, are nontraded goods. Increasingly, the shortcomings of the narrow welfare concept have been acknowledged. Assuming a formal welfare concept, the availability of environmental amenities with a direct impact on the well-being of the population may also be considered as a welfare attribute (refer to Figure 6.3). As noted above, on the cost side, basic resources comprise both manmade and natural capital. It has recently been proposed to differentiate also between objectives regarding irreversible vis-à-vis reversible environmental problems (Hedman 1990).

Traditionally, the techniques of cost-benefit analysis have been applied as a policy tool, whereby prices serve as socioeconomic weights. If available and a true reflection of the value to society, market prices are applied. If markets are imperfect, generate external effects, or are considered distorted, shadow prices may be applied. The latter approach, among other things, sets project appraisal for developing countries apart from approaches for developed countries. More recently, various types of multi-criteria analysis have been applied to project and plan evaluation in developing countries (Nijkamp et al. 1990; Van Pelt 1993). Clearly, because the evaluation of urban development in the developing countries has to consider market and nonmarket aspects simultaneously, conventional evaluation methodologies tend to lose their relevance and applicability in a broader urban plan assessment methodology.

Equity. The equity aspect of urban problems refers to the distribution of positive factors (e.g., income and access to medical care) in the city, as well as to the negative factors (e.g., environmental pollution, lack of waste disposal facilities, and unacceptable water quality). The dual nature of developing countries is often reflected in disintegrated neighborhoods, social segmentation, and differences in housing quality standards, which often form a spatial mapping of unequal distribution of resources and amenities.

Distributional equity is a major ingredient in urban sustainability analysis in developing countries. The equity motive has not only spatial, but also temporal aspects. In traditional project appraisal, usually a time horizon encompassing not more than one generation is assumed. The frequently applied discounting technique implicitly assigns consequences of projects affecting future generations a negligible or zero weight. In view of the long-term focus implied by sustainability concerns, it is also necessary to emphasize intergenerational equity, i.e., the distribution of welfare among successive generations. Sustainability concerns draw particular attention to long-term ecological risks, some of which may have various specific characteristics (Quiggin and Anderson 1990), particularly since probabilities associated with various possible events often cannot be estimated. Some authors (e.g., Reijnders 1990) argue that long-term ecological risks are unacceptable. This implies an assigned weight of one to the environmental risk criterion. In this context, "no regret" strategies try to avoid highly uncertain but potentially disastrous events and surprises by embarking on measures that can also be justified on the basis of their impact on related, but more predictable fields.

Speaking about risks to sustainable urban development, Khosh-Chashm (1991, 246) argued: "Safety regulations for roads, houses, workplace etc. are not observed. One of the most fundamental detriments to the environment and the city's health is the lack of a proper legal framework and the ability of the system to safeguard the rights, safety and well-being of their citizens." Khosh-Chashm also claimed: "Poverty has probably much more adverse impacts on environment and health than any other factor. To alter people's self-esteem and, consequently the betterment of their life and environmental quality, the major task for the 1990s will be to create enough jobs to employ billions of new workers throughout the developing world" (p. 248).

Sustainability. Plan and program evaluation for cities and regions often does not include constraints on the use of environmental resources. Implicitly, any use of natural resources could be permitted, provided compensation is offered in the form of a larger production of manmade goods and services. However, while environment criteria often assume a subordinate role in sustainability-oriented project appraisal, urban sustainability should respect the critical role of environmental and health conditions for present and future generations, for instance, by imposing certain threshold levels regarding the use of environmental capital (or the total stock of capital, comprising manmade capital as well). The more data-demanding forms of sustainability criteria do involve measurement of the degree of sustainability on a cardinal or ordinal scale, which expresses the relative difference between normative threshold levels and actual resource use (Opschoor and Reijnders 1989).

The choice of threshold levels for sustainable resource use depends to a large extent on how the present generation judges its responsibilities to future generations (the so-called "trustee" principle), including assessment of risks and possibilities for technological substitution in production functions (intergenerational equity).

Environmental sustainability should not be regarded as a luxurious policy motive, but as one of fundamental importance for developing countries, most especially since urban populations in these countries are suffering from a high illness and mortality rate which is geared to low environmental conditions. For example, as water quality and infant mortality are two closely related phenomena in the poorer segments of the cities in the developing world, urban poverty, urban mortality, and urban sustainability cannot be treated as separate issues. Improvement of urban environmental quality (e.g., discouragement of the use of toxic materials, improvement of water quality standards and housing quality, and improvement of waste treatment) must run parallel to urban economic development programs.

Environmental Quality in Asia's Megacities

Environmental quality, or lack thereof, in Asia's megacities is the result of various factors: demographic growth, socioeconomic inequality, extreme density of poor people, topography, meteorology, lack of abatement equipment for industrial pollution, old car fleet, absence of water sewage systems, lack of proper waste incineration technology, and poor enforcement of environmental regulations. The sources of pollution are manifold and affect, among other areas, the quality of the air, water, soil, and residential well-being.

Air Pollution. High urban air pollutant emissions are caused by energy consumption as a result of cooking, heating, lighting, transport, and industry in the city (UNEP/WHO 1992). In particular, the use of fossil fuels leads to a high concentration of various types of direct and indirect air pollution, such as sulphur dioxide, nitrogen oxides, carbon monoxide, volatile organic compounds, suspended particulate matter, and lead. In many cities, motor vehicles appear to be the main source of air pollution. Besides the well-known pollutants, an increasingly large number of toxic and carcinogenic chemicals are also being detected, such as heavy metals, trace organics, radionuclides, and fibers. Such chemicals are emitted by various sources such as waste incinerators, industrial production, building materials, and urban transport. While information on air pollution is often not systematically gathered and monitored in the developing countries, and information on the above chemicals is rare, a recent study by UNEP/WHO (1992) contains air pollution data on various megacities (Figure 6.4).

Urban air pollution has wide-ranging impacts. Human health is affected via respiratory and cardiovascular systems as a result of inhalation, drinking water or food contamination, as is the natural environment via acid deposition which causes soil and fresh water acidification, crop losses, forest damage, and destruction of terrestrial ecosystems. Although the health impacts have not been precisely measured, some indicative figures exist (Table 6.2).

The WHO has established air quality standards for many pollutants, allowing assessment of the ambient air quality levels within the framework of public health. Though many cities have adopted such guidelines, lack of financial and/or organizational resources has impeded their full adoption and implementation. In addition, there are insufficient (technological or market-driven) incentives in place to enforce compliance with the standards.

As is clearly shown in Figure 6.4, environmental policy has often failed. Each of the nine cities for which data are shown exceeds at least one of the air quality standards set by the WHO. Also, the trend of air pollutant emissions is not diminishing on a significant level and, in many cases, it is rising, so that severe problems can be expected regarding the achievement of urban sustainability in those cities. Despite this alarming conclusion, some optimism is justified. A UNEP/WHO (1992, 43) report notes that:

"... in some of the megacities studied the severe air pollution conditions observed today could have been much worse if certain

Table 6.2
Health Impacts Attributed to Ambient Air Pollution in Selected Cities

City	Pollution Source	Impact
Bangkok[a]	Particulates	51 million restricted activity days (including 26 million work loss days) and 1,400 excess deaths in 1989
	Carbon monoxide	20,000–50,000 people at risk of increased angina pain/day; 900,000–2,300,000/day at risk of minor effects such as headaches
	Lead (all sources)*	200,000–500,000 cases of hypertension/year; 300–900 heart attacks and strokes/year; 200–400 deaths/year; 400,000–700,000 IQ points/year lost in children
	Air toxin (mobile sources)	90–100 cancer cases/year**
	Air toxins (at city dumpsite)	less than one cancer case/year
Bangkok[b]		900,000 cases of respiratory illness
Beijing[c]		Lung cancer rates increased 145 per cent from 1949 to 1979
Bombay[d]		Tuberculosis and respiratory diseases are the major killers in the city
Calcutta[d]		60 per cent of residents suffer from respiratory diseases
Chinese cities[d]		Lung cancer mortality is 4–7 times higher in cities than in the nation as a whole
Chinese cities[c]		High rates of chronic bronchitis and chronic respiratory infections in the cities as opposed to the rural areas
Delhi[e]		30 per cent of the population suffers from respiratory diseases; 12 times national average 30 per cent decrease in crop yield and poor quality of grains; millions of rupees lost in engineering materials, textiles, building materials, and leather goods
Manila[f]		471,100 cases of upper respiratory tract infection and 79,400 cases of bronchitis reported in 1988

[a] USAID 1990a. Impacts are not empirical, but are calculated using standardized risk formulas.
[b] *Bangkok Post*, 11 September 1990.
[c] Krupnick and Sebastian 1990.
[d] Hardoy and Satterthwaite 1989; WHO 1988.
[e] *India Today*, 31 August 1991.
[f] Hechanova 1990.
* Airborne lead may account for about 40 per cent of the lead intake of adults and 70 per cent of that for children.
** Recalculated with the authors' adjusted unit risk.
Source: ESCAP 1990, pp. 5–19.

Figure 6.4
Air Pollution Data for Selected Asian Cities
(annual mean concentrations of sulfur dioxide [SQ$_2$]
and suspended particulate matter [SPM])

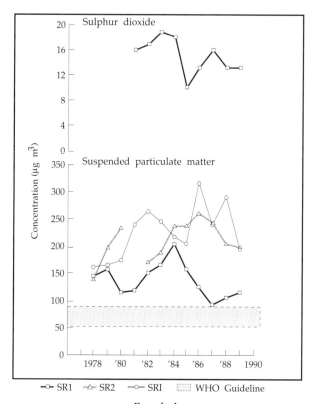

Bangkok

Note: Sulphur dioxide is not a problem in Bangkok as there is no winter heating season. Suspended particulate matter exceeds WHO guidelines in all three monitoring sites. In the city center of Beijing, WHO guidelines for SQ$_2$ are exceeded by a factor of two, and SPM exceeds the guidelines at all four stations. In Bombay, planning control measures and the introduction of natural gas have reduced sulfur dioxide emissions; ambient concentrations are well below WHO annual guideline levels. SPM annual mean exceeds WHO guidelines at all stations, however. In Calcutta, SQ$_2$ levels are below WHO guidelines, owing to the low sulphur content of local coal. SPM from industrial burning of coal represents the greatest air pollution problem in Calcutta. In Delhi, SQ$_2$ concentrations regularly exceed annual and daily WHO guidelines at commercial and industrial sites. SPM concentrations are well above WHO guidelines. In Jakarta, SQ$_2$ presents no problem, but SPM values indicate a potential for health problems. In Manila, SQ$_2$ does not appear to be a problem, but SPM substantially exceeds WHO annual mean guidelines. In Seoul, the widespread use of coal causes extensive SQ$_2$ and SPM pollution; WHO annual mean guidelines are consistently exceeded. In Shanghai, both SQ$_2$ and SPM are well above WHO guidelines
Source: UNEP/WHO 1992.

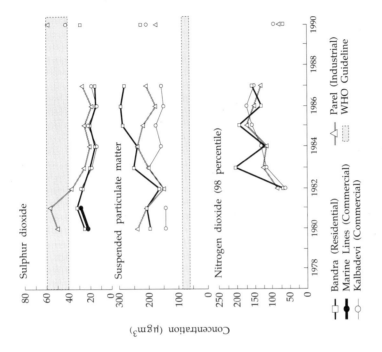

Bombay

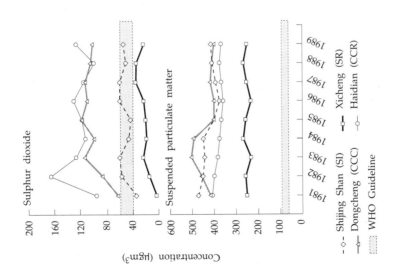

Beijing

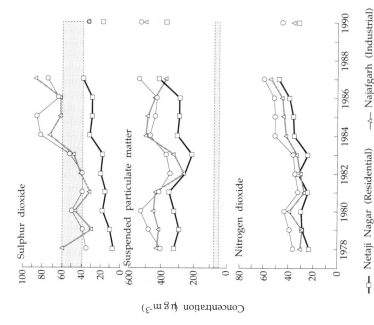

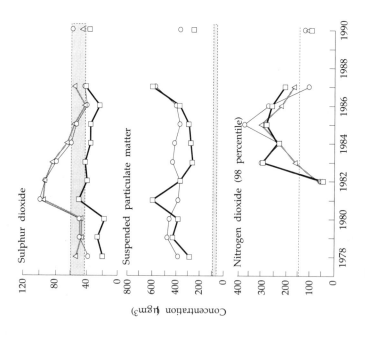

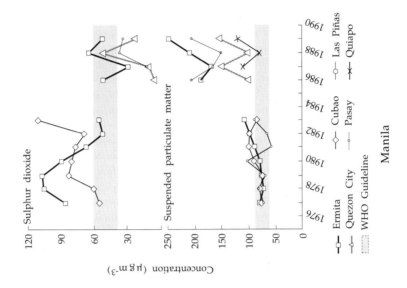

Manila

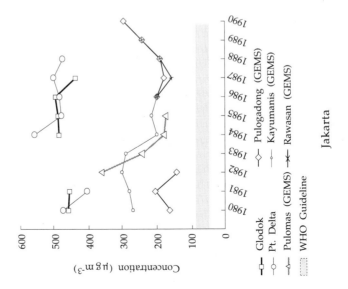

Jakarta

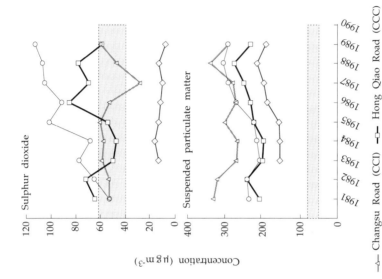

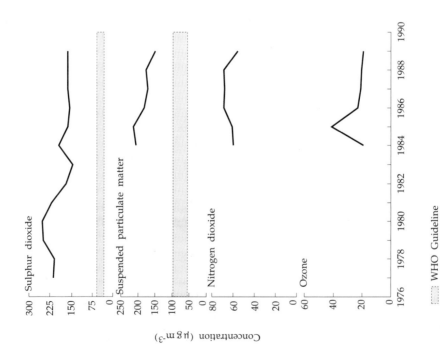

control measures had not already been introduced. Examples are Beijing, Delhi, Seoul and Shanghai where, because of controls, the rise in air pollution levels has been slowed and, in some cases, stabilized before they could reach the high air pollution levels which, for example, were found in London 40 years ago. Over the past 30 years, London, Los Angeles, New York and Tokyo have reduced their air pollution dramatically.

It appears that many cities in the developing countries follow the historical pattern of large cities in the developed countries: i.e., after a period of moderate pollution, the transition towards industrialization, motorization, and high density concentration causes a rapid rise in air pollution. Gradually growth declines or is stabilized, and pollution control measures and programs are implemented. Given the massive scale of urban environmental pollution, and its consequences for human health and implications for local and global sustainability, such urban environmental policies should be instituted without delay.

Residential Quality. Besides air pollution, the cities in the region are also suffering from low residential quality (or even lack of shelter). In general, considerable segments of the urban population face a lack of basic urban services, nonexistent or insufficient social and medical care, inadequate housing, unemployment, lack of water and of modern sewage systems, and environmental deterioration. In addition, the fleet of vehicles in the developing countries are usually old, causing air pollution and increased noise and congestion, which adds to a diminished quality of life. Some data on demographic, socioeconomic and environmental conditions are presented in Table 6.3 and Box 6.1 to illustrate these conditions. (Refer also to Chapter Five of this volume.)

Unplanned and uncontrolled growth of squatter settlements causes most of the above problems. Lack of enforcement of those environmental, land use, and building regulations that do exist exacerbates the situation.

Further, urban policies have failed to provide safe drinking water, sewage systems and waste disposal, which further degrades the quality of life for the urban poor. Finally, the distribution of environmental costs is not shared equally by all residents. The poorer segments of the urban population are further disadvantaged by this unequal distribution.

Table 6.3
Incidence of Poverty and Marginal Settlements in Four Asian Metropolises

	Manila	Jakarta	Calcutta	Madras
Total Population (millions of persons)	6.4	8.0	9.2	5.0
Area (square kilometers)	646.0	550.0	800.0	1,170.0
Urban Density (persons per hectare)	98.0	200.0	115.0	43.0
Urban Growth Rate (per cent)	3.8	4.0	3.0	3.5
Average Household Size (number of persons)	5.4	5.0	5.1	5.2
Average Annual Income (US$ per capita per year)	296.0	132.0	104.0	104.0
Absolute Poverty Level (US$ per capita per year)	266.0	124.0	132.0	132.0
Percentage of Population Below Absolute Poverty Level	35.0	60.0	60.0	45.0
Percentage of Population in Substandard Housing (slums)	45.0	40.0	33.0	60.0
Percentage Living in Squatter or Illegal Settlements	30.0	...	...	25.0
Education Levels (literacy rates)	85.0	78.0	65.0	66.0
Percentage of Labor Force in the Informal Sector	50.0	65.0	54.0	60.0
Percentage with Access to Water (house connection)	43.0	47.0	48.0	40.0
Percentage of Garbage Collected Daily	70.0	25.0	55.0	78.0
Percentage with Access to Human Waste Disposal Systems	60.0	42.0	45.0	58.0

Note: Although the data are drawn from the most authoritative and reliable sources, they may not be internationally comparable because of the lack of standardized definitions and concepts used by different countries when collecting data. The data are, nonetheless, useful to describe orders of magnitude to indicate trends, and to characterize certain significant differences among countries.
Source: Lea and Courtney, eds. 1986.

POLICIES

Framework for Environmental Policies

There is a definite need for clear, feasible, and effective urban sustainability policies, which should be initiated and implemented without delay. The failure of public policies to achieve urban environmental management in the short run will severely aggravate urban environmental quality problems in the longer term and cause dramatically high social costs in terms of health, quality of life, natural environment, cultural heritage, and social tension.

Environmental policies should have a wide coverage. They should focus on both short-term, realistic strategies at alleviating or reducing local and small-scale urban environmental problems (e.g., better water sewerage, strict rules on the quality of drinking water sold by private vendors, expansion of piped-water systems so as to serve public water distribution points, and better collection and processing of garbage) and long-term, structural initiatives and preventive measures to improve water and air quality and, in general, urban quality of life (investments in public infrastructure, effective energy savings programs, and recycling of urban waste).

The private sector (including NGOs) may play an important role in developing more satisfactory urban sustainability policies. All initiatives, both private and public, that aim to minimize the use of renewable and nonrenewable resources in the city so as to keep environmental quality conditions within the carrying capacity of the city should be encouraged. Of course, this cannot be the case without an action-oriented and effective urban environmental policy.

In a recent UNESCO study, Young (1992) offered various guidelines for a general environmental policy for use by developing countries. These guidelines are presented in Box 6.2.

Though the guidelines are relevant insofar as they affect policy formulation, the nature of (un)sustainable cities is significantly different in developing countries, especially as far as the political dimension is concerned. Hardoy et al. (1992, 23) note that:

> Most environmental problems are political problems. They arise not from some particular shortage of an environmental resource such as land or fresh water but from economic or political factors which deny poorer groups both access to it and the ability to demand changes. In most cities, poorer groups' lack of piped water supplies is not the result of a shortage of fresh water resources but the result of governments' refusal to give a higher priority to water supply (and the competent organizational structure its supply, maintenance and expansion requires). There are some cities or metropolitan areas with critical shortages of fresh water resources (for instance Mexico City) but rarely are supplies so constrained that they prevent piping sufficient supplies for health to poor households. The same is true for land; most cities or metropolitan areas in the Third World have

Box 6.1
Inadequacies in Water Supply and Sanitation in Selected Asian Cities

Bangkok: About one third of the population has no access to public water and must obtain water from vendors. Only 2 per cent of the population is connected to a sewer system; human waste is generally disposed of through septic tanks and cesspools, with the effluents, as well as wastewater from sinks, laundries, baths and kitchens, discharged into stormwater drains or canals.

Calcutta: Some three million people live in *bustees* and refugee settlements which lack potable water, endure serious annual flooding, and have no systematic means of disposing of refuse or human waste. Some 2.5 million others live in similarly blighted and unserviced areas. Piped water is only available in the central city and parts of some other municipalities. The sewage system is limited to only a third of the area in the urban core. Poor maintenance of drains and periodic clogging of the system have made flooding an annual feature.

Jakarta: Less than a third of the population have direct connections to a piped water system; around 30 per cent depend solely on water vendors whose prices per liter of water are up to 50 times that paid by households served by the municipal water company. Over a third of the population rely on shallow wells (most of which are contaminated), deep wells, or nearby river water. Over half of all dwellings have no indoor plumbing and much of the population has to use drainage canals for bathing, laundry, and defecation. The city has no central waterborne sewage system. Septic tanks serve about 68 per cent of the population with 17 per cent relying on pit latrines or toilets which discharge directly into ditches or drains, 6 per cent using public toilets (generally with septic tanks), and about 9 per cent with no formal toilet facilities.

Karachi: Only 38 per cent of the population have water piped to their homes; 46 per cent rely on standpipes and a further 16 per cent purchase it from vendors who supply it from water tankers. In most areas served with a piped supply, water is only available for a few hours a day.

Madras: Only two million of the 3.7 million residential consumers within the service area of the local water supply and sewerage board are connected to the system. On average, they receive some 36 liters per day per capita. The rest within the service area must use public taps which serve about 240 persons per tap. Another million consumers outside the service area must rely on wells, but supplies are inadequate also because of falling groundwater levels. The sewage system serves 31 per cent of the metropolitan population.

Manila: Only 15 per cent of the population is served with sewers or individual septic tanks. Some 1.8 million people lack adequate water supplies, and educational, health, and sanitary services.

Source: Hardoy et al. 1992, p. 40–42.

sufficient unused or underutilized land sites within the current built-up area to accommodate most low-income households currently living in very overcrowded conditions. The many poor households who live in settlements on dangerous sites such as floodplains or steep slopes choose such sites not in ignorance of the dangers but because the authorities failed to plan for and allocate more suitable sites. Again, there are cities with critical land shortages because of special site characteristics but even here, governments could do much more to reduce risks for those in hazard-prone areas.

It is clear that while all of the items listed in Box 6.2 are relevant when developing an effective urban sustainability policy, those related to the policy failures of governments require special consideration, especially as such failures are a major cause of worsening environmental quality conditions in urban areas. Avoidance of government failures and adherence to market-based environmental policy principles accompanied by a strict enforcement of regulations offers a most effective policy strategy. Policies that ensure a higher quality of drinking water, better sanitation facilities and sewerage systems, avoidance of unnecessary air pollution (both indoor and outdoor), upgraded health care services, better planning of housing and land use, and adherence to sound environmental policy principles should be encouraged. A change in policy priorities in favor of the environment and a more equal distribution of and access to environmental goods and services is essential for urban sustainability. According to Hardoy et al. (1992, 23–24):

A failure of governance underlies most environmental problems—failure to control industrial pollution and occupational exposure, to promote environmental health, to ensure that city-dwellers have the basic infrastructure and services essential for health and a decent living environment, to plan in advance to ensure sufficient land is available for housing developments for low-income groups and to implement preventive measures to reduce environmental problems or their impacts. This is often, in turn, linked to the national economy's weakness; effective governance in ensuring a healthy environment for citizens is almost impossible without a stable and reasonably prosperous economy. Strong support for efficient resource use, minimum waste, cities and urban systems which limit the need for private automobiles and maximum recovery of materials

Box 6.2
Environmental Policy Guidelines

Constraint	Prescription
1. Maintain environmental quality:	conserve nutrient and material cycles; limit waste emission; and maintain landscape amenity.

2. Efficient resource use:	make users (consumers) pay;
	make polluters (consumers) pay;
	compensate for the production of
	    positive nonmarket benefits;
	allocate and enforce use rights;
	couple resource security with
	    environmental security;
	avoid selective price distortions;
	do not mask ecological signals with
	    subsidies;
	pursue technical efficiency; and
	promote recycling/product durability.

3. Avoid government failure:	use market mechanisms; promote resource stewardship; tax resource extraction and use; package decisions to favor the poor; and maintain political and economic stability.

4. Maintain future options:	off-set environmental degradation;
	when ecologically uncertain, take a
	    precautionary approach;
	increase ecological, social, and economic
	    diversity; and
	maintain low, stable interest rates.

from waste streams can ensure that increasing prosperity does not also mean increasing environmental degradation.

Critical Success Factors for Urban Sustainability

A number of factors are critical to the development and implementation of successful sustainable development policies. These are best illustrated using the pentagon model shown in Figure 6.5 which takes for granted the existence of five crucial conditions which must be achieved to ensure the feasibility of a given policy directive. This pentagon prism has been applied to various policy analyses, such as

Box 6.2 (continued)
Environmental Policy Guidelines

Constraint	**Prescription**
5. Stop population growth:	create self-replacing population; and make primary and secondary education compulsory (especially for girls).
6. Conserve natural capital:	employ replacement cost pricing; invest to enhance conditionally renewable resource productivity; harvest at no more than the regeneration rate; and off-set conditionally renewable resource degradation and depletion.
7. Maintain the aggregate value of mineral stocks and conditionally renewable resources:	reinvest rent; and complement conditionally renewable resource productivity.
8. Redistribute wealth to per capita-poor countries:	promote free trade; set equivalent trading standards; reduce rent in per capita-poor countries; and facilitate wealth transfer to per capita-poor countries.

Source: Young 1992.

those in infrastructure, environment, energy, and public services. In this discussion, the pentagon model is geared toward developing urban sustainability policy particular to the developing countries, and includes five elements.

Hardware. This is the development of customized technical skill and technologies for pollution and waste treatment drainage and, *inter alia*, route guidance for traffic in urban areas. A particularly weak element in many cities is the frequent absence of basic infrastructure, such as the provision of sanitation services. While the development of such services has recently been given greater attention in various countries (e.g., Pakistan and Thailand), and organizations frequently emphasize such development in their projects (ADB 1991), more needs to be done in this area. From the perspective of sustainable development, the provision of quality housing and of fundamental public services such as education, socio-medical care, and pollution abatement is critical. Modern technology may be pivotal in generating the necessary technical equipment for addressing such concerns as urban pollution control, appropriate waste treatment plants, industrial pollution control equipment, hazardous waste control, environmental biotechnology, and clean energy production (ESCAP 1992). Hardware success stories do exist, most notably in Singapore where 96 per cent of the population is served by modern sanitation through an extensive network of public sewers with a total length of over 2,000 kilometers, controlled by a computer-based automation system.

Socioware. This requires the development of and access to community-oriented socio-medical and related urban support systems (e.g., community organizations, NGOs, and nonprofit foundations) to effectively combat poverty and degradation of quality of life. Especially necessary are decentralized service delivery systems which focus on specific groups (e.g., children or elderly). Socioware factors would often be based on private or semi-public initiatives. Several countries (e.g., India, the Philippines and Sri Lanka) have implemented successful "socioware" factors; among these, decentralized policies seem to be the most successful (ADB 1991). Decentralized solid waste disposal and decentralized heating systems are also good examples of socioware factors oriented towards the needs of local communities in large cities. A necessary condition for socioware is the provision of adequate environmental education, the enhancement of environmental awareness, the development of environmental campaigns, and the design of environmental communication networks (ESCAP 1992). Examples are the Magic Eye anti-littering campaign in Thailand and the campaign to keep Singapore clean.

Orgware. This is the development of an efficient, alert and pro-active administrative system with sufficient coordination and cooperation among different institutions (e.g., community-based organizations) aimed at improving urban quality of life by means of viable development programs or in-situ slum upgrading projects. Cooperation between local community leaders and local developers is of critical importance, especially as ownership issues become part of a restructuring process. Because of the multiplicity of needs (e.g., shelter, water supply, public transportation) a flexible institutional framework for achieving urban sustainability must be designed. Participatory service delivery systems, self-help community-based programs, and private-public community development programs offer great potential in this context. As discussed earlier, a major weakness in most developing country cities is a lack of administrative competence, which might lead to a mobilization of all public and private forces for enhancing urban environmental quality. Indonesia, Republic of Korea, Philippines, and Thailand recently developed initiatives to integrate environmental concerns into regional and local economic development planning (ESCAP 1992).

Ecoware. This entails sufficient recognition of environmental interests and presence of a legislative and institutionalized system ensuring adequate incorporation of environmental interests in urban development planning. In particular, the development of monitoring mechanisms and emissions registration procedures deserves serious attention (including environmental impact assessment). Simple and rapid methods for air quality monitoring and assessment could be adopted, as could environmental risk management and environmental accounting procedures. Sufficient attention would have to be given to the needs of the urban poor in terms of quality of life, healthy living and working conditions, and clean water. Physical planning measures—including an efficient transport infrastructure—are also important: much of the environmental damage and annoyance in cities is related to the poorly designed spatial layout of urban areas and outdated urban infrastructure which causes unnecessary spatial movement. Finally, water quality is a critical factor which is of decisive importance for health and quality of life in cities in the developing world. A good example of how this factor can be incorporated in policy comes from Indonesia where a team from the World Resources Institute developed a framework for natural resource accounting. The method advocated followed the one used in national income accounts, except that the method led to the calculation of net GDP, which was derived by subtracting estimates of net national resource development from GDP.

Finware. This is the development of an economic and financial support system which is able to generate the necessary financial resources for those urban development and environmental projects (or programs) which have a net positive social benefit. This factor concerns not only the (quantitative) size of scarce financial resources, but also the institutional competence for allocating these resources from various sources and decision levels. A main challenge would be to develop savings mechanisms among the local population to stimulate the financing of basic community infrastructure (e.g., financing medical care based on matching grants). Decentralized community-based initiatives would then be necessary so as to generate sufficient interest (and hence financial resources). Examples of such initiatives can be found in Indonesia, Republic of Korea, Pakistan, and Philippines. Of course, local tax revenues (preferably based on user charge principles) could also play an important complementary function (e.g., fuel tax, property tax, and telephone tax). Finally, local financial management and expenditure administration must be improved. Clearly, both the private and public sector could play an important role here, especially as governments are short of capital. A link between the informal sector and privatization of environmental services might be encouraged, provided strict quality standards are imposed and enforced.

Feasible Urban Environmental Policies

The above considerations on critical success factors are still fairly general and ought to be translated into economically and ecologically meaningful strategies for urban sustainability in developing countries. In the general area of global sustainability policies, various guidelines have been proposed. An example can be found in Box 6.3.

While the list of criteria offers various economic principles for effective sustainability strategies with a strong emphasis on market principles, whether such principles can be applied at the urban level in developing countries, where cities have often turned into "pollution havens," remains to be seen. Given the nature of the environmental problems in Asian cities, as noted earlier, it would appear that such general economic guidelines are insufficiently customized.

A necessary condition for effective and efficient urban sustainability policy is the existence of a competent, representative, nonbureaucratic and action-oriented government, which is able to cooperate closely with NGOs and the private sector to mobilize all forces for successful urban environmental management. A joint effort is needed to reduce poverty and to improve environmental quality conditions in cities by improving housing and living conditions, by supporting proper environmental technologies and pollution abatement systems, by providing better public infrastructure (including waste treatment,

Figure 6.5

A Pentagon Prism with Necessary Conditions for Policy Success

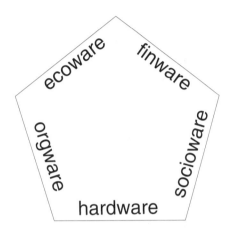

sewerage and drinking water) to all urban residents, by offering training and educational programs on the environment, by involving the poorer segments of the urban population in decision-making, by strengthening urban institutions dealing with environmental protection, and by strictly enforcing land use and environmental regulations.

This is an enormous task for Asian cities, but is a task that cannot be ignored; the social and environmental costs of doing so are just too great. Further, the "growth-first" strategy adopted in many countries and cities offers short-term benefits at high long-term costs (Kobayashi 1991). Some first signs of the recognition of the short and long-term benefits of a coevolutionary strategy can be found in Taipei,China, which adopted a policy to cope with environmental degradation that reduces social welfare and a program for rigorous environmental clean-up.

A limited set of fields where sustainable policies may be effective are discussed below, using the pentagon model and the above guidelines as a framework. These fields include (i) urban resources and waste management; (ii) urban quality of life; (iii) urban transport; and (iv) urban sustainability policy finance.

Urban Resources and Waste Management. Cities are concentration points of economic and social activities. Related negative externalities of urban compactness should preferably also be coped with on the basis of strategies based on scale economies (e.g., centralized waste treatment). This means that policies to increase the efficiency of raw materials, energy and waste treatment have to be stimulated and implemented. For instance, cities offer unique possibilities for selective recollection, recycling, and reuse of materials, or for district heating (or perhaps district cooling) or industrial co-generation. Illegal dumping of waste has to be strictly prohibited, and environmental standards in industrial processes, waste treatment plants, and water sewage systems have to be initiated. Several cities in the developing countries offer good examples of environment-conscious strategies, *inter alia*, by using intensive publication campaigns to increase local awareness. Thus education and communication related to socioware are—besides appropriate hardware equipment—necessary to the achievement of sustainable urban development.

In general, a source-oriented environmental policy is more effective and less costly to implement than effect-oriented measures, although curative policies may be necessary in concert with preventive environmental policies. A strict market-based enforcement of "polluter-pays" principles is a necessary condition for coping with environmental externalities in cities in the developing world. An interesting example can be found in Malaysian palm and rubber factories, where fees are levied on palm-oil and rubber factories for the discharge of polluting effluents (ESCAP 1992, p. 190).

In addition, there is a need to develop rapidly and efficiently implemented environmentally sound policies for the low-income groups, using market-oriented strategies. Polluter-pays principles, user charges, and matching grants fit these criteria.

Urban Quality of Life. Urban quality of life is related to the quality of the housing stock, availability of shelter, prevailing land use patterns, availability of socio-medical care, and, in general, an entire package of urban infrastructure services. Land use and housing are critical issues in cities in developing countries as illegal land use and squatter settlements are common phenomena. Low-income groups tend to become victims of semi-institutional and informal changes in land use and ownership conditions. The needs of the poor must, therefore, be reconciled with the public need to enforce laws on land use and ownership. Improved urban quality of life achieved on the basis of community participation is one way to meet this need, but this is a long-term process, and must be approached as such.

Institutional rigidity and public inertia may be detrimental to an effective quality of life policy, but an equally important factor is the lack of funds to pay for the services needed. A variety of mechanisms

---

Box 6.3
Economic Guidelines for Sustainability Strategies

1. Employ policy targets for all areas where pollution is a problem and a phased strategy for the eventual elimination of these problems.

2. Emphasize a mixed-policy approach to ensure that investment and resource use are efficient, equitable, adaptable to change, and dependable, and that they encourage innovation, promote continuing improvement beyond the policy target, have low information requirements, are administratively feasible, are not vulnerable to swings in public opinion, and are politically acceptable.

3. Employ no subsidized resource use and no price-support schemes that mask market signals.

4. Ensure that resource prices reflect the user-pays and polluter (consumer)-pays principles.

5. Ensure that regulations and safe minimum standards underpin a wide array of resource-right and other economic instruments.

6. Rely on self-enforcing policy mechanisms which are backed by an administrative structure not prone to regulatory capture and corruption.

7. Employ a widespread use of fees, levies, and charges to ensure that prices paid by consumers include the costs that their purchases impose on other people and the administrative costs of pollution prevention and control.

8. Ensure the existence of off-set policies that encourage developers to either off-set any loss of environmental services, landscape amenity and other similar considerations, or pay for the cost of replacing these functions.

9. Use deposit-refund and security-deposit schemes, especially for heavy metals and other chemicals which do not readily assimilate into the natural environment.

10. Be prepared to compensate people who maintain environmental services backed by resource-right systems which ensure that the benefits from such services are maintained in perpetuity.

Source: Young 1992.

can, in principle, be envisioned, ranging from local taxes or central government transfer payments to self-financing service revenues, but in most developing country cities, the financial possibilities are extremely limited. Consequently, alternative modes of quality of life services have to be envisaged as well, such as self-help, participatory and community-based serviced delivery systems, and improved technologies. Thus, a mix of hardware, socioware, finware, and orgware is essential for a more satisfactory quality of life.

Urban Transport. Most cities in the developing countries face severe transport problems which not only cause unacceptable negative social externalities (e.g., congestion, pollution, health effects, and fatalities), but also negatively affect the economic performance of these cities. There is no easy solution to these problems. In general, financial resources for implementing infrastructure investments are lacking or insufficient. Further, this lack means that efforts to improve the efficiency of public transport services and to reduce economic losses caused by traffic jams are even more serious in developing countries, given the foreseeable rise in car ownership and car use in the next decade. In a recent study (ESCAP 1990) it was found that finware (i.e., lack of funding for urban transport investment) was perceived to be a main problem in Indonesia, Pakistan, Philippines, and Thailand, whereas orgware and hardware (i.e., lack of technological skills and lack of appropriate coordination channels) appeared to cause a major bottleneck in Hong Kong and the Republic of Korea.

A major problem is that urban transport policy is often regarded as a (segmented) traffic management issue, whereas in reality this is closely connected with land use policy, housing policy, and industrialization policy.

It is clear that—in view of the central economic position of cities in developing countries—more investments in transport infrastructure are warranted (possibly to be paid out of user charges). Also, appropriate training schemes for traffic managers, public transport operators, and infrastructure owners/managers are needed. Finally, a more thorough economic basis for fare structures and investment decisions on all infrastructure development is necessary to avoid inefficient spending of scarce public financial resources. The same applies to fuel taxes, vehicle taxes, and vehicle regulations. Clearly, public transport needs a drastic upgrading (a "quality jump") in almost all Asian cities. Such improvements may range from large-scale mass transit systems to small-scale adjustments (e.g., separate bus lanes, priority for buses on traffic lights, better information provision on routes and destinations of public transport, and more (light) rail investments for medium and long distances). Price distortions must be avoided in all cases, and cost recovery principles must be strictly applied to offer the quality products needed by the market.

While many possibilities exist to improve local traffic conditions, for the immediate future, a broad combination of charges or taxes combined with the establishment and enforcement of environmental or technological standards would be the most appropriate strategy for alleviating the high social costs of urban transport in cities in the developing world.

Urban Sustainability Policy Finance. The pentagon model lists finware as one of the most critical conditions for substantial improvement of urban quality of life. The question arises as to whether an urban sustainability policy can generate sufficient "value for money" to justify a mobilization of huge financial resources. Similar questions have also recently been raised in the context of other "nonproductive" assets such as housing, infrastructure, and culture (Montanari and Petraroia 1991; Struyk et al. 1990). Despite the indigenous merits of housing, infrastructure, and culture, investments often need to be justified based on their contribution to social welfare.

It is evident that net positive socioeconomic benefits are absolutely essential to justify public intervention in the urban environment. Such benefits comprise both primary economic benefits (e.g., extra tourist revenues as a result of a strict urban environmental policy) and secondary benefits (e.g., new enterprises attracted by a pleasant urban climate). Clearly, the distributional effects have to be considered as well, ensuring a careful analysis of the beneficiaries (and externalities) of environmental policies favoring a sustainable city.

For example, in industry, the implementation of new technologies and the installation of better insulation may lead to a considerable rise in energy efficiency, albeit with a long lead time under normal circumstances. In the residential sector, housing insulation programs may also lead to drastic energy savings for both space heating and air conditioning (e.g., by means of better insulation, heat pumps, solar energy installations, wind turbines, and economizers for central heating systems). On a more integrated and meso-level of urban energy planning, various possibilities are offered by central heat distribution, by recycling of energy from heat, by combined heat and power either in district heating or in co-generation, or by using urban/industrial waste as fuel for generating plants. Especially at a local level these energy saving options are likely to be more efficient than on a more regional level, as in general such options require fairly high densities of energy demand.

In the transport sector, considerable savings are also possible, for example, through more energy efficient engines, vehicle weight reduction or, in the long run, through more energy-efficient physical planning aimed at a reduction of commuting distance and/or a shift of the modal split in favor of public transport (see also Button 1992). In addition, land use zoning and physical planning might also provide some of the regulatory regions for environmental policy.

In all cases, environmental programs are expensive. Because of severe public budget constraints and deficits of governments at all levels (national, regional, and local), increasingly private financing of public programs or projects must be sought, especially after deregulation. In most cases, however, dependence entirely on private financing is not feasible or desirable. More often programs are financed through various types of public/private partnership configurations. Such cooperative agreements face two problems: institutional setting and financial arrangements.

The institutional setting in which an urban environmental and energy policy would have to operate is of paramount importance for the feasibility and effectiveness of such a policy. For example, public/private-oriented district heating systems, private-based industrial co-generation systems, and private (but collective) solar and wind energy systems are becoming popular, but require clear and well set agreements among all parties involved. Synergy in urban environmental and energy policy measures will certainly increase the viability of urban sustainability.

In general, urban environmental and energy planning may comprise a set of different and complementary environmental and energy policy strategies ("packaging" of policy measures), such as industrial co-generation, district heating, combined heat and power generation (using steam turbines, internal combustion engines, gas turbines, or combined-cycle gas turbines), combined urban waste management and energy production, transport policies, load management, and institutional reforms in the structure of utilities. A number of European cities provide good examples of the potential of urban energy planning (e.g., Amsterdam, Berlin, Gothenburg, Grenoble, Odense, Rennes, and Torino), which might be emulated in Asia.

Financial arrangements also affect the success of public/private partnerships, and a significant part of the success of environmental and energy conservation policies in many cities can be attributed to various financial incentive programs. For example, in industry, grants to stimulate discrete conservation investment, tax incentives to encourage energy efficient production processes, and loans to stimulate less energy-intensive capital investments have been used successfully. In the residential/commercial sector, grants to help develop energy conservation schemes, tax incentives to encourage the installation of building insulation, and loans for specific energy conservation purposes have been used with good results.

In addition, in various countries, information programs (e.g., publicity campaigns, residential and industrial energy audits, appliance labeling or transportation fuel efficiency information) and regulation/standard systems (e.g., building codes, appliance efficiency standards, and fuel economy standards for new passenger cars) have been introduced as effective policy tools to increase environmental and energy awareness.

Traditional economic theory teaches that the expected financial revenues of new urban environmental programs would induce a willingness to pay among those involved. However, because of the poverty levels in many cities in the developing countries, willingness to pay is not always a plausible financing option, thus, a cooperative agreement where governments or public authorities provide a leverage of private support is more likely. A system of matching grants between the public and the private sector may work. Schuster (1989) makes a distinction between three types of matching grants: cofinancing, challenge grants, and reverse matching grants.

Despite the potential of matching funds, governments nevertheless have to generate the necessary financial resources. Money from the public budget may originate from fees or charges levied on the use of environmental facilities. Specific pollution abatement measures may also be based on polluter-pays principles (for industries, households, and transport) and may be complemented with command and control regulations for achieving urban sustainability.

CONCLUSION

The nodal position of cities in all economies, including those of developing countries, necessitates careful analysis and thorough policy attention regarding the socioeconomic potential of these cities. Urban sustainability may be regarded as an appropriate motive for effective and efficient strategies to achieve a balance between growth, equity, and environment. This means that local government capacity has to be strengthened, so that environmental considerations are integrated in urban development plans.

The particular conditions of Asia's urban areas, characterized by massive urbanization, poverty, low levels of public services and a dual economy, increase their vulnerability and affect their ability to initiate policies aimed at environmental sustainability. The close connection between urban poverty and urban environmental conditions reinforces the trend to seek short-term solutions without reducing, and sometimes even exacerbating, the long-term problems. Governments are faced with extremely difficult and delicate choices in finding a balance between the fulfillment of urgent needs and the necessity to work toward sustainability. The paradox which emerges in many countries is that the increase of welfare levels of the poor will lead to more pollution and waste, and hence will erode the urban basis for sustainable development. In this context, a keen combination of hardware, socioware, orgware, ecoware, and finware measures must be found.

It is evident that, besides improved welfare prospects and related behavioral changes, technology development in the area of environmental management and pollution abatement is also essential. At both national and local levels, effective steps have to be undertaken to discourage the use of polluting technologies. At the same time, because many abatement technologies and other industrial or household technologies with a polluting nature are acquired from countries outside Asia, part of the solution to the (urban) pollution problem in Asia may be found in the developed economies. Thus, there is a need for an international code for preventing the transfer, trade, or export of polluting technologies and products, and the development of agreements with multinational companies or exporting companies must become a high priority. Also, the use of polluting products by households at the local level (e.g., plastic bags and CFCs) must be discouraged. Hardware and ecoware would need to become a mutually supportive mechanism, for instance, by developing products incorporating indigenous natural raw materials and by favoring recycling schemes. This strategy would also reduce urban poverty and unemployment.

Also, the active role of the private and public sector in reducing pollution from all economic activities and energy use must be taken into consideration. Price and tax schemes on fuel, electricity, and gas have to be properly applied so as to ensure an efficient use of scarce resources in combination with a sufficient availability of such resources for the low-income groups. In general, inappropriate pricing of environmental resources and services has to be avoided. Also, positive stimuli have to be provided to safeguard the urban environment (e.g., tree replantation schemes, maintenance of urban parks, selective/controlled disposal of waste and garbage, installation of drainage and sewage systems, and construction of flood control systems) to upgrade the urban environment.

Finally, the positive role of the city in developing countries must be emphasized. A city is a node of economic activity, entrepreneurial spirit, and social renewal. Not only industrial and service activities should be promoted in the city, but also many other activities which increase urban sustainability. For instance, many Asian cities house collections of monuments and cultural amenities which could attract tourists. Various cities have been successful in exploiting this indigenous resource, but in many cities in developing countries such resources remain largely untapped. In this context, a more market-oriented approach to the development of tourist amenities would have great potential. Further, a proper mix of ecoware, finware, and socioware would greatly improve the competitive position of cities in the developing world.

In conclusion, Asian cities are not concentration points of socioeconomic despair but can be focal points for sound sustainable development. The five critical success factors mentioned in this study, viz. hardware, socioware, orgware, ecoware, and finware must be implemented and respected in proper combination to ensure long-term sustainability.

Notes

1. For a review of urban sustainability policies in Europe, see Nijkamp and Perrels (1993).
2. For interesting local and urban applications of GIS, see also Fischer and Nijkamp (1993); Giaoutzi and Nijkamp (1993); and ESCAP (1992).

References

Agarwal, A.K. 1992. "International Trade and Sustainable Development from a Southern Non-governmental Perspective." In *International Trade and Sustainable Development*, edited by J.W. Arntzen, I. Hemmer, and O. Kuik. Amsterdam: Free University Press.

Andersson, A., and U. Strömquist. 1989. "The Emerging C-Society." In *Transportation for the Future*, edited by D.F. Batten, and R. Thord. Berlin: Springer. pp. 43–64.

Archibugi, F., and P. Nijkamp (eds). 1989. *Economy and Ecology: Towards Sustainable Development*. Kluwer, Dordrecht.

Asian Development Bank. 1991. *The Urban Poor*. Manila: Asian Development Bank.

Bergh, J.C.. 1991. *Dynamic Models for Sustainable Development*. Amsterdam: Free University.

Berry, R. 1985. "Islands of Renewal in Seas of Decay." In *The New Urban Reality*, edited by P. Peterson. Washington, DC: The Brookings Institution. pp. 123–140.

Button, K.J. 1992. "Transport Regulation and the Environment in Low Income Countries." In *Utilities Policy*. pp. 248–257

Carley, M., and I. Christie, 1992. *Managing Sustainable Development*. London: Earthscan.

Cloke, P.J., and C.C. Park. "Integrated Management Strategies." In *Rural Resource Management*. Andover, Hants: Croom Helm. pp. 408–448

Daly, H.E. 1991. *Steady State Economics*. Washington, DC: Island Press.

ESCAP. 1990. *Identification of Major Problems on Urban Transport in the ESCAP Region*. Bangkok: ESCAP.

_____. 1992. *State of the Environment in Asia and the Pacific*. Bangkok: ESCAP.

Fischer, M.M., and P. Nijkamp (eds.). 1993. *Geographic Information Systems, Spatial Modelling and Policy Evaluation*. Berlin: Springer Verlag.

Fuchs, R.J., G.W. Jones, and E.M. Pernia (eds.). 1987. *Urbanisation and Urban Policies in Pacific Asia*. London: Westview Press.

Giaoutzi, M., and P. Nijkamp. 1993. *Decision Support for Regional Sustainable Development*. United Kingdom: Gower, Aldershot.

Hardoy, J.E., D. Mitlin, and D. Satterthwaite. 1992. *Environmental Problems in Third World Cities*. London: Earthscan.

Hedman, S. 1990. "Reversibility as a Weighting Factor in Integrated Least Cost Planning Methodologies." (revised version) Paper Presented at the International Congress on The Ecological Economics of Sustainability. The World Bank, Washington DC. University of Maryland, College Park.

Heggie, I.G. 1992. "Can Charging for Negative Externalities Help Finance Improved Urban Transport Facilities: The Case of Developing Countries." In *Public/Private Partnerships in Urban Mobility*. Paris: OECD. pp. 207–217.

International Institute for Applied Systems Analysis (IIASA). 1992. *Science and Sustainability*. Laxenburg: IIASA.

Kairiukstis, L. 1989. "Ecological Sustainability of Regional Development: Background to the Problem." In *Ecological Sustainability of Regional Development*. Laxenburg: International Institute for Applied Systems Analysis. pp. 1–5.

Khosh-Chashm, K. 1991. "Man and City Environment in Developing Countries." *Cities and the Global Environment*. Dublin: European Foundation for the Improvement of Living and Working Conditions. pp. 242–257.

Kobayashi, H. 1991. "Shortcomings of the Growth-First Strategy." *Economic Eye*. vol. 12, no. 4. pp. 9–12.

Lea, J.P., and J.M. Courtney (eds.). 1985. *Cities in Conflict: Studies in the Planning and Management of Asian Cities*. Washington, DC: The World Bank.

Lichfield, N. 1990. *Economics of Conservation*. Cambridge: Cambridge University Press.

Linn, J.F. 1983. *Cities in the Developing World*. New York: Oxford University Press, New York.

Little, I.N.D., and J.A. Mirrlees. *Project Appraisal and Planning for Developing Countries*. London: Heinemann Educational Books.

Lo, Fu-chen. 1992. "Growth and Management of the Third World Megalopolis." *Comprehensive Urban Studies*. no. 45. pp. 189–202.

Lo, Fu-chen, and K. Salih (eds.). 1978. *Growth Pole Strategy and Regional Development Policy*. Oxford: Pergamon Press.

Lovelock, J. 1979. *Gaia: A New Look at Life on Earth*. Oxford: Oxford University Press.

Marahrens, W., C. Ax, and G. Buck. 1991. *Stadt und Umwelt*. Basil: Birkhaüser.

Montanari, A., and P. Petraroia. 1991. *Polluted City*. Roma: Instituto Poligrafico.

Nijkamp, P. (ed.) 1990. *Urban Sustainability*. United Kingdom: Gower, Aldershot.

_____ . 1991. "Evaluation of Environmental Quality in the City." *International Journal of Development Planning Literature*. vol. 6. no. 4. pp. 119–134.

_____ . 1993. "Towards a Network of Regions: The United States of Europe." *European Planning Studies*. vol. 1, no. 2., pp. 149–168.

Nijkamp, P., P. Lasschuit, and F. Soeteman. 1992. "Sustainable Development in a Regional System." In *Sustainable Development and Urban Form*, edited by M. Breheny. London: Pion. pp. 39–66.

Nijkamp, P., and A. Perrels. 1993. *Sustainable Cities in Europe*. London: Earthscan.

Nijkamp, P. and A. Volwahsen. 1990. "New Directions in Integrated Regional Energy Planning." *Energy Policy*. October. pp. 764–774.

Nijkamp, P., J. Vleugel, R. Maggi, and I. Masser. 1993. *Missing Transport Networks in Europe*. United Kingdom: Avebury: Aldershot.

Opschoor, J.B., and L. Reijnders. 1989. "Duurzaamheidsindicatoren voor Nederland." Draft Paper Discussed at IVM/RIVM Workshop, Utrecht, October 30, 1989.

_____ . 1991. "Towards Sustainable Development Indicators." In *Search of Sustainable Development Indicators*, edited by O. Kuik, and M. Verbruggen. Dordrecht: Kluwer. pp. 7–29.

Organisation for Economic Co-operation and Development (OECD). 1978. *Urban Environmental Indicators*. Paris: OECD.

Orishimo, I. 1982. *Urbanisation and Environmental Quality*. Dordrecht: Kluwer.

Pearce, D., A. Markandya, and E.B. Barbier. 1989. *Blueprint for a Green Economy*. London: Earthscan.

Pelt, M.J.F. van. 1993. "Sustainability-oriented Project Appraisal for Developing Countries." Ph.D. Thesis, Wageningen Agricultural University.

Pelt, M.J.F. van, A. Kuyvenhoven, and P. Nijkamp. 1990. "Project Appraisal and Sustainability: Methodological Challenges." *Project Appraisal*. vol. 5, no. 3. pp. 139–158.

_____ . 1991. "Sustainability, Efficiency and Equity: Project Appraisal in Economy." Research Memorandum 1991–1996. Department of Economics, Free University, Amsterdam.

Pezzy, J. 1989. *Economic Analysis of Sustainable Growth and Sustainable Development*. WP15. Environment Department. Washington, DC: The World Bank.

Porter, M. 1990. *The Competitive Advantage of Nations*. New York: Free Press.

Quiggin, J., and J. Anderson. 1990. "Risk and Project Appraisal." Paper Presented at the World Bank Annual Conference on Development Economics. 26–27 April 1990. Washington, DC.

Reijnders, L.. 1990. "Normen voor Milieuvervuiling Met Het Oog op Duurzaamheid." *Milieu.* vol. 5, pp. 138–140.

Schuster, J.M.D., "Government Leverage of Private Support. "*The Cost of Culture,* edited by M. Wyszomirski and P. Clubb. New York: American Council for the Arts. pp. 63–97.

Simon, H.A. 1967. *Models of Man: Mathematical Essays on Rational Human Behaviour in a Social Setting.* New York: John Wiley.

South Commission. 1990. *The Challenge to the South.* Oxford: Oxford University Press.

Squire, L. 1989. "Project Evaluation in Theory and Practice." In *Handbook of Development Economics,* edited by H. Chenery and T.N. Srinivasan. vol. II. Dordrecht: Elsevier Science Publishers.

Squire, L., and H.G. van der Tak. 1975. *Economic Analysis of Projects.* Baltimore: Johns Hopkins University Press.

Struyk, R.J., M.L. Hoffman, and H.M. Katsura. 1990. *The Market for Shelter in Indonesian Cities.* Washington, DC: The Urban Institute Press.

United Nations Environment Programme/World Health Organization (UNEP/WHO). 1992. *Urban Air Pollution in Megacities of the World.* Oxford: Blackwell.

UNIDO. 1972. *Guidelines for Project Evaluation.* New York: United Nations: United Nations Industrial Development Organization.

Ward, B. 1976. *The Home of Man.* New York: Norton.

Wegelin, E.A. 1993. "Urban Shelter, Municipal Services, and the Poor Issues and Policy Measures." Paper Presented at the Finalization Meeting. ADB, Manila (appears as Chapter Five of this Volume).

World Commission on Environment and Development (WCED). 1987. *Our Common Future.* (Bruntland Report) World Commission on Environment and Development. Oxford: Oxford University Press.

Young, M.D. 1992. Sustainable Investment and Resource Use. Paris: UNESCO.

Author Index

Subject Index